# BRITISH POETRY IN THE AGE OF MODERNISM

If modernist poetry dominated the early twentieth century, what did it mean for British poets like Thomas Hardy, Edward Thomas and Wilfred Owen not to be modernist? This is the first critical account of how non-modernist poetry responded to the modernist revolution. Peter Howarth uncovers the origins of the battles over poetic style still being fought today, and connects the early twentieth-century controversy about poetic form with contemporary social and political developments and the trauma of the First World War. Howarth argues that at the heart of the division between modern and traditional poetic form are different ideas of freedom, power and individuality. Scholars and students of twentieth-century poetry will find this an informative and inspiring account of the themes and debates that have shaped British poetry of the last hundred years.

PETER HOWARTH is a Lecturer in the School of English Studies at the University of Nottingham. He has published in *English Literature in Transition, The Wordsworth Circle* and the *Times Literary Supplement.*

# BRITISH POETRY IN THE AGE OF MODERNISM

PETER HOWARTH

CAMBRIDGE
UNIVERSITY PRESS

CAMBRIDGE UNIVERSITY PRESS
Cambridge, New York, Melbourne, Madrid, Cape Town, Singapore, São Paulo

Cambridge University Press
The Edinburgh Building, Cambridge CB2 2RU, UK

Published in the United States of America by Cambridge University Press, New York

www.cambridge.org
Information on this title: www.cambridge.org/9780521853934

First published 2005

Printed in the United Kingdom at the University Press, Cambridge

*A catalogue record for this book is available from the British Library*

*Library of Congress Cataloguing in Publication data*
Howarth, Peter, 1973–
British poetry in the age of modernism / Peter Howarth.
p. cm.
Includes index.
ISBN 0-521-85393-1
1. English poetry – 20th century – History and criticism. 2. Modernism
(Literature – Great Britain. I. Title.
PR605.M63.H69    2005
821′.91209112–dc22        2005017948

ISBN-13 978-0-521-85393-4 hardback
ISBN-10 0-521-85393-1 hardback

*For my family, old and new*

# Contents

# Acknowledgements

During this book's long voyage to publication I have been grateful for the navigation, forecasts and steerage supplied by Catherine Phillips, Eric Griffiths, Louis Menand, Heather Glen, Tom Paulin, Ray Ryan and the anonymous readers of Cambridge University Press. I owe intellectual debts to an embarrassing number of people, but Victoria Coulson, Mark Robson and Jennifer Wallace in particular have been unfailingly stimulating and thoughtful friends to test out my latest ideas on. Nor would this book have been possible without the practical support of the Robbins family, Liz Sanville, and my friendly colleagues in the School of English Studies at Nottingham. For assistance with manuscripts I am indebted to the librarians of King's School, Canterbury, King's College, Cambridge, the Dorset County Museum, Cambridge University Library, the Bodleian Library, Oxford and the British Library. Particular thanks are due to the staff of the Berg Collection at the New York Public Library.

This book was written during research leave funded by the University of Nottingham and extended by the Research Leave scheme of the Arts and Humanities Research Board. For permission to reproduce unpublished material, I am grateful to Mrs Myfanwy Thomas, Professor Jon Stallworthy, the Society of Authors, King's School, Canterbury, and the executors of the H. M. Davies Trust. Citations from material in the Berg Collection of English and American Literature, the New York Public Library, Astor, Lenox and Tilden Foundations appear by permission. A version of chapter 3 has appeared in *English Literature in Transition 1880–1920* 46 (2003), and parts of chapter 1 in a different format in *The Wordsworth Circle* 34 (2003).

# Introduction: the poetry wars

Among its lists of publishing opportunities, grants and fellowships, the 2003 edition of *The Writer's Handbook* offers a solemn warning for today's aspiring poet:

> It would be great in 2003 to report an end to the poetry wars. Or indeed the end of any kind of war. But those disagreements on poetic style and metrical direction which began so long ago are still very much around. As ever, the battle is between the insiders and the outsiders, the left vs. the right, with both sides convinced they are the ones who own the true poetic grail. The insiders are the ones who write what new readers often imagine real poetry to be. They are clear, crisp and immediately comprehensible. They represent the Georgian line of narrative in verse that runs from Hardy through Betjeman and Larkin to Tony Harrison, Andrew Motion, Wendy Cope, Carol Ann Duffy, Sean O'Brien and the other bestsellers of the present day. The outsiders are the experimenters, the chancers, those of innovative texts. They are the ones who embraced the difficult modernism of Eliot and Pound and then took poetry off to those rarefied places where, apparently, the public never bother to go. They made it new. Wallace Stevens was central. John Ashbery is his heir. Over here Edwin Morgan, Roy Fisher, Tom Leonard, Allen Fisher and others continue the process. Poetry should be different. It should generate sparks when you engage with it. Comprehension comes later.[1]

It would be nice to imagine the aspiring poet reading this, immediately resolving not to be co-opted by either side, and encouraging herself by the thought of half-a-dozen contemporary poets who don't fit into such either/or generalisations. What would the poetry wars make of Alice Oswald's *Dart*, for example, a complex modernist collage of voices and a Wordsworthian landscape narrative at the same time? Of Paul Muldoon or Derek Walcott, neither 'immediately comprehensible' but both popular by poetry's standards? But the easier it is to show how war is not the answer, the more difficult it becomes to explain how contemporary poetry got itself stuck with such a rigid opposition in the first place. This book is set at the beginning of the poetry wars, the revolutionary decade between

1912 and 1922 when Eliot and Pound introduced the poetic styles and cultural values that would change the rest of the century's poetry for good. Its focus, however, is on the other side, Hardy and the 'Georgian line' of Edward Thomas, Wilfred Owen, Walter de la Mare and W. H. Davies, poets who read, reviewed and wrote in the context of modernism, but who remained unconverted. How much did the modernist revolution affect them, and how might we read their poetry in its light? Trying to understand what those disagreements about 'poetic style and metrical direction' originally were, though, makes this also a book about what poetic form means, a question debated more forcefully in this period than for the previous hundred years, and one whose disagreements have set the agenda for the next hundred years of the poetry wars. After modernism, it was impossible to think of form as an aesthetic box for the content or to dissociate a rhythm from questions of personal integrity and audience engagement. But although many books have been written about the meanings of modernist form, there are none about what it meant to their non-modernist contemporaries, writers whose work has also mattered a good deal for the century that followed. What did they have to say which could not be said in the forms of their modernist contemporaries?

The fact that there are very few books about the relation of the two sides at all is also a result of the poetry wars, of course. The notion that modernist art was a world whose intellectual and aesthetic concerns were largely unique to itself was encouraged by both modernists and later their opponents, and the division between them has been articulated in various oppositions over the century: popular vs. professional poets, school vs. university, traditional vs. avant-garde, rootedly national vs. exiled inter-national, unified vs. fragmented, formal vs. free. None of these antitheses are true of the situation as it was back in 1912, but if they reflect the basic division that literary criticism has always drawn between modernist poetry and its contemporaries – a division which this study will always have cause to cross – they also indicate how any account of this period always has the rest of the twentieth century peering over its shoulder. Turning to face that century directly, two things seem clear enough. Firstly, that a good deal of great twentieth-century British, Irish and Commonwealth poetry owes as much or more to Thomas and Hardy's example than it does to Pound and Eliot. As the century has progressed, the work of W. H. Auden, Philip Larkin, Seamus Heaney and Derek Walcott, to name simply the heavyweights, has testified to their enduring influence and in doing so, shifted the anthologies' centre of gravity: it is noticeable how since the 1970s, almost all have given as much space to Thomas, Hardy and Owen as to their modernist counterparts. And the same interest is evident in the poetry-reading public; in the 1995 BBC survey of the nation's favourite poems, all of the poets in this volume had entries in the top forty, and apart from Davies, all have been continuously in print since publication.[2] The number of people for whom Thomas and Owen's poetry matters for its own sake means no critical account of the period which leaves them as not-quite-modernists will do them justice. Even when the aim has been to rescue them for a middle ground between conservatism and revolution, that middle is still a degree on the scale set up by the *ne plus ultra* of modernism.[3] By situating their work in its modernist context, my aim is to give the non-modernist poets a place on their own terms.

But secondly, it is also certain that British poetry has been irrevocably changed by modernism. Not only did modernism introduce new styles and languages for poetry, it also ensured that there could be no way to hear the old ones in the same way. A generation later, Philip Larkin was to anathematise Pound and all his works, and his most infamously shocking line, 'They fuck you up, your mum and dad', is in perfect iambic tetrameter. But the poem would not have its Oedipus-for-Dummies mockery were that rhythm not heard as both stupidly obvious and flatly inevitable, and it can be heard as such partly because Pound made the unpredictability and self-direction of free verse a major force in English poetry. If, as Eliot argued in his 'Reflections on *Vers Libre*', free verse's covert reference to the metre it breaks makes it continuous with all traditional poetry, then it follows according to the logic of 'Tradition and the Individual Talent' that the arrival of free verse has, if ever so slightly, altered the whole tradition of poetry, including the poetry written expressly to ignore it.[4] It is therefore also important not to treat Thomas or Hardy as if they were living in a different world to Pound or Eliot, because modernism caused poetry to be heard differently ever after, and none more so than the work of its contemporaries. This book is an attempt to hear that difference as it emerges.

Writing about modernists and non-modernists together, however, runs almost immediately into a minefield of terminology and personnel, and a long list of writers who should be accounted for but aren't. This study is not a survey of all the different non-modernist poets, or of the many varieties of modernism in Europe and America.[5] Focusing instead on the place and decade when these definitions were first being formulated, it asks how those poets whose work has subsequently become emblematic of the poetry wars actually related to one another. Hence 'modernist' in this book means largely those Pound saw as part of his movement, the creators of a new sort of verse in and around literary London in the decade of the First World War, and 'non-modernist' means the poets of the same decade (and often the same magazines and the same parties), whom literary history has subsequently opposed to them, only sometimes because the modernists wanted to be remembered like that. This is not to claim that the configurations of the poetry wars are the real and only way to understand modernism in Britain, of course, nor that these particular outsiders to it are the only ones worth studying. Rather than make a general survey of poetic responses to modernism, my aim is to show how vividly the work of these particular poets demonstrates the vicissitudes of the battle that would come to be fought in their name – through its literary impact, in the case of Thomas, Hardy and Owen, and/or the way it exemplifies the twists and turns of the debate over the values of modern poetry, in the case of Davies and de la Mare. Given the charged history of the hundred years since, this dual focus on the poetry as itself and as it has been remembered is unavoidable; the tension between historicity and uniqueness is also, as I shall argue, a major concern for the poets themselves, not least as the question of poetic form. In this sense, the problem of a satisfying collective noun for them is a small but symptomatic one. Calling them simply non-modernists suggests that what they all really had in common were the poets they weren't, which is unfair to their individual positions. Calling them simply Georgians, though, is complicated by history; only two were published Georgians, and the broader sense of 'Georgian' still excludes Hardy, but includes a very wide range of poets, not all of whom knew or liked each other. There were those who were made by their appearance in *Georgian Poetry*, such as Wilfrid Gibson, Lascelles Abercrombie and Rupert Brooke; those whose work had been successful beforehand, for example de la Mare and Davies, and those like Edward Thomas and Robert Frost who were friends with the Georgians but disliked much of their poetry. Wilfred Owen called himself a Georgian because he was thrilled to be held peer by Robert Graves and Siegfried Sassoon, although he was actually published in the Sitwells' modernistic anthology *Wheels*. Worse, the word also has to cover the post-war coterie of poets led by J. C. Squire, whose conspicuous anti-modernism attracted some of Eliot's most stinging attacks on Georgian complacency, but who were generally loathed or ignored by the surviving original Georgians.[6] My compromise is to call these poets 'Georgians' when their work is aligned with the general aims of the earlier Georgian anthologies, 'non-modernists' when I need to distinguish their particular work from the substantial morass of bad poetry in those anthologies, and to give the closest attention I can to the particular affiliations of each poet.

Hopscotching over the terminological cracks like this, though, is itself a consequence of the perpetual tendency of the poetry wars to present the two sides as mirror images of each other, rather than acknowledge the more asymmetrical alignments of the time. What really connected the poets in this study was an intricate, casual and shifting network of friendships, friend-of-friendships and admirations, rather than their following a common style, becoming a self-declared movement like the Imagists, or issuing a counter-modernist manifesto. Partly this is because they did not share an identical relation to individual modernist poets. Hardy had worked out his poetic before Pound or Thomas began to write, and with his mind on the battles of another era, was rather surprised (and pleased) to find out how important his work had become to the generation of the First World War. But while Pound praised his eye on the object, Eliot excoriated him for naked self-absorption.[7] After Owen's death, Eliot admired 'Strange Meeting' (with its uncanny prescience of *The Waste Land*) and Yeats damned him as 'all blood, dirt & sucked sugar stick'.[8] Hardly anyone paid attention to Thomas at all. And these divergent reactions indicate the other reason for the absence of a definitive non-modernist movement, the fact that in this decade there was no very clear-cut thing called 'modernism' to defy either.[9] What became modernist and what was left outside it has been to a degree retrospectively defined by the poetry wars, and one of the larger themes this book traces is the degree of contact between groups separated too absolutely by the later needs of such reconstructions, particularly Pound and Eliot's battles with Squire after the war, or Larkin's attempts forty years later to find an English tradition unsullied by modernism. A good recent study shows the poetry wars in action around 1919:

As many literary historians have observed, one tool moderns used to draw the line [between modernist and non-modernist] was the work of those who had published and represented the values of the relatively traditional work published in Harold Monro's Georgian Anthologies. The critic Arthur Waugh (father of Evelyn), for example, after he had denounced the *Catholic Anthology* (which contained Eliot's 'The Love Song of J Alfred Prufrock') as a collection of 'unmetrical, incoherent banalities' composed by 'literary "Cubists"', argued that 'the humour, commonsense, and artistic judgement of the best of the new "Georgians"' would save contemporary letters. Directly opposing these kinds of sentiments was John Middleton Murry, husband of Katherine Mansfield and editor of the journal *Athenaeum*, in whose pages he regularly attacked Georgian writing. After attending a lecture by Eliot, Murry, undoubtedly agreeing with

Pound's description of Waugh's writing as 'senile slobber', exultingly described the two encamped armies that had gathered at the talk: 'The anti-*Athenaeums* – Munro [*sic*], Jack Squire etc – present in force. There's no doubt it's a fight to the finish between us & Them – them is the "Georgians" en masse.'[10]

Extraordinary what a difference a war makes; in 1912 it had been the editor of the Georgian anthologies, Eddie Marsh, who stepped in to save Murry and Mansfield's little magazine *Rhythm* from bankruptcy. Arthur Waugh's original *Quarterly Review* article bracketed *Georgian Poetry* and the *Catholic Anthology* together in an 'atmosphere of empirical rebellion', whose anarchistic creed it was to 'draw the thing as we see it for the God of things as they are' instead of 'an eternal idea expressed in flawless language', and specifically criticised the Georgians' 'deliberate defiance of metrical tradition', 'incoherent violence' and attempts at free verse.[11] His review began the 'drunken helots' tag that Pound paraded gleefully as evidence of the age's critical stupidity in *The Egoist* and Eliot remembered eighteen years later in *The Use of Poetry*, but it was originally aimed equally at the other side.[12] And Harold Monro actually offered to publish the *Catholic Anthology*, but Pound turned him down since Monro was a contributor to it as well.[13] In addition to *Georgian Poetry*, Monro had published the first Imagist anthology, *Des Imagistes*, followed by Aldington's *Images*, Flint's *Cadences*, and was compiling manuscripts for a Futurist anthology when the War interrupted everything. So when Pound wrote worriedly to John Quinn in 1918 that there was a shortage of modernist French writers, that only Jules Romains 'would be with us, rather than with the Poetry Bookshop and the Georgian Anthologies, Abercrombie Eddie Marsh etc', his neat division of the modernist 'movement' from Monro's Poetry Bookshop/Georgian circle was being strategically forgetful.[14] The Bookshop's lodgings had housed arch-Georgians such as Wilfrid Gibson, but also T. E. Hulme and Jacob Epstein, not to mention the not-yet-famous Wilfred Owen. And it was in the pages of the Bookshop's literary magazines that much of the new modernist programme for poetry had been publicised; Pound's Imagist 'Prolegomena' and the lecture that became Hulme's 'Romanticism and Classicism' were both first printed by Monro's *Poetry Review*, and their work was promoted by the magazine exactly because it was consonant with the ideas about a new, utterly direct, utterly sincere poetry being worked out by non-modernist poets on the same pages. Both purported to loathe the excesses of 'Romanticism' and manifested it at all levels; both wanted an immediate, stripped-down poetry without ornament, and both summed up these tendencies in a crusade against rhetoric, which is the starting-point for this book. For it is in this struggle against rhetoric that the non-modernists and modernists set the agenda for so much subsequent twentieth-century poetics on both sides of the division, be it Plath's heart-stopping confessions or Auden's light verse, Larkin's aggressive ordinariness or J. H. Prynne's dismantling of humanistic perspective, a development of Eliot's own radical solution of dissolving the boundaries of the individual voice, and with them, the possibility of an original self to be false to.

Demonstrating the poetry wars' shifting battle-lines over common ground, though, invites the charge that this book should have gone further, shown the basic error of being exclusively on one side or the other, and paid much more attention to great poets who in some degree belong to both, such as D. H. Lawrence, Robert Graves, Charlotte Mew, or W. B. Yeats. Although my approach is basically sympathetic to such peace-making ideals, the division between modernist poetry and its contemporaries that crystallised around these problems of rhetoric and integrity was a real one, even if the answers do not correspond exactly to the official affiliations of the protagonists, and any dissolving of oppositions needs first to explain the force with which they operated in this first decade or so. Certainly, the values of one side reappear translated into the vocabulary of the other (the Imagist-style justifications for W. H. Davies discussed in chapter 4, for example), but equally certainly, the quest to eliminate rhetoric involves a number of values that are not always consistent: private integrity and public communicability, for example, or authenticity and transparency. What modernists and non-modernists share is more a common set of problems to do with these issues of autonomy and engagement bequeathed them by the Romantic poets, and any attempt to claim a middle ground has first to recognise the seriousness of the different answers and their far-reaching implications. It is the arguments about rhetoric, for example, that underpin the disagreements about metrical direction rather than the other way round. However tempting it is to caricature the relationship between modernist and non-modernist poets as a simple opposition between free-verse poets committed to creative liberty and law-abiding formalists, the opposition will not hold: Thomas and Owen wrote free verse, and even Abercrombie, Pound's literary *bête-noire*, tried his hand at a series of haiku and unrhymed odes (one even had a Greek title) which were only published posthumously.[15] And of course Pound and Eliot wrote free verse, formally regular verse and all shades in between. In fact, in 1917 when they first properly accused their Georgian contemporaries of rhetoric and justified their own poetics by its elimination, those poetics were then the return to classicism, 'rhyme and regular strophes' as Pound recalled it, not free verse.[16] The opposition between free and formal in this era is actually only one version of the more fundamental argument about the poet's integrity expressed in the *Poetry Review*; rhetoric, in its pejorative post-Romantic sense, implies a gap between inner core and outer expression, the essential and the excessive, an inorganic relation of language to thought. It was by convicting the Georgian anthologies of rhetoric that modernism made critical opinion lose interest in them and anyone associated with them, and so successful was this attack that for decades afterwards, non-modernist poets had to be divorced from Georgian poetry to be taken seriously. Even when Ross and Stead wrote books designed to rehabilitate the Georgians in the 1960s, they chose to emphasise Georgian directness and fidelity to actual experience in concrete language – naturalising, in other words, the values of Imagism at the same time as they were describing an alternative to it.[17] Important as these studies were in giving Hardy or Thomas a literary context of which they did not have to be ashamed, they also ducked the larger issue as to what 'rhetoric' actually means, and what being free from it would entail. This is the story of the first chapter, which traces the way certain key modernist ideas about avoiding it – the Image, 'Classicism', the fragment and the Tradition – have their roots in the Romantic demand that poetry's form express perfect self-determination, a freedom from any influence or law outside the poem. But by writing a poetry that in the context of modernist demands cannot but look artificial, generic or forced, poets like Thomas and Hardy register the problems of agency this autonomous poetic entails, as Wordsworth had made it uncomfortably present for Coleridge a hundred years before. Their work registers the perpetual struggle with what was not chosen but contingent, with exterior influence, and their tangled relations of dependence and freedom, private and public are the theme of the chapters that follow. For the question of how much one chooses and how much one is pushed, how much one acts and how much acted through is crucial for Hardy's poems about guilt and responsibility, for de la Mare's exploration of the haunting power of poetry, for Edward Thomas deciding whether to go to the front or not, and for Wilfred Owen, facing the appalling consequences of doing so.

Given his importance for Pound and Eliot *and* his principled defence of formal pattern, a century's hindsight might interrupt here to suggest that since Yeats's poetry has been such a monumental influence for poets on both sides of the poetry wars, his theories about poetic form (in development throughout the period here, although most publicly formulated only in 1937 as the *General Introduction for my Work*) must surely transcend the division, and offer the best hope for common ground. But although proper discussion of their complex of politics, philosophy and occultism would require an entire book to itself, a brief survey may illustrate what is at stake in my reading of Owen or Hardy's form as a site of historical conflict, rather than its resolution, and why Yeats is not the mediator he appears in this respect. Despite his friendship with Pound, Yeats disliked the latter's free verse, and defended the necessary artifice of traditional forms because he felt their impersonal patterns enabled the artist to transcend his contingent, changing self, whereas free verse simply reproduced the moment as it was: 'If I wrote of personal love or sorrow in free verse, or any rhythm that left it unchanged, amid all its accidence, I would be full of self-contempt because of my egoism and indiscretion. I must choose a traditional stanza, even what I alter must seem traditional.'[18]

The direction of Yeats's next few sentences, however, illustrates why this argument is rather closer to Pound's programme than might be supposed, for his justification of traditional forms is based on a metaphysic much more akin to the multiple voices of Pound's montage and the impersonal ideal of Eliot's 'Tradition and the Individual Talent':

Talk to me of originality and I will turn on you with rage. I am a crowd, I am a lonely man, I am nothing. Ancient salt is best packing. The heroes of Shakespeare convey to us through their looks, or through the metaphorical patterns of their speech, the sudden enlargement of their vision, their ecstasy at the approach of death... The supernatural is present, cold winds blow across our hands, upon our faces, the thermometer falls, and because of that cold we are hated by journalists and groundlings. There may be in this or that detail painful tragedy, but in the whole work none. (522–3)

The crowd and the individual voice seem equal and simultaneous possibilities here, with the result that, like Pound's justifications for free verse, Yeats's traditional forms also rule the possibility of rhetoric out of court, only this time by *dissolving* the boundaries of self and crowd, original and copy, living and dead into a greater whole. For him, traditional form is not the heteronomous constraint on self-expression the free versifiers declared, but a ritual which introduces the real occult forces that underlie all existence; patterns which allow the self to play out a psychic drama with its spiritual opposites/doubles/unconscious and thus manifest in the well-formed poem the energy of those trans-historical oppositions that organise Yeats's cosmogony. The occult theology behind these conflicts thus has a profound effect on their concept of finite agency, particularly visible in Yeats's insistence that the privations of personal suffering are details and should never affect the completed whole. In a move echoing modernism's shift from Imagism to 'Tradition and the Individual Talent' discussed in chapter 1, Yeats rejects the autonomous, singular self of free verse (as did Thomas, Hardy or Owen) only to replace it with a dramatic self which, in its dyadic struggle with its anti-self, 'the being that bears my likeness but is without weariness or trivial desires', becomes reborn as 'something intended, complete', unified and autonomous.[19] When *A Vision* describes this principle of unity-in-opposition throughout the revolving phases of world history, their centre is the phase of 'unity of being', which is tellingly described as the acceptance of this 'struggle with no conquest', a state where 'fate and freedom are not to be distinguished'.[20] Here the dramatic, apparently contested conception of self through traditional form becomes a unity where there is no division between interior and exterior, compulsion and freedom; if rhetoric is what results from the quarrel with others, as Yeats famously remarked, then implicitly otherness is what has been removed here in order to have the quarrel with self that produces poetry. By contrast, Hardy, Thomas or Owen's work presents situations where its speakers are vulnerable, where the forces of heteronomy (death, war, time) are not symmetrical to those selves or recuperable by any transcendental opposition (which is why Yeats so disliked Owen's verse) – and consequently, where the form may not fit, where rhetoric is a structural possibility, exactly because this disparity is the price of poetic selves being finite, contingent and fallible.[21]

These questions of agency and integrity are also at the heart of the sociological disagreements over difficulty, popularity and nationhood that were to prove so important for the next phase of the poetry wars. *Georgian Poetry* was commercially successful and artistically bankrupt, Eliot had argued in various settings between 1919 and 1922, because it pandered to 'the General Reading Public, which knows no tradition, and loves staleness'.[22] It was a travesty of true artistic integrity because it was dominated by the middle-class, insular, mass-produced sensibilities it was written for; difficult, professional poetry, on the other hand, would resist exactly those homogenising blandishments by opening poetry to new influences and forms. The egalitarian climate of post-war Britain, however, did not see popularity with the ordinary reader as a hindrance, and the rise of the Movement poets provided artistic justification for a reassessment of modernist values – but, ironically, using exactly the same principles of self-determining integrity reapplied to the borders of the public, rather than the borders of the individual talent. The reappraisals of Davies, de la Mare, Owen, Hardy and Thomas collected in Larkin's *Required Writing* are part of his aim to rewrite the history of modern poetry, so that modernism becomes not a triumph over Georgian sentimental nostalgia, but 'an aberration', whose foreign 'culture-mongering' has lost poetry its audience.[23] By implication, the non-modernists are the native tradition which runs from Wordsworth and Clare through Hardy, Thomas and Owen to himself, a line whose English form had to have a more natural, popular relation to the public than an imported, subsidised one. Bolstered by the rise of Seamus Heaney, Philip Hobsbaum went further to insist that the 'English tradition' is alien to the montage, discontinuity and free verse more natural to 'the American language', a prospect which, if true, was bad news for Blake and Frost alike, not to mention Heaney's own loyalties.[24] But Eliot was perhaps more present in this process than Larkin would have liked, for if the arrival of Larkin's verse prompted the discovery of an English tradition to back it up, it was doing exactly what Eliot insisted all 'really new' poetry did: alter our perception of the 'relations, proportions, values of each work of art towards the whole', so that the past can be seen to have always already contained the genesis of the present.[25] And if Eliot can be seen to be structuring the method, Pound's isolation of modernism from the corruptions of the Poetry Bookshop is all too easily maintained in Larkin's separation of a normal, native English tradition from alien influence. Despite its tweed-jacket image, the idea of an English tradition is really a post-modernist assertion of the values of locality and limitation against modernist polyglot internationalism, a modernism cast more in Eliot's mould than that of Yeats or MacDiarmid, say.[26] But by discounting the shared context of modernist and non-modernist poetry and the history of Romantic poetics behind them, characterising Hardy and the Georgians by their native Englishness displaces the period's actual arguments about rhetoric onto a problem of national identity, while preserving all the problems with the principle of pure self-determination behind that argument. When Thomas criticised Pound's verses as 'so extraordinary, dappled with French, Provençal, Spanish, Italian, Latin and old English', it was because he thought Pound was trying too hard to establish his own extraordinariness; when Eliot criticised Georgian insularity in return, it was because he thought a European sensibility essential to avoid being victim to one's own poetic clichés.[27] Of course, England was under threat in this period – but as far as Thomas and Owen were concerned, from German soldiers rather than foreign cultural prestige and a surfeit of free verse. Owen's aesthetics were strongly influenced by French symbolism, and the last chapter will explore the dilemma he found reconciling their aesthetic with writing about war. Hardy's notebooks are full of French and German poets, as well as Nietzsche and Schopenhauer; de la Mare wanted his poems to be English haiku, and Edward Thomas announced his newly found poetic vocation to its chief encourager, the American Robert Frost, in a quotation from Verlaine's 'L'Art poétique': 'I want to wring the necks [*sic*] of all my rhetoric'.[28]

Rather than separate them off into an *ex post facto* English tradition, then, this study will place Owen, Thomas or Hardy back into the same context as their modernist counterparts, the historical situation of the first decades of the twentieth century and their literary-critical inheritance of post-Romantic aesthetics. To write about any kind of non-modernist poetics, though, equally means to register the incontrovertible power of modernism; this book is not an argument with modernist poetry (there is no arguing with *The Waste Land* or 'Mauberley') but with some of the justifications used for it, the principles of self-defining integrity which kept the poetry wars running. By returning the modernist debate about prosody in turn to the original Romantic debate about the limits of power and freedom, however, this book also provides a reading of poetic form opposed to the isolation of formalism. My argument throughout is that a poem's formal structure, its way of spacing time and sound, is inseparable from its connections to history and agency, although it is not reducible to them. Bourdieu has characterised formalism as a forgetting of 'the historical process through which the social conditions of freedom from "external determinations" get established': by taking some time to trace the origins of the idea of prosody and autonomy back to its sources in Coleridge and the German Romantics, my aim is to show how 'external determination' is exactly the argument about form itself in modern and modernist poetics in the first place.[29] Seen historically, in other words, the debate about poetry's autonomy is not only cast in terms of its social responsibilities, but equally in terms of its formal structures, and the fact that the principle covers both makes prosody an inescapable part of post-Romantic poetry's historical and social relations. This perspective makes prosody opposed equally to aesthetic ideology and the recent anathemas against it, which have left critics with no option other than to treat poetry as ideal historical data, promptly reinstating the aestheticist split of form and context in reverse. For in a curious way, the critic who treats poetry without thinking about its form in the name of resisting the anti-contextual, anti-historical seductions of aesthetic 'freedom' is, in fact, recapitulating the situation of the later Romantic Idealists who valued it for just that reason. Romanticism initially celebrated poetry as the archetypal art form because the arbitrary character of its medium – language – ensured the maximum amount of freedom from material constraint. 'No content is in principle unavailable', as J. M. Bernstein puts it, so that 'the arbitrary sign's systematic distance from materiality converges with the freedom of the imagination in a way that is the inverse of the convergence of the syntactical constraints of materiality with the holistic logic of physical beauty'.[30] Hence poetry was elevated above all plastic arts. But rhyme, stress and rhythmic pattern all refuse the complete disappearance of the material qualities of the word in the freedom of the imagination. Poetic form sets up an aesthetic frame in which the external-ity of sound, vowel, consonant and inherent stress-pattern is heard as meaningfully organised. It matters that the poem has these words and no others, not only because the combination of their ideal content is unique, but because their sound combination makes them untranslatable. Hence by asserting the *insistent* materiality of the sign, poetic form ultimately became seen as opposed to the undetermined freedom of the imagination. For the Jena Romantics discussed in chapter 1, the idea of poetry culmin-ates in the novel, because prose collapses the opposition between the words' particular material form and their meaningful content, and hence offers more expansive possibilities of expression.[31] For Hegel, the material of poetry was something ultimately to be discarded in art's progress towards absolute Spirit:

Art frames laws which are supposed every time to harmonize in general with the character of the material to be presented, but in detail they preclude both longs and shorts and the accent from being solely determined by the spiritual meaning and from being rigorously subject to it. But the more inward and spiritual the artistic imagination becomes. . . it is so concentrated in itself that it strips away the, as it were, corporeal side of language and in what remains emphasises only that wherein the spiritual meaning lies for the purpose of communication, and leaves the rest as significant by-play.[32]

Or in other words, poetry's 'spiritual meaning' is free from any de-pendence on the words themselves, the poem is nothing but its mental meaning, and can therefore be translated without loss, as Hegel infam-ously goes on to argue. Criticism that pays attention to the patterns and rhymes of poetry, on the other hand, would always be an acknowledge-ment of the tension between a poem's irreducible particularity, its fini-tude, and the multitude of situations and meanings to which it might ideally be related. The price of paying attention to that particularity, however, is the poem's resistance to being subsumed under any reading, including all the ones in this book. But if the poem's form emphasises the resistance of the letter to any final critical judgement, it is by the same token unable to communicate without such judgement.[33] In reading the meanings of poetic form, that tension animates the many others to which this book tries to do justice: private and public, free and determined, poetic and historic and, not least, modernist and non-modernist.

Finally, in specific readings of the rhythm of such forms, I have adopted Derek Attridge's distinction between a beat (the places where the metre of the poem leads the reader to expect a stress) and the stress itself.[34] This distinction not only makes it easier to discuss the effects of free and formal verse in the same breath, it puts the focus of rhythmic analysis on mental processes rather than on an abstract standard of correctness, which after all was one of the cardinal reasons for romantic and modernist experiments in prosody. It was the mission of Coleridge, and of Pound after him, to ensure that a rhythm was exactly congruent with the passions that created it, and the following chapter examines the problems they had, problems that began with Wordsworth.

# CHAPTER I

# Inside and outside modernism

Like many of the *Lyrical Ballads*, Wordsworth's 'Simon Lee' ends with a sense of disappointment, just as it promises. After describing for nine stanzas the hopeless situation of a poor and weak old huntsman increasingly unable to support himself and his wife, the poem abruptly reins itself in, and apologises for going nowhere:

> My gentle reader, I perceive
> How patiently you've waited,
> And I'm afraid that you expect
> Some tale will be related.
> O reader! had you in your mind
> Such stores as silent thought can bring,
> O gentle reader! you would find
> A tale in every thing.
> What more I have to say is short,
> I hope you'll kindly take it;
> It is no tale; but should you think,
> Perhaps a tale you'll make it.[1]

This moment of self-awareness is simultaneously a hope and a warning. It expresses faith in the power of well-stocked minds to make a meaning from the most unpromising materials. But then, why write this particular poem, if the reader can find a tale wherever he or she looks? On the other hand, if the poem 'Simon Lee' is necessary to making some sort of tale – for moral sense-making, for the 'salutary impression' Wordsworth's 1800 Preface promised this poem would offer – it is also a warning that whatever tale we make of it will not be faithful to the poem's own nature, for 'it is no tale'.[2] In effect, this is a poem about a problem with integrity, for to ensure some sense of narrative and moral completion in the gentle reader's mind, the poem must remain its disappointing, lacking self. This little ethical lesson about the virtue of feeling let down is a preparation for the ending of 'Simon Lee', of course, where the speaker's 'mourning' refuses to be gratified by Simon Lee's gratitude or to feel smug about being charitable. But it is also a version of a much larger question about integrity which is at the heart of Coleridge's disappointed criticisms of this poem, criticisms which set the agenda for the modernist revolution a century later: how does the poem's aesthetic unity relate to the personal integrity of its author?

These problems with integrity become evident in the poem's last stanza. Simon Lee is not strong enough to chop down an old tree, so the speaker of the poem does it for him easily; the old man is grateful, the bonds of human fellowship are renewed and tears are being shed in reciprocal sympathy, yet in the last few words the speaker is unhappy:

> The tears into his eyes were brought
> And thanks and praises seemed to run
> So fast out of his heart, I thought
> They never would have done.
> – I've heard of hearts unkind, kind deeds
> With coldness still returning;
> Alas! the gratitude of men
> Has oftner left me mourning.

What begins as a tale of sympathy ends in sorrow and indignation at the sufferings of Simon Lee, the combination of age and circumstance that has reduced him to penury, and the contrast between his intractable difficulty and the ease with which the speaker helped him. The moral that suggests itself here concerns the injustice of Simon Lee's situation. His gratitude leaves the speaker mourning because it is so out of proportion to the effort it took; evidently Simon was not expecting help because he had not often been given it, yet if his old age can be eased so simply, why has this not happened more often, and what sort of society is it that leaves him to struggle?

However, there is something else amiss in this last stanza. Hitherto, the poem's short ballad metre has ensured a very regular and strong three beats in each stanza's fourth and eighth line, with some flexibility about the second and sixth lines. But in order to make the fourth line have the innocent meaning, 'I thought his tears would never finish', a reader has to add a slight extra stress on 'have' to match the natural double stress in the phrase 'have done with it'. For a reading stressed exactly with the beats suggests something else, that his tears 'néver wóuld have dóne', that they were improper for any socially respectable situation. With this hint at the respectability of the audience addressed ('my gentle reader'), and the inner sense of social propriety in the speaker, the rhythm suggests another source of disquiet that has been there all along, namely the inseparable presence of self-congratulation alongside the act of charity or the call for justice. So eager is the narrator to emphasise the sufferings of the poor that his stage-whispered asides have frequently dipped his subject into undignified bathos:

> He says he is three score and ten,
> But others say he's eighty.
>
> For still, the more he works, the more
> His poor old ancles swell.

Simon Lee is poor and old, but 'poor old' does not distinguish itself sufficiently from the patronisingly familiar: it might be Simon Lee's own words ('as he to you will tell'), but whether the distance between the speaker and Simon Lee can be so lightly leaped over is begging the poem's whole question. The repeated deixis of 'he' shows the speaker's determination to keep pointing Simon Lee and his infirmities out:

> His hunting feats have him bereft
> Of his right eye, as you may see . . .
>
> He has no son, he has no child
> His wife, an aged woman . . .
>
> And he is lean and he is sick,
> His little body's half awry . . .

And as the reader becomes more aware of the respectability of the speaker's mental audience, such crusading on behalf of the dispossessed starts to sound more like a means of demonstrating how much the speaker cares, which would explain the curiously anguished bounciness of verses like this:

> Beside their moss-grown hut of clay,
> Not twenty paces from the door,
> A scrap of land they have, but they
> Are poorest of the poor.
> This scrap of land he from the heath
> Enclosed when he was stronger;
> But what avails the land to them,
> Which they can till no longer?

Jingles and clichés such as 'poorest of the poor' and, earlier, 'sole survivor' betray a certain ready-to-hand terminology that sits uncomfortably with a poem about charity. Similarly, the jollity of the double rhymes such as stronger/longer, weighty/eighty, merry/cherry, Ivor/survivor and so on feels too comically well resolved for the distress they disclose. The poem's form is mismatched to its content, like someone singing the lyrics of 'A slumber did my spirit seal' to the tune of 'I'm the King of the Swingers'. So when the final stanza closes with a sudden off-rhyme of 'mourning' and 'returning', those preceding double rhymes ensure the change is palpable. It suggests that the speaker has realised that Simon Lee's gratitude is out of proportion, that both have been playing their part in a bad, eighteenth-century sentimental poem where charity is rewarded with floods of tears and mutual gratification. There are, in effect, two tales which might be made here, one that believes in charity and wonders about justice, and one that is radically suspicious of the self-interest behind charity, making sympathy with the poor an expressive opportunity for rich self-congratulation. When the pathos of the poem topples over into bathos, it exposes the whole economy of this kind of sentimentalism. Hence the disappointment felt at the end of the poem would be an immunisation against the vanity of charity, which is parasitically dependent upon the social structures of human unkindness which have left Simon Lee poor.[3] Unintentionally, the speaker has participated in injustice at the same time as relieving its effects.

Yet self-suspicion also has its implications, for it is not certain that making the poem a cautionary tale about the vanity of charity would be less selfish or patronising than making it one about kindness. Mourning one's own complicity could be a peculiarly enjoyable moment of grittiness, the self-isolating comfort of knowing oneself one's own sharpest critic. And Simon Lee really was helped: if his thanks and praise are just false consciousness, then to mourn the way that the poor have been indoctrinated into gratitude instead of being angry at systemic injustice has the effect of robbing him of any right to his own emotions, which would patronise him still further. Simon Lee is grateful for a kind act whatever the speaker's underlying motives, unless the reader is *really* suspicious about those tears. Worrying about one's own kindness would perpetuate the self-absorption the poem was to expose, and regretting an act of charity in itself simply maintains the status quo. The poem's disappointment, in fact, might be prompted not only by injustice and selfishness, but the necessary failure of any transparent justification of motivations and acts, because its speaker is always too involved.

Coleridge also felt let down by this poem, but on account of its aesthetics rather than its moral uncertainty. In *Biographia Literaria*, he numbered it among those specimens of Wordsworth's poetry that 'notwithstanding the beauties which are to be found in each of them where the poet interposes the music of his own thoughts, would have been more delightful to me in prose'.[4] The passage occurs during the famous chapter on the function of poetic metre, in which he argues that metre is not an abstract system for organising words into art, but depends on the import of those words for its own appropriateness. The trouble with 'Simon Lee' was that the absence of a tale has left nothing important enough to warrant Wordsworth's making a poem out it. For 'poetry, Mr Wordsworth truly affirms, does always imply PASSION ... The very *act* of poetic composition *itself* is, and is *allowed* to imply and to produce, an unusual state of excitement, which of course justifies and demands a correspondent difference of language' (71–2). If '*metre itself* implies a passion, i.e. a state of excitement, both in the Poet's mind, & is expected in that of the Reader', as Coleridge wrote to Sotheby in 1802, then the poem's emotional content must match the metre, and that of 'Simon Lee' does not.[5] It is classed alongside 'The Sailor's Mother', whose rhymes furnish a sense of 'oddity and strangeness' at 'finding *rhymes at all* in sentences so exclusively colloquial' (70). If the metre arouses expectation and the words do not fulfil it, 'there must needs be a disappointment felt; like that of leaping in the dark from the last step of a stair-case, when we had prepared our muscles for a leap of three or four' (66).

This disappointment is not merely a local flaw in 'Simon Lee', however, because Coleridge then puts the 'same argument in a more general form' (72), one that will apply to the whole of the aesthetic:

*All* the parts of an organized whole must be assimilated to the more *important* and *essential* parts. This and the preceding arguments may be strengthened by the reflection, that the composition of a poem is among the *imitative* arts; and that imitation, as opposed to copying, consists either in the interfusion of the SAME throughout the radically DIFFERENT, or of the different throughout a base radically the same. (72)

Wordsworth's disjunction between prosaic content and metrical form has broken the fundamental organisational principle of art, which is imitation rather than copying. Coleridge's confusing distinction becomes clearer when it is understood that the difference is less about the realism or abstraction of art than its internal consistency. The work of art does not draw its purpose from pretending to be a natural object (such as wax fruit), but from the way it coheres according to its own internal principles while imitating something else, the same in the different. A copy has insufficient difference from an exterior model, but an imitation is structurally independent of the thing it respectfully imitates. Coleridge's idea of 'imitation' is here drawing on the idea of living form in Schiller's *Aesthetic Education* and behind that, Kant's *Critique of Judgement*, for which 'art can be called fine [schön] art only if we are conscious that it is art while yet it looks to us like Nature'.[6] That is, it is art in so far as it seems to appear on its own account, as Schiller glosses Kant's passage:

> First of all, we must know that the beautiful thing is a natural object, that is, that it is through itself; secondly, it must seem to us as if it existed through a rule, since Kant says that it must look like art. The two claims *it is through itself* and *it is through a rule* can only be combined in a single manner, namely if one says: *it is through a rule which it has given itself.* Autonomy in technique, freedom in artfulness.[7]

In imitation, the formal rules are not exterior to the content but coextensive with it; 'Simon Lee' is bad art because the pathetic content is too patently being pushed around by a metrical form which does not derive from its nature. True art is thoroughly 'assimilated' into unity, and because unified, free from external determination.

This violation of the true poem's autonomy lies at the heart of all of *Biographia Literaria*'s complaints against Wordsworth. By thinking of the Cumbrian peasantry as somehow poetic in and of themselves, he has failed to see that 'poetry as poetry is essentially *ideal*, that it avoids and excludes all *accident*' of individual circumstance (46), because the accidental would mean there was a point in the art in which the form of the art work did not determine itself. Claiming that rustic language is more naturally poetic suffers the same problem, because the uneducated labourer is likely to '*particularize*' his feelings, rather than reflect on them, and it is through the operation of reflection that any sense of freedom from immediate circumstance is gained (54). 'There is a want of that prospectiveness of mind, that *surview*, which enables a man to foresee the whole of what he is to convey, appertaining to any one point' (58), and without such freedom of expression, the diction will be determined by local circumstance. On the same principle, throughout chapter 18 of *Biographia Literaria*, Coleridge takes issue with Wordsworth's idea that there '*neither is nor can be any essential difference between the language of prose and metrical composition*', because it would imply that metre was simply external to the language used, rather than the poem being an inseparable unity of the two (60). The point he particularly objects to is when Wordsworth, having conceded that rhyme and metre obviously do make a difference to ordinary language 'of themselves', insists that the difference does not 'pave the way to other distinctions' between prose and verse language. 'The distinction of rhyme and metre is voluntary and uniform', he writes, 'and not like that produced by (what is called) poetic diction, arbitrary and subject to infinite caprices, upon which no calculation can be made'.[8] Quoting this part of the sentence, Coleridge explodes, 'But is this a *poet*, of whom a poet is speaking? No surely!' (81). True poets are never arbitrary or capricious, and if we do not trust the poet's genius, as Wordsworth implies we must not, it implies there is a rule for harmony, which would be the antithesis of art: 'Could a rule be given from *without*, poetry would cease to be poetry, and sink into a mechanical art. It would be μόρφωσις [morphosis] not ποίησις [poiesis]. The *rules* of the IMAGINATION are themselves the very powers of growth and production' (83–4). Poiesis creates; morphosis merely shapes from the outside. This principle applies to metre as well, for the sentence of Wordsworth that Coleridge interrupted continues to insist that unlike poetic diction, 'the metre obeys certain laws, to which the Poet and Reader both willingly submit'. But there is no language of submission to law in Coleridge, for when he suggests the psychological origins of metre at the beginning of the chapter, he describes it as a union of '*spontaneous* impulse' and '*voluntary* purpose' (65). The essential tension or balance of metre is derived from the poet's impulse and his willing control of it, not between his desires and an external system to which he must submit.

Situated where it is in *Biographia Literaria*, Coleridge's aesthetic complaint against 'Simon Lee' thus involves considerably more than simple aesthetics. For drawing on Schiller's idea of art as an aesthetic education, *Biographia Literaria* proposes a model of poetry in which the freedom from external determination that guarantees the poem's completeness of being makes it a guide for human progress and education.[9] Simply copying the real language of men (as Wordsworth claimed to have taken a line 'word for word' from Simon Lee), or bolting on a metre to something unpoetic ( as Coleridge accused Wordsworth of doing) makes the work dependent on exterior events or rules, whereas it is precisely its imaginative autonomy, its unity with itself through reconciling 'opposite or discordant qualities' which makes it free and the ideal, 'graceful and intelligent whole' that is the goal of human development (16, 17).[10] These considerations underlie Coleridge's famous adaptation of A. W. Schlegel's ideas about organic form. A poem's form is organic when it 'is innate, it shapes as it develops itself from within', as opposed to being formed from outside with a 'pre-determined form, not necessarily arising out of the properties of the material', like moulded clay.'' Thinking of the work of art as internally organised, organicism rejects the subordination of any part as a means to an overall end, and hence any poem where the form is conspicuously determining the content. Rather, content and form are inseparable, and organicism is thus of a piece with autonomy for a poetic which makes the characteristic quality of the true work of art its freedom from all *exteriority*. In its brief criticisms of the form of 'Simon Lee', *Biographia Literaria* expresses for English readers the dominant political motif of European Romantic aesthetics, which made the work of art of supreme importance because it models the highest possibilities of human development, freedom and self-determination.

Yet on Coleridge's own logic, Wordsworth could have replied that if 'Simon Lee' were not a strictly organic poem, neither is it an inorganic one. For a problem with self-determination is exactly Wordsworth's point: its speaker thinks he is doing a kindness, yet on second reading turns out to be playing out a prescriptive sentimental fantasy which in turn derives from unequal social relations. Hence the poem's form here occupies a strange position as both interior to and necessarily somewhat exterior to the content. The double rhymes, for example, are inseparable from the poem's entire meaning, and to change them would be to change that meaning. But part of that meaning is that finally they are revealed as an external force which has been pushing the poem along in a direction in which it does not, finally, want to travel. In a sense, the poem confirms everything a militant organicist would argue against over-regular form, that it is rhythmic exteriority that inevitably leads to moral coerciveness. And yet this ability to pitch form against content, to give Coleridge his sense of disappointment, is precisely what allows the poem to indicate that something is wrong, that the speaker has been saying one thing and meaning another. The remorselessly jolly rhymes and bouncy metre suggest very well the emotional briskness which would treat poor people as objects to be assisted. And the flat, awkward ending is made possible because the regular form makes the reader expect a double rhyme and then not get it, which makes the present moment of disappointment then ironise everything that precedes it. Were the form always simply doing what the content was saying, such internal divisions could not occur. But because its regular pattern can make non-syntactic, non-linear links between elements of the poem, can play off one part of the poem against another, it offers a sense of several different forces working at once, pulling and dividing the material in different directions, in mixed emotions or divided loyalties; the poem is not wholly autonomous because the situation it talks about is not. Its formal exteriority is thus also 'within' the poem, as Coleridge put it, and this indeterminacy between within and without renders exactly the moral difficulty of 'Simon Lee', namely, how much of our action is self- determined and how much determined by exterior structures which create the conditions of that self's possibility. And Wordsworth's questioning of the borders of personal and formal autonomy has implications for the more usual sense of the 'autonomy' of the aesthetic, its freedom from moral or philosophical subsumption; for if, as Nigel Leask and others have suggested, Coleridge's aesthetics rework the anti-authoritarian implications of self-legislation into a conservative isolation of the aesthetic from wider society, then Wordsworth's internal externality implicitly refuses such an absolute separation.[12] Intransigently, Wordsworth's poetic form raises the vexed question of *agency*.

This unresolved debate about what is within the poem and what from outside it prefigures the relations between modernism and its contemporaries with uncanny foresight. For the question of poetic form that arises in the twentieth century is, as with Coleridge, always at the same time a debate about how to write poetry which is true to itself and to the self that created it, and thus implicitly involves the question of where those selves begin and end. The test that Pound and Eliot consistently applied to justify their own distinctive forms – and to criticise the Georgians' – was that of total integrity; poetry meant the elimination of all external agency, be it using other people's forms, second-hand thinking or simply 'rhetoric', and this demand provides one of the hidden continuities between Pound's predominantly individualist aesthetic and Eliot's anti-individualist one. Wordsworth's difficulties with agency, on the other hand, suggest a reason why Hardy, Thomas and Owen should be interested in a degree of aesthetic artificiality and awkwardness, a certain irresolvable formal dissonance from their content.

Such dissonance, however, gains its particular acuteness from its place in a literary period in which there was a wider movement against rhetoric, custom and convention in poetry than just the modernists, a movement in which Hardy, Thomas and Owen were a vital part. Like the disagreements between Wordsworth and Coleridge, the story of the poetry wars does not make sense without understanding how close the two sides originally were. The sections that follow explore the way that between 1912 and 1914, Georgians and Imagists alike were devoted to the ideal of direct and immediate poetry and, under the auspices of the Poetry

Bookshop, were both theorising about the sort of poetic mind that would produce such poems, without cliché, self-consciousness or convention, a realism premised on removing the filters of custom. What this boils down to is a common desire for a poetry whose agency would be utterly singular: that is, it would have its own voice, rather than borrowed words, thoughts or morals, and would thus be necessarily fresh and immediate – literally, un-mediated. But like Wordsworth's case for the real language of men, many Georgians tried to find this singularity by imitating sensibilities they imagined to be unified because they were unconventional – reprobates such as John Masefield's Saul Kane, Wilfrid Gibson's working people, or Lascelles Abercrombie's peasants. Their shock tactics of horrible subject-matter (corpse-washing, frog-crushing, sea-sickness) are similarly a resistance to anything that would filter or dissipate the poem's impact. Imagism, however, took a more Coleridgean line by insisting what mattered was not the authenticity of the poem's extra-poetic sources or the nature of the subject-matter, but its unity with itself. Most obviously, it is organic form's claim that metre be derived from within the poetic content, or the poet's interior intention, that sponsors the Imagist introduction of free verse.[13] Drawing on Coleridge's pervasive plant imagery, Pound published an Imagist 'Credo' for the readers of Harold Monro's *Poetry Review* in 1912:

I think there is a 'fluid' as well as a 'solid' content, that some poems may have form as a tree has form, some as water poured into a vase. That most symmetrical forms have certain uses. That a vast number of subjects cannot be precisely, and therefore not properly rendered in symmetrical forms.[14]

The kerfuffle when Pound changes course mid-sentence from discussing 'content' to 'form', and then switches back again at the end to make water both form and content is, in the end, only consonant with his point that there should be no identifiable divergence between the two. Pound was not, of course, arguing that free verse was the only permissible kind of poetry, since unlike some of his fellow Imagists, he was no enemy of traditional form for its own sake. 'There is great freedom in pentameter', he insisted in 1915, 'and there are a great number of regular and beautifully regular metres fit for a number of things, and quite capable of expressing a wide range of energies and emotions'.[15] Nor, he was keen to point out to the poetry-reading public, was Eliot a one-trick poet: 'If the reader wishes mastery of "regular form", the *Conversation Galante* is sufficient to show that symmetrical form is within Mr Eliot's grasp. You will hardly find such neatness save in France; such modern neatness, save in Laforgue'.[16]

Rather than eradicating traditional verse forms, modernist poetry changed the justification for them. In order to argue for free verse's rightful place, the criteria for verse-form had to become the entire appropriateness of the form to the meaning, and here Pound was simply putting Coleridge's poetics into practice. 'Since Dryden', declared Coleridge, 'the Metre of our Poets leads to the Sense: in our elder and more genuine Poets, the Sense, including the Passion, leads to the metre'.[17] Or as Pound put it: 'Poetry is a composition or an "organisation" of words set to music. By "music" here we can scarcely mean much more than rhythm and timbre. The rhythm form is false unless it belong to the particular creative emotion or energy which it purports to represent.'[18] And in free verse, the idea was that the exterior form would *necessarily* be in perfect correspondence with the interior content: there could be no manipulation of the latter to fit any prearranged pattern, and hence the poem itself would be true to what it talked about, and embody a sensibility utterly at one with itself. Hence when Pound accused his neo-Wordsworthian contemporaries of rhetoric and inaccuracy, his argument essentially repeated Coleridge's strictures against Wordsworth, only with a neater pun; Eliot's work, he sighed thankfully, is 'a great and blessed relief after the official dulness and Wordsworthian lignification of the "Georgian" Anthologies', where 'lignification' combines turning to wood and making a line. Wooden form typifies poetry whose perspective is borrowed ('official dulness') and in consequence, untrue to itself.[19]

Nevertheless, because Georgian and Imagist poets shared basically similar goals, they ran into the same difficulty, for by trying so hard to make the poem the expression of a singular or unified consciousness, both groups actually ended up promoting the poet's self rather more than the poem. As Eliot noted, the effort to avoid rhetoric itself became a convention, and his way out of convention was not to ignore other poets but to find oneself through them, a process he later called 'Tradition'. The great shift in modernist poetics from a model of poetry as unfettered self-expression (subsequently labelled 'Romantic') to one that is explicitly anti-Romantic and anti-individualist (or 'Classical') stems from a reaction to this problem of writing a truly free poetry. In distrusting the individualism of Amy Lowell's brand of free verse, Classicism formed a theoretical anchor for the return to strict quatrains in Pound and Eliot's poems after 1916, and in its formulation as 'Tradition', almost simultaneously the fragmented polyphony of what were becoming the *Cantos* and *The Waste Land*. But what is concealed by this shift of terms is the way that modernist classicism is in fact based on the same Coleridgean ideas about autonomy as the Romanticism it despised, for the very terms of the opposition are taken from two of Coleridge's most influential sources, Schiller and Schlegel. Schiller's influence is evident in the way T. E. Hulme first uses the terms, where 'classicism' turns out not to mean submission to higher authority, but organic poetry based on Schiller's concept of the classically 'naïve' poet. Similarly, 'Tradition', in Eliot's formulation, does not mean common custom, but something much closer to Schlegel's idea of the Romantic fragment poem – a polyphonic space where all possible tension between what belongs to an individual poem or poet and what is exterior to it would dissolve in irony, and where it forms, in Eliot's subsequent discussion, an 'organic whole'.[20] By tracing Hulme and Eliot's sources to these arch-Romantic German idealists, it becomes possible to see the continuity between what look like wildly differing concepts of poetry, modernism's simultaneous attraction to minimalism (the elimination of the superfluous) and maximalism (the incorporation of hugely various cultures and influences). 'Romanticism', Eliot admonished his students in 1916, 'stands for *excess* in any direction'; but it was excess, in the sense of any kind of externality of form or influence, that both Romantic and modernist poetics were designed to make impossible.[21] The rest of the book is about why non-modernist poets might have found it useful.

Tracing these early stages of the poetry wars, however, is made more difficult by the way that there was no great showdown between Thomas, Hardy and Owen and their modernist counterparts, and their individual responses to modernism have to be reconstructed from hints and guesses; by the time Eliot published 'Tradition and the Individual Talent', two of them were dead and the others were sufficiently established to have little interest in justifying their work in a theoretical way. But like Wordsworth, that did not mean that in conspicuously retaining a sense of exteriority, their poetry might not ask awkward questions about the self-enclosure of organic, autonomous poetics. For Hardy, Thomas or Owen's poems are about situations that are not self-determined, where the exterior or alien is very much at work. Yet they are not the less Romantic for doing so; rather, they suggest a reason for seeing tension between what belongs and what is extraneous to the poem not as a failure, but as a truth which is also visible in the freest verse, and the most truly organic.

2

The Poetry Bookshop was always an awkward institution for those wishing to dissociate modernist poetry from its contemporaries. By 1915, not only had its proprietor, Harold Monro, published the first Imagist anthology, *Des Imagistes*, followed by Aldington's *Images* and Flint's *Cadences*, as well as a Futurist anthology, but two volumes of *Georgian Poetry*, on whose success *Des Imagistes* had been based. Pound had actually given Monro's own work a place in the next Poetry Bookshop publication, the *Catholic Anthology* (along with Eliot and Joyce), but after the war took the opportunity to lambast him for his eclectic publishing policy: 'Only *HELL* – you've never had a programme – you've always dragged in Aberbubble and Siphon, and Wobblebery and wanted to exploit the necropolis . . . One always suspects you of having (and knows you have had) sympathy with a lot of second-rate slopp – and never knows when the ancient sin will break out again.'[22]

But Monro could honestly reply that hitherto he had not seen quite what was so uniquely compelling about Pound's own programme. In a 1915 article on the Imagists, he had remarked: 'It has never become very clear in what particular respects they may be considered innovators', and drawing their avant-garde sting, adduced Jonson, Dryden, Addison, Burke, Coleridge and Arnold in support of the Imagist goals of 'accuracy of vision, precision of language, and concentration'. Nor, he declared, are they particular innovators within their own time, being 'one of the latest groups in the forward movement of English poetry – not the only one'.[23] This criticism evidently hurt, because a swift reply in the next issue from the Imagist May Sinclair argued that Monro had a problem with labels. The poet H. D., she protested, doesn't need Jonson, Shakespeare, Wordsworth or Arnold, for her verse 'stands by itself in its own school'.[24] Unfortunately, this also meant that H. D. was not an Imagist either, and the absurdity of justifying Imagism because none of its poets actually belonged to it underlines the threat that Monro's comment represented. For Imagism's foremost commandment had been 'direct treatment of the thing', and if it could be shown that such 'direct treatment' had a tradition behind it, it could not be as direct as all that.[25] Worse for Sinclair, it was Monro himself who had done the most to make the general reader aware that Imagism did not differ unequivocally from the company it kept, because he was the editor of the first magazines in which Imagists and non-Imagists had alike made their case for brevity, precision and accuracy.

In 1912, for example, Monro's *Poetry Review* provided the British reader with several key staging-posts in what was to become modernism. In February, it printed Pound's 'Prolegomena', a programme for what was to be announced as Imagism, along with some new Imagist poems by Pound. In July it sponsored T. E. Hulme's lecture 'The New Philosophy of Art as Illustrated in Poetry', which was republished as 'Romanticism and Classicism', the essay whose call for classical dryness and hardness

began a second phase of modernist poetics, associated with abstract geo-
metric art and Eliot's impersonal poetry.[26] In October it provided the first
English appearance of William Carlos Williams's poetry, with commentary by Pound. But the *Poetry Review* was not a modernist house organ, it
was an outgrowth of the Poetry Bookshop, and the Georgian poets are
equally in evidence. 'Prolegomena', for example, is followed by reviews
of Lascelles Abercrombie; in the August issue Richard Aldington reviews on the same page as Rupert Brooke, and most of the magazine is
taken up with Flint's exhaustive survey of 'Contemporary French Poetry',
whose appearance should be contrasted with Eliot's accusation that Georgian verse 'takes not the faintest notice of the development of French verse
from Baudelaire to the present day'.[27] This mixture carried on when the
*Poetry Review* seceded to Stephen Phillips in 1913 and Monro began *Poetry
and Drama*, which provided regular exposure for works by the Georgian
anthologists (awarding a prize to Rupert Brooke's 'Grantchester'), and at
the same time, to Pound's circle and other avant-garde movements, so
that Futurism and Imagism were each given a whole issue to promote
their poetry and manifestos. In fact, Hulme was one of the Brooke prize
judges. A reader of *Poetry and Drama* in December 1914 could see poems
by Frost, Davies, Pound, Aldington and Lawrence and prose by Edward
Thomas and Rémy de Gourmont, the Symbolist critic whom Pound
admired and Eliot named one of his two perfect critics. The Imagist
special issue puts Flint's 'French Chronicle' and Pound's new poems
alongside Edward Thomas on the art of bad reviewing, and Monro in
praise of W. H. Davies. The June 1914 issue contains Thomas on reprints,
Hulme's 'German Chronicle' with its important recantation of his previous Imagism, and almost in summary of the mix, a reprinting of work
from both *Des Imagistes* and *New Numbers*, the self-publicising magazine
set up by Brooke, Gibson, Abercrombie and Drinkwater. What with its
Imagist issue, Futurist issue, Flint's up-to-the-minute 'French Chronicle'
and Hulme's introductions to German Expressionism, the subscribers to
*Poetry and Drama* (who included Thomas Hardy) would probably have
been better informed about new movements in European modernism
than anyone else in the country, as well as thoroughly familiar with the
Georgian poets. Such catholicism may simply reflect Monro's uneven
taste, as Pound thought, but actually looking at the articles themselves
reveals that Monro's editorial policy was rather more consistent than was
convenient for Pound's retrospective self-fashioning.

In January, the first number of his editorship of the *Poetry Review*,
Monro set forward his programme, declaring boldly that 'it is now at last

absolutely necessary for the fetters of stereotyped poetic language to be shaken off.[28] In order for modern poetry to be modern, 'the modern poet's equipment must include, apart from the natural adoration of beauty, a clear and sound grasp upon facts, and a stupendous aptitude for assimilation':

The goal is nothing less than the final re-welding of metre to meaning, and it cannot, in the nature of things, be achieved until man has attained a second innocence, a self-obliviousness beyond self-consciousness, a super-consciousness; that condition, in fact, produced only by a complete knowledge of his own meaning . . . a fastidious selection of topic, language and form . . . it must be packed and tense with meaning; no line may be thin, no link may rattle.

(11–13)

When the magazine published Pound's 'Prolegomena' in the February issue, therefore, a subscriber to the *Poetry Review* would not have noticed any sudden swerve in editorial policy. Pound's demand for 'the trampling down of every convention that impedes or obscures' (73) corresponds to Monro's unfettering of stereotyped poetic language, or his declaration in 'Freedom' that 'a new diction is demanded . . . the Modern poet will be free, at all hazards, from the conventions of his predecessors'.[29] Pound's belief in 'an "absolute rhythm", a rhythm, that is, in poetry which corresponds exactly to the emotion or shade of emotion to be expressed' (73) accords with Monro's 're-welding of metre to meaning' above. Monro's 'fastidious selection' and dislike of thin lines resembles Pound's whittling down of 'In a Station of the Metro' from thirty lines to two in the cause of 'maximum efficiency of expression'.[30] Both Monro and Pound are announcing a programme of poetry based on expelling any-thing extraneous, for just as Pound's 'absolute' rhythm is an 'uncounter-feiting, uncounterfeitable' record of the poet's sensibilities, so Monro's 'complete knowledge of his own meaning' implies there is nothing about the poet's materials which is beyond his ken – as Pound put it a few months later, '"good writing" is perfect control'.[31] Pound printed '$\Delta\acute{\omega}\varrho\iota\alpha$' to show what he meant by 'austere, direct' poetry (76), but he had been forestalled: in the January issue, the Georgian W. W. Gibson was praised for his diction of 'direct and unadorned austerity' and then censured for taking it too far, from 'an austere simplicity to baldness'.[32] A few pages later, ironically, Pound was criticised by his fellow Imagist Flint for his second-hand work; despite Pound's praise of Daniel and Cavalcanti's 'testimony of the eyewitness' and their 'first hand' symptoms, thought Flint, 'so much of his inspiration seems bookish, so much of his attraction lies in the vivid picturesqueness of his romance-besprinkled page'.[33] It was not only Monro's articles that resembled Pound's Imagism. In the March 1912 issue, Pound's Georgian foe Lascelles Abercrombie wrote a long article on 'The Function of Poetry in the Drama', arguing that poetry requires a different attitude to character, for poetry allows its speakers 'a certain powerful simplification and exaggeration, so that the primary impulses of being are infinitely more evident' and their speech has an 'intense unobstructed significance'. In poetry alone, he continues, 'the primary emotional urge of our being is conveyed directly, immediately into our apprehension'.[34] Less significant than the truth of his ideas is the key Imagist vocabulary of intensity, directness and immediacy to describe the essence of poetic communication; compare Pound's 'direct treatment' and instant presentation of the Image, or his clarification that 'an image, in our sense, is real, because we know it directly'.[35] Just as Abercrombie believed that this direct poetry would allow the 'primary emotional urge' to be transmitted, so Pound's '$Δώρια$' is also, in Flint's words, 'a perfect translation of pure emotion', H. D.'s work that of a poet who 'will accept nothing that has not come to her direct, that has not sprung immediately out of her own contemplation'.[36] Consequently, the Imagist justifications for free verse based on direct transmission of the impulse sound remarkably similar to Georgian justifications for metre. Imagism was for free verse because it allowed 'the precise rendering of the impulse', in Pound's terms.[37] Or, as Richard Aldington expanded:

The old accented verse forced the poet to abandon some of his individuality, most of his accuracy and all his style in order to wedge his emotions into some preconceived and sometimes childish formality; free verse permits the poet all his individuality because he creates his cadence instead of copying other people's, all his accuracy because with his cadence flowing naturally he tends to write naturally and therefore with precision, and all his style because style consists in concentration, and exactness which could only be obtained rarely in the old forms.[38]

Needless to say, Aldington does not heed his own advice about style being concentration and not wedging your style into a preconceived formality, as his sentence's inordinate length is entirely determined by its ternary parallelism. But his overall focus is clear: free verse allows the poet to be natural, at one with himself, his individuality never compromised by convention. Such absence of convention also allows him to write accurately and precisely. Ironically, this was exactly the same argument that Abercrombie used for regular metre:

Metre gives to the poet's words a *form* which is itself a direct expression of the emotion which the words enclose. Not only does the underlying consistent beat keep our answering emotions in the necessary state of excitation, but the sudden varieties and modulations of metre, the momentary deviations from consistency, are most powerful suggesters of shifting changes and unexpected upward rushes of emotion.[39]

The difference in technique only makes the criteria of complete unity of form and feeling more obvious. 'What the Imagists are "out for" is direct naked contact with reality,' explained May Sinclair in response to Monro's summary of Imagism's faults in *The Egoist*.[40] In the article that follows Abercrombie's, Gibson summarises neatly: 'Poetry is not the decorating or disguising, but the unveiling of truth . . . the most direct, trenchant, terse and intimate of the arts.'[41]

These similarities suggest that, rather than veering in several directions, Monro saw himself editing a publication whose overall slogan was direct transmission of the poetic impulse. Unsurprisingly, there are strong similarities in the terms of approval and disapproval on both sides. Rupert Brooke wrote that Gibson, 'with an almost terrifying severity' abstained from '"romantic" devices' with a 'careful pruning of every unnecessary part . . . every superfluous ounce removed'.[42] This stripped-down verse reflects Gibson's accuracy, for 'perfect technique in poetry consists in keeping carefully before the mind the precise shade of feeling of the idea you want to evoke': compare Pound's continual insistence on rendering subjects 'precisely . . . whether of external nature or of emotion'.[43] Edward Thomas praised the Georgian Ralph Hodgson's *Eve and Other Poems* because their lack of Victorian decoration meant there was 'nothing between their beauty and the reader', allowing Thomas to 'recall what poetry was before Keats and Tennyson had so adorned it that it could run and ring too seldom'.[44] Walter de la Mare thought Hodgson's work 'bare, vivid, wasteless – as near action as words can be'. His speech is 'clean and incisive as a blow', because 'it does not argue, it does not dissect or explore or teach or attempt to criticise life', a criticism which sounds remarkably like Pound's explanation that the image is 'constatation of fact. It presents. It does not comment . . . It is not a criticism of life.'[45] Such similarities of argument only underscore the difference in the actual poetry, of course. But when Monro does make a comparison of *Des Imagistes* with Abercrombie's latest publication in the Imagist number of *Poetry and Drama*, the expected terms are reversed. Far from being direct and immediate, the Imagists are 'Faint, shadowy, cool, almost, it must be said, mellifluous, their few words enmesh images, hint,

imply, suggest; seek, while never too hotly pursuing; find, but never
definitely articulate; hold you out their meaning, but withhold it before
your grasp.'[46]

This flowing, indefinite netting of images deliberately ironises
Aldington's demands for poetry with 'a hardness of cut stone', or
Pound's hatred of 'slush' and 'mushy technique'.[47] For Monro, their
gentle vagueness contrasts violently with Abercrombie's 'End of the
World', which sounds like a generic description of a modernist poem:
'It is the precise opposite of impressionism. Detail brims over from its
lines. It is difficult, hard, tough. One imagines the average reader baffled
by it.'[48] While on the Imagists' side, Flint praised Frost for his 'direct
observation of the object and immediate correlation with the emotion'.[49] Pound too admired Frost's ability to 'paint the thing, the thing
as he sees it', although Frost stubbornly resisted the latter's attempts to
get him to write free verse.[50]

Familiar with such a mixture, the reader of Monro's publications
would perhaps have not have thought it remarkable to find that the *Poetry
Review* was sponsoring a lecture by T. E. Hulme in 1912 – a lecture which
became 'Romanticism and Classicism' with its famous call for poetry to
be a 'compromise for a language of intuition which would hand over
sensations bodily', a language only one remove from neurotransmission.[51]
This language Hulme defined as 'Classical', against 'Romantic' indirection and imprecision, and in doing so, presaged the movement against
'personality' in modernist criticism which culminates in Eliot's 'Tradition
and the Individual Talent'. But it is the anti-Romanticism of this very
essay that has helped disguise the most obvious common factor between
the Georgian and Imagist programmes: their mutual reliance on Romantic thought, and especially Wordsworth's Preface to *Lyrical Ballads*.
Pound's insistence that 'the "image" is the furthest possible remove from
rhetoric' echoes Wordsworth's famous calls for 'simple and unelaborated
expressions', a style of 'nakedness and simplicity' with 'little of what is
usually called poetic diction'.[52] As Eliot himself said in 1942, without
drawing out the implications: 'Every revolution in poetry is apt to be, and
sometimes to announce itself as, a return to common speech. That is the
revolution that Wordsworth announced in his prefaces and he was right
. . . and the same revolution was due again something over a century
later'.[53]

The image as incarnation of all directness finds its ancestor in
Wordsworth's assertion that 'there is no object standing between
the Poet and the image of things': indeed, Wordsworth summarises

triumphantly, 'Poetry is the image of man and nature' (752). No wonder that Monro's article on Imagism remarked that 'Wordsworth (if Christ was a Socialist) might almost be called an Imagist in theory'– a sly thrust at Imagist separatism, since Wordsworth was patently the tutelary genius of the Georgians. Abercrombie's peasants, Gibson's working poor, Brooke's sunny youth, Masefield's ne'er-do-wells, Thomas's tramps and de la Mare's children all manifest the *Lyrical Ballads'* fascination for a subject who would speak without compromise or convention: since W. H. Davies actually was a beggar and a tramp, he simply wrote as himself, an irony whose implications I will pursue in chapter four.[54] Yet this little stab also carried the justification for Monro's inclusive editorial policy, because it links the Wordsworthian subjects favoured by Georgian poets with the Wordsworthian aims of Imagist technique; in 1917 Pound himself was to call Wordsworth 'a silly old sheep with a genius, an unquestionable genius, for imagisme'.[55] Like Wordsworth, both group's strictures against rhetoric are made the cause of a poetry whose expression would be true to the 'primary laws of our nature' and 'the essential passions of the heart' (743), as exemplified by the humble and rustic who live without the influence of 'social vanity' (744). However implausible its sociology, the Preface to *Lyrical Ballads* opens with a model of personal sincerity uncompromised by social falsehood, and Coleridge criticised Wordsworth's ideas about technique because he felt they failed to live up to Wordsworth's own principles about such sincerity; most obviously, the latter's disastrous idea that metre was an 'intertexture of ordinary feeling . . . not strictly and necessarily connected with the passion' (755), which would make Wordsworth's form foreign to his expression of the 'essential passions of the heart'. Or, as Pound declared to the *Poetry Review* readership, 'I believe in technique as a test of a man's sincerity'.[56] Free verse is the opposite of rhetoric, for Aldington, because nothing would impede 'some real observation, some accurate expression of emotion'.[57] Pound's direct, cut-down poetics are about unimpeded emotional accuracy:

Poetry is the statement of overwhelming emotional values[,] all the rest is an affair of cuisine, of art. On n'émeut que par la clarté. [One writes movingly only by clarity.] Stendhal is right in that clause. He was right in his argument for prose, but Poetry also aims at giving a feeling precisely evaluated.[58]

When this rhythm, or when the vowel and consonantal melody or sequence seems truly to bear the trace of emotion which the poem (for we have come at last to the poem) is intended to communicate, we say that this part of the work is good. . . from the other side, ideas, or fragments of ideas, the emotion and concomitant emotions of this 'Intellectual and Emotional Complex' (for we have come to the intellectual and emotional complex) must be in harmony, they must form an organism, they must be an oak sprung from one acorn'.[59]

Behind this slightly breathless claim that the emotional value of poetry is both overwhelming and precisely evaluated, we might also hear the more familiar Wordsworthian formulation that poetry is both the 'spontaneous overflow of powerful feelings' and 'emotion recollected in tranquillity'.[60] Ultimately, it was for emotional insincerity that Pound and Eliot criticised Georgian poetry, for the words didn't have any basis in real feeling: the Georgians were looking for 'des sentiments pour les accommoder à leur vocabulaire' [feelings to suit their vocabulary].[61] And nowhere was this Romantic emphasis on sincerity more clearly shown than in Hulme's essay, which is premised on the fact that a truly Classical poem means not adherence to a set of principles, but a truly sincere poem and poet. Far from being an accident of publishing history, it is entirely appropriate that Hulme's anti-Romantic document should have been sponsored by a magazine committed to a new Wordsworthian revolution in poetry.

Hulme always seemed to be a forerunner of the various strands of modernism. It was he who in 1908 first called for a version of Imagism in free verse, although Pound disputed his claim to be the sole source of the Imagist school of 1912. He translated Bergson, whose philosophy of direct intuition of the unique rather than a comparative analytic method of science provided philosophical underpinning for Imagism's hatred of conventions. Yet just as the burgeoning English free-verse movement was putting his 1908 demand for 'the maximum of individual and personal expression' into practice, with his rejection of regular metre as 'rhetorical', 'cramping, jangling, meaningless, and out of place', 'Romanticism and Classicism' called for order, discipline and restraint.[62] It presaged a new geometrical, anti-humanist art exemplified in Hulme's advocacy of Wyndham Lewis, Gaudier-Brzeska and Jacob Epstein, and its argument for the 'original sin' of mankind and the necessity of restraint and limitation in art as well as politics led T. S. Eliot to call him 'the forerunner of a new attitude of mind, which should be the twentieth-century mind'.[63] M. H. Levenson has placed this essay as a fulcrum between early modernism based on impressionism and the personal, and the later modernism based on order and impersonality, and Richard Shusterman has seen it as the beginnings of modernism's decisive turn to scientific objectivism.[64] But 'Romanticism and Classicism' is not such a *volte-face* as critics have thought, for on closer reading the same impulse that drove Hulme's earlier call for personal individual expression is still vividly present in the turn to discipline and the subsequent rejection of all humanist art; the complete self-determination of the poet and the poem.

Hulme begins with a rejection of Romanticism, which he defines as Rousseau's belief that man is a creature of unlimited potential held back by social convention. To this he opposes Classicism, which holds that 'man is an extraordinarily fixed and limited animal whose nature is absolutely constant', and 'it is only by tradition and organisation that anything decent can be got out of him'.[65] Romanticism is a false religion, which has appropriated the divine realm of infinity for the human, and blurred fundamental boundaries: 'the concepts that are right and proper in their own sphere are spread over, and so mess up, falsify and blur the clear outlines of human experience' (62). This messing up and blurring is also exactly the trouble with Romantic poetry. It is vague in its outlook because it is so concerned with the infinite, whereas Classicism is concerned with 'the earthly and definite'. But 'so much has romanticism debauched us, that, without some form of vagueness, we deny the highest' (66), he laments; 'particularly in Germany, the land where theories of aesthetics were first created, the romantic aesthetes collated all beauty to an impression of the infinite involved in our being in absolute spirit . . . it is quite obvious to anyone who holds this kind of theory that any poetry which confines itself to the finite can never be of the highest kind' (68). Hulme's remedy is a sense of limit, 'small, dry things', expressed with accuracy: 'the great aim is accurate, precise and definite description' (68).

The fact that Hulme is arguing for earthly finitude from a theological standpoint indicates, of course, that being accurate and down-to-earth has just as much metaphysics behind it as being vague and infinite: accuracy is no more a goal in itself than infinity. And despite his disparagement of Hegel, the progress of Spirit is very much in evidence as Hulme continues, for Hegel's goal of self-determination and autonomy is where Hulme's accuracy now unexpectedly leads. Precise description involves language, and 'language is by its very nature a communal thing; that is, it expresses never the exact thing but a compromise – that which is common to you, me and everybody' (68). Regardless of this *a priori* impossibility, Hulme then says that precise description is possible but must involve a wrestling with language's conventions, like an architect bending an approximately curved piece of wood to get 'the exact curve that he sees whether it be an object or an idea in the mind' (69). Accuracy, he sums up, is

First the particular faculty of mind to see things as they really are, and apart from the conventional ways in which you have been trained to see them . . . Second, the concentrated state of mind, the grip over oneself which is necessary . . . to prevent one falling into the conventional curves of ingrained technique, to hold on through infinite detail and trouble to the exact curve you want. Wherever you get this sincerity, you get the fundamental quality of good art without dragging in infinite or serious. (69)

The fact that Hulme has called for 'infinite detail' to demonstrate an art which would not drag in the infinite is more than a slip: it is indicative of the way his criteria for accuracy are utterly consonant with the very Romanticism he despises, with Coleridge his master (67). Classical accuracy is 'sincerity', perfect expression of the vision one sees without the mediation of common forms of language, and requires perfect self-determination in the artist. The criteria for true objectivity, discipline and order in the work of art turn out to be in an *internally* autonomous state of mind which will allow no interference from convention. Such internal transparency is the correlative of Hulme's perfectly Kantian definition of seeing aesthetically: 'The object of aesthetic contemplation is something framed apart by itself and regarded without memory or expectation, simply as being itself, as end not means, as individual not universal.'(70). This internalisation of poetic accuracy is confirmed by Hulme's expansion of the idea of 'sincerity' towards the end to include Coleridge's notion of the organic. A work whose analogies do not quite fit, and have 'a certain excess' to them, is inferior. But when it is 'sincere in the accurate sense, when the whole of the analogy is necessary to get out the exact curve of the feeling or thing you want to express – there you seem to me to have the highest verse' (71). This sincerity Hulme then defines as the 'vital or organic': in a sincere, accurate work of art, the exact correlation between the public analogy and the private thing expressed is such that there is no difference between them (72). Hence every single part of the analogy is needful, and if any one part were removed then the meaning of the whole would alter. This inseparable reciprocity between the poem's meaning and its expression, and by extension between its form and content, shows how over the course of a few pages, Hulme's classical ideal of discipline and order has morphed into one of Coleridge's key doctrines, the organicity of the work. What provides a unifying strand throughout these constant reformulations of 'accuracy', though, is the drive to eliminate the extraneous. The classical limitation prevents humankind from blurring boundaries: man is in his proper, fixed, limited place as himself. Accuracy is truth to the emotion or thing, and this means that no external conventions mediate between the artist's vision and his expression of that vision. Organicism means that there is no excess of analogy to meaning, form to content, and hence no structuring principle that does not arise from the character of the work itself. Each part alters every other part, so that there is complete internal unity of the work, an idea to which Hulme then surprisingly adduces Ruskin as a witness. In fact, Hulme's metaphor of 'the motion of a snake's body', which 'goes through all parts at once' and whose 'volition acts at the same instant in coils which go contrary ways' (72) is taken almost word for word from the second volume of Ruskin's *Modern Painters*, where it is an analogy for the seamlessly synthesising work of the Imagination.[66] The metaphor was first suggested, however, by Coleridge's *Lectures* as an illustration of the sinuously diverse nature of Shakespeare's genius, 'writhing in every direction, but still progressive' towards his artistic goal.[67]

The approving use of Coleridge and Ruskin should make it clear that Hulme's essay is by no means anti-Romantic, and the lurking presence of Romantic genius is entirely consonant with the use Hulme makes of Bergson in the final paragraphs to amplify his point about the difference between an organic and a mechanical unity. 'Now all this is worked out in Bergson', continues Hulme cheerfully, 'it is all based on the clear conception of these vital complexities which he calls "intensive", as opposed to the other kind which he calls "extensive" . . . to deal with the intensive you must use intuition' (72). Hulme is elliptically referring to Bergson's contrast between kinds of knowledge that the analytical, scientific or 'extensive' approach could give, and that afforded by what he called the 'intuitive'. Bergson thought that analysis can only see the object in terms of comparison with a conventional measurement, and therefore is blind to the unique internal landscape of that object. 'Intuition' rejects such exteriority for an '*intellectual sympathy* by which one places oneself within an object in order to coincide with what is unique in it'.[68] This rejection of convention to see the object on its own terms was a primary intellectual source behind the Imagist desire for an undecorated poetry, whose form would be as unique and singular as its content. Bergson called his intuitive knowledge of the object an 'absolute', because it was not relative to anything else, and the idea undergirds Pound's belief in an 'absolute' rhythm, a rhythm which would be incommensurable with anything else – thus, emphatically, not a regular rhythm – and hence as singular and unique as the personal artist. 'The creative-inventive faculty is the thing that matters', declared Pound, 'and that the artist having this faculty is a being infinitely separate from the other type of artist who merely goes on weaving arabesques out of other men's "units of form"'.[69] Bergson compared his absolute perspective to reading a novel:

The author may multiply the traits of his hero's character, may make him speak and act as much as he pleases, but all this can never be equivalent to the simple and indivisible feeling which I should experience if I were able for an instant to identify myself with the person of the hero himself. Out of that indivisible feeling, as from a spring, all the words, gestures and actions of the man would appear to me to flow naturally.[70]

'Indivisible' is the vital word, or in Pound's terms for Bergson's intuition, 'that which presents an intellectual and emotional complex in an instant of time'.[71] The Bergsonian poem would be *indivisible from itself*: the emotion inseparable from the reflection, the description from its object, the formal 'how' of the presentation inseparable from the 'what' of the content. Removing the inessential and imprecise would leave an indivisible, singular core, an absolute.

Bergson's philosophy of the irreducible and incommensurable object underwrote a good deal of Imagist theorising on poetry.[72] But there was also a Bergsonian review of the visual arts, *Rhythm*, run by Middleton Murry and Katherine Mansfield, which printed work by Picasso, Derain, Kandinsky and Gaudier-Brzeska alongside its regular selection of work by the lesser-known British and American Fauvists Fergusson, Peploe, Rice and Dismorr. The magazine's enthusiastic opening editorial put forward its belief that Bergson's philosophy was an 'open avowal of the supremacy of the intuition, of the spiritual vision of the artist':

The artist attains to the pure form, refining and intensifying his vision till all that is unessential dissolves away . . . he must return to the moment of pure perception to see the essential forms . . . modernism . . . penetrates beneath the outward surface of the world, and disengages the rhythms which lie at the heart of things.[73]

To demonstrate such stripped-down purity of perception, it printed stories by Mansfield and D. H. Lawrence. But when the magazine became more serious about its poetry section in 1912, it was the Georgians they printed. Murry praised Gibson's work for its 'direct presentment of the author's sense of reality, so direct, so sympathetic', without 'prettiness'.[74] The *Georgian Poetry* editor Eddie Marsh had recently stepped in with a loan to save *Rhythm* from bankruptcy, so Middleton Murry's praise may have been tactical: nonetheless, the fact that Marsh stepped in at all is a sign of his interest in some kinds of modernist art (he owned four Gaudier-Brzeskas), and Murry's choice of adjectives indicates no change of editorial policy. Shortly afterwards, Rupert Brooke informed Gwen Raverat that he, de la Mare, Gibson, Abercrombie and Davies were 'the staff poets' of the magazine, and their work featured in almost every subsequent issue alongside painting's international avant-garde.[75] The *OED* gives the first instance of the adjective 'modernist' applying to a movement in the arts as 1927; in 1912, however, *Rhythm* was advertising itself in *Poetry Review* as 'the Unique Magazine of Modernist Art'. It is a historical irony, but perhaps an understandable one, that the Georgians appeared under the banner of 'modernism' – in the sense we would use it today – long before the Imagists ever did.

3

Shortly after writing 'Romanticism and Classicism', Hulme changed his mind about Bergson. His initial attraction had been based on the way Bergson promised a way out of the late nineteenth-century deterministic and mechanistic view of the world: if it were composed entirely of atoms acted upon by physical forces, there had seemed no phenomenon that was not ultimately determined by those forces, including human beings. Bergson's argument for a uniquely incommensurable object of knowledge provided philosophical underpinnings for a reassertion of individuality – and ironically, it was this that provoked Hulme's subsequent rejection of him. As he explained it to readers of the *New Age*, 'I had no sooner sat down in this hall and felt the almost physical sensation produced by the presence all around me of several hundred people filled with exactly the same kind of attitude to Bergson as my own, than I experienced a complete reversal of feeling . . . I was immediately repulsed by what before had attracted me'.[76] Hulme's biographer calls this a 'trivial and subjective reason', but it is also truly Bergsonian in its assertion that the absolute truth of things cannot be accessible to common standards.[77] And although Pound damned Bergson as 'frog diarhoea', his own rejection of the common was equally heartfelt, for since 'poetry is the expression of overwhelming emotional values, no rattle of formulae, Christian, pagan or socialistic will compass this force of expression'.[78] Just as *Blast* dedicated art to the individual, so Pound declared in 1917 that 'there is no respect for mankind save in respect for detached individuals', and quoted John B. Yeats's dictum that 'poetry is the last refuge and asylum of the individual of whom oratory is the enemy' approvingly.[79] Poetry is the opposite of rhetoric because poetry is truly individual, and obviously must therefore be entirely true to itself. Hence his strictures on rhetoric, on indirection and on a mismatch of form and content have a politics attached to them, that the individual psyche must not be compromised by the common. And so what in Coleridge is a freedom that art promises for everyone becomes in Pound a freedom which constantly needs to be asserted against everyone else. This hatred of any interference in the individual's rights has been traced to sources as various as Yeatsian ideas of nobility, Emersonian self-reliance and Jamesian pragmatism, but it is certain that Pound also found much support in the philosophy of Max Stirner which lies behind the title of the magazine he sub-edited, *The Egoist*.[80] Stirner's basis was his belief that the perfect uniqueness of each self is compromised by its relations with anything outside it, and is irreducible to any common terms of morality or social concern, because they require a part of the ego to be thought about in terms other than itself, which would threatens that uniqueness. Effectively, in its criticism of those who believe in a 'higher being' as 'involuntary egoists', Stirner's philosophy is a plea against government and law on the basis of a plea against self-division:

Developing yourself, you get away 'from yourself,' that is from the self that was at that moment. As you are at each instant, you are your own creature, and in this very 'creature' you do not wish to lose yourself, the creator. You are yourself a higher being than you are, and surpass yourself. But that *you* are the one that is higher than you, that is, that you are not only creature, but likewise your creator – just this, as an involuntary egoist, you fail to recognize; and the 'higher essence' is to you – an alien essence. Every higher essence, such as truth, mankind, and so on, is an essence *over* us.[81]

There is a direct continuity between Stirner's belief that higher essences are falsifications and Pound's unhesitant declaration that 'humanity is a collection of individuals, not a *whole* divided into segments or units', despite the fact that the etymology of the word 'individual' contradicts him.[82] The poetics and politics of autonomy come together in Pound's assessment of the relation of art to government: 'The Renaissance . . . rose in a search for precision and declined through rhetoric and rhetorical thinking, through a habit of defining things always "in the terms of something else".'[83]

Yet Pound's verdict unconsciously reveals the problem with its own policies. For what use is definition, if it is not in terms of something else? A world of unique items is an utterly indescribable world, and paradoxically, a world where there is less individuality, not more. Presented with a group of singular things which are entirely incommensurable, it becomes a matter of indifference to choose between them.[84] Paradoxically, a world of utter individuals would be as homogeneous as a world of identical people, because there would be no common criteria to distinguish them from one another, and the poetics of individualism has the same problem, for the more that the poetry is unique, the less possibility there is that we could ever know it. As Frank Kermode first pointed out in *Romantic Image*, for the unique poem to be recognisable as such, it must use a common, discursive language.[85] Hulme's idea that 'poetry is compromise for a language of intuition' admitted what Pound would not when he declared that 'the Image is the word beyond formulated language'.[86] Language is not language unless it is to some degree formulated, and the concepts of accuracy, sincerity and organicity are meaningless without the threat of some kind of formula. If the absolute or individual is ever to be appreciated as such, it depends to some degree on the common.

This is not, of course, a problem unique to Hulme, Pound or Bergson. It can be plausibly traced to the contrary demands placed upon the very idea of the aesthetic itself in Kant's *Critique of Judgement*, where aesthetic must be judged as itself, without reference to concepts or categories (or it would be reducible to an example of something else) and simultaneously stand as an example of such indeterminate freedom in order to be the education in the '*sensus communis*', the reconciliation of freedom and universality that Kant's project aims for.[87] But not the least of the many ironies in Hulme's essay is that its entire programme for the undivided Classical psychic unity is itself based on a Romantic essay which addresses exactly this paradox of uniqueness and dependency, Schiller's *On the Naïve and Sentimental in Literature*. There is no direct record of Hulme reading Schiller (though Pound tells us he read Kant and Hegel in the original), but the distinction between Classical and Romantic common in Victorian poetics – Arnold is the most obvious example – was first formulated as an opposition between a unified 'naïve' aesthetic and an infinitely divided, 'sentimental' one by Schiller's essay.[88] It was Coleridge's lectures on Shakespeare that introduced that essay's terms to the English-speaking public, just as they introduced the concept of organic form to which Hulme draws his reader's attention, and although Coleridge adapted both from his reading of A. W. Schlegel's *Lectures in Dramatic Art and Literature* (it was Schlegel's brother Friedrich who first called modern art 'Romantic'), he had, like Schlegel himself, derived the substance of his opposition from reading Schiller.[89]

Nevertheless, the essay's importance for twentieth-century poetics has hitherto been mostly overlooked in favour of Schiller's more prominent reworking of Kant in the *Aesthetic Education*, whose English editors make a strong case for its prescience of modernist thought.[90] In these letters, Schiller advocates the aesthetic as an education in unity, which enables humankind to experience the harmony that modern political, intellectual and social divisions have denied him, and his broad programme is visible not only in *Biographia Literaria,* but Eliot's diagnosis of the 'dissociation of sensibility' in modern thinking, or Pound's assertion above that in the Image, emotion and ideas are a single 'organism'. *On the Naïve and Sentimental,* however, is a serious questioning of the conditions of possibility of such aesthetic unity, but its revisionary import for English poetics has been rather disguised by Coleridge's adaptation of it. Although careful recent detective work has revealed that he knew the essay by 1802 and possibly earlier, when he drew on its terms in 1819 he combined it with the Schlegel brothers' historicising emphasis to make 'naïve' and 'sentimental' terms of chronological succession: pre-Christian poets are naïve and post-Christian ones sentimental.[91] Schiller's original distinction, however, is between two distinct modes of sensibility, and importantly for Hulme, turns on a definition in which the supposedly indivisible and unique naïve poet turns out to be thoroughly dependent on the disunified sentimental one. Where Hulme sees Classical and Romantic as polar opposites and votes firmly for the Classical, Schiller's essay is less certain that the distinction can be made absolute at all.

Like Hulme, Schiller describes the naïve almost interchangeably as a mode of sensibility and a type of poetry, but both perpetually manifest 'the law of harmony'.[92] The naïve is fundamentally characterised by its direct relation to the world and the unity within itself, in contrast to the modern world split by market-based specialisation and the divisions of thought and feeling. Schiller's prime example of the naïve is how children think and feel. But *naïveté* also provides us with the best guide to the sensibility of the perfect artist, the genius, for 'every true genius must be naïve or he is no genius' (189). And hence the genius is able to create art which will transcend the divisions of modern society, for by being 'unacquainted with the rules, those crutches of feebleness and disciplinarians of perversion', he is 'guided solely by nature, or instinct'. Exterior rules would compromise the inner harmony of the naïve, just as formal rules of pattern or diction are anathema to the Imagists because they impede the truth-to-itself of the image.

Consequently, Schiller's naïve stands behind a number of famous modernist statements about the autonomy of art and artist. The naïve poet will write work that avoids the mediating, compromising function of words themselves: 'While the sign always remains different from and alien to what is signified in the case of scholastic understanding, the language of genius springs from thought as by an inner necessity and is so one with it that even concealed by the body, the spirit appears as though exposed. . . the sign completely disappears in what is signified' (190–1). The modern desire for precision, accuracy, and the *mot juste* is directly related to this desire to make the sign disappear: 'language in a healthy state', said Eliot in an unwary moment, 'presents the object, is so close to the object that the two are identified'.[93] 'Direct treatment of the thing' was Pound's way of putting it.[94] Schiller's naïve genius also has no trouble with the division of spontaneous overflow of feeling and reflection in tranquillity evident in Wordsworth's *Preface*: 'He operates as an undivided sensuous unity and as a harmonising whole. Sense and reason, receptive and spontaneous faculties, have not yet divided the task between them; still less do they contradict one other'(200). Derived, of course, from Kant's *Critique of Judgement*, the idea of the artist operating as a unity of reason and intuition is the cornerstone of *Biographia Literaria*'s theory of Imagination. But its idea of an immediate unity can be traced forward to Pound ('one, as a human being, cannot pretend fully to express oneself unless one express instinct and intellect together'), and from Pound to Eliot's admiration of 'the amazing unity of Greek, the unity of concrete and abstract in philosophy, the unity of thought and feeling, action and speculation, in life', his disparagement of the post-civil war dissociation of sensibility and his demand in 'The Metaphysical Poets' that poets ought to 'feel their thought as immediately as the odour of a rose'.[95]

Most crucially for modernist technique, such a unity of person in the naïve poet means there is no corresponding split between an artist's form and content, matter and manner, for 'naïve poetry never lacks for content, since its content is already contained *in the form itself*'.[96] Or as it appears in Walter Pater's famous proto-modernist formulation, inspiration for generations of abstract painters and free verse poets: '"*All art constantly aspires towards the condition of music*". For a while in all other kinds of art it is possible to distinguish the matter from the form, and the understanding can always make the distinction, yet it is the constant effort of art to obliterate it.'[97]

Such is the inseparability between how the naïve poet sees and what he sees that he is also, to all extents and purposes, impersonal. 'The *naïve poet* is the work and the work is the *naïve poet*', declares Schiller, and 'you have to be unworthy of the work or not up to it or have already had your fill of it, to ask only about *the poet*' (197). By having no critical distance between the work and the sensibility of its author, the poem is simultaneously totally personal and wholly impersonal, a paradox which reappears undiminished in Pound's discussion of the Imagist-Vorticist poet in 1915:

By bad verse, whether 'regular' or 'free', I mean verse which pretends to some emotion which did not assist at its parturition. I mean also verse made by those who have not sufficient skill to make the words move in rhythm of the creative emotion. Where the voltage is so high that it fuses the machinery, one has merely the 'emotional man', not the artist. The best artist is the man whose machinery can stand the highest voltage. The better the machinery, the more precise, the stronger; the more exact will be the record of the voltage and of the various currents which have passed through it.[98]

In order to make the poem nothing but the purest record of the pulsations of creative emotion, the artist himself is reduced to a machine for recording them. Even Hulme's call for a 'dry, hard' classical verse based on limitation and finitude has a distinct resonance of the naïve poet's 'dry, matter-of-fact way' of treating things.[99] In short, Hulme's classicism is Schiller's naïve rewritten, and the naïve provides an ideal for some of the cardinal doctrines of Imagist poetics.

As the title indicates, however, Schiller's essay is written not simply in praise of the naïve, but in contrast to its opposite, the sentimental. Within the sentimental poet, 'the agreement between his feeling and his thinking . . . is no longer in him but rather outside him', in an 'ideal yet-to-be-realised state' (201). He no longer operates as an 'undivided sensuous unity', but constantly oscillates between immediate feeling and reflection, yearning for their reconciliation but never able to achieve it on his own. The naïve poet *is* nature, the sentimental poet just seeks it, and as a consequence remains permanently divided, writing always not of his object but of the felt distance between self and object. Nevertheless, Schiller intimates that this division indicates that the sentimental poet has one thing which the naïve poet does not, namely freedom to choose. The naïve poet's unity means he has 'a single relation to his object', whereas the sentimental 'always has to do with two conflicting images and feelings' (204). Yet this conflict arises because of the disparity between 'the actual world as a limit and his idea as something infinite', in other words, inherently free. As the essay progresses, Schiller claims that the future of poetry lies not in a return to the naïve, but in enabling the sentimental poet to join his freedom with the undivided unity of the naïve and soar onwards to greater poetry than has yet been written. Contradicting his earlier assertion that 'naïveté alone makes someone a genius' (189), he describes the 'sentimental genius' (235) who would draw his power from his infinite inward capacities and join them to the sensuous, natural but unfree powers of the naïve.

Yet this triumphant future reconciliation of the naïve with the sentimental is proclaimed in terms that keep collapsing, as if such a thing were by definition necessary, desirable but also impossible.[100] 'Knowing how to restore nature in its original simplicity within himself is precisely what constitutes the poet' (224), but if a poet 'knows' how to restore simplicity, by definition he can't be simple, nor will he be able to restore it. The naïve person can never know they're naïve, since if they did, they wouldn't be naïve any more. The person without divisions cannot know that they are without divisions, because to know this would mean to know the difference between thinking and feeling, and for that to happen, one would have to understand what it would be to split them, and so on. In other words, the naïve and sentimental is an essay whose very terms of analysis are predicated on the impossibility of the naïve person ever writing such a thing. As Schiller admits, this means that only the sentimental can recognise the naïve, but the logical consequence of his argument is less often pursued, that the naïve *cannot actually exist* as a concept without its sentimental opposite. That which is characterised by its own internality, structured on its own terms, 'being at each moment a self-sufficient and complete whole' (233), cannot actually be recognised without the externality it was supposed to exclude. And this has important implications for the subsequent history of all verse that is premised on its naïve capacities – that somewhere, somehow, the presence of the admiringly sentimental will be detectable in the vicinity, and the self-division that the naïve was to eliminate will reappear with it.

Just such a division is powerfully evident in one of the creeds that was designed to prevent it, Pound's famous announcement of the rules for Imagist poetry:

1. Direct treatment of the 'thing', whether subjective or objective.
2. To use absolutely no word that does not contribute to the presentation.
3. As regarding rhythm: to compose in the sequence of the musical phrase, not in sequence of a metronome.[101]

The first two words are mutually contradictory. If poetry is a 'treatment' of a thing, then it is by definition not direct, unless 'direct treatment' is one sort of treatment among others, which would reduce it to a stylistic device. Pound later commented that he had learnt a great deal from Hardy's 'absorption in *subject* as contrasted with [*sic*] aesthetes' preoccupation with "treatment".[102] 'Treatment' has one eye on the audience and one on the subject, and so cannot be wholly 'direct'. And such 'treatment' is evident in the second part of the sentence, 'whether subjective or objective'. By accepting both halves of the opposition, Pound renders the distinction meaningless; if it doesn't matter whether the thing is subjective or objective, why bother to make the distinction? The clause is there to amplify the first clause as if the reader could not be trusted to understand, and in that sense is also 'treatment'. The second tenet's determination to use 'absolutely no word that does not contribute' simply violates itself. 'Absolutely' is an intensifier that contributes nothing further to the prescription except Pound's concern that the reader should take this clause very seriously; again, it is treatment, not subject. The same is true of the anaphora in the third tenet, whose second 'in sequence of' could be removed without changing the meaning of the command.

Pound's offhand indifference to 'whether subjective or objective' is true of each phrase in its combination of a statement of objective principle amplified by a personal worry about being misunderstood. The three tenets are rhetorical in the modern sense because they use useless words, according to a strict criterion of directness. What makes them not at all useless, of course, is that they are indicative of rhetoric in the old pre-Romantic sense, of Pound's need to persuade his audience. The same issue is evident in this classic statement of Imagistic impact:

Constatation of fact. It presents. It does not comment. It is irrefutable because it doesn't present a personal predilection for any particular fraction of the truth. It is as communicative as Nature. It is as uncommunicative as Nature. It is not a criticism of life. I mean it does not deal in opinion. It washes its hands of theories.[103]

We are to know that the Image has been 'presented' by the absence of comment, personal predilection and opinion; we have to feel the white space round the tiny Imagist poem, the intense neutrality of every line. Such criticism displays a personal predilection of its own, since Pound has to explain, amplify, clarify and refine his definition by telling us just what the Image isn't, with a certain mistrust of his audience. Here, the telling adjective 'irrefutable' suggests a mental audience of philosophers reading poetry in order to argue with it, or perhaps an Imagist poet whittling away until he or she gets to the poem's core, discarding far more than is kept – as the paragraph of negatives itself proceeds by elimination. That suspicion of the audience manifests itself in a self-consciousness that inevitably draws attention to itself, and what we get, in truth, is less the fact than the constatation of it: all those negatives draw attention to its presentation, not to the fact itself. If the Image simply, actually, did present itself, Pound wouldn't need to write a thing. Any appreciation of the directness of something has the paradoxical effect of drawing attention to the mode of presentation, rather than the subject presented. Directness is a *theatrical* mode in denial.

Such theatricality is nowhere more in evidence than in the shock value of an Imagist poem that obeys all of Pound's rules, H. D.'s 'Hermes of the Ways'. First published by the Poetry Bookshop, it begins:

> The hard sand breaks,
> And the grains of it
> Are clear as wine.
>
> Far off over the leagues of it,
> The wind,
> Playing on the wide shore,
> Piles little ridges,
> And the great waves
> Break over it.[104]

The unique rhythmic pattern of the free verse makes its beginning as direct and unstereotyped as Pound could want. Yet free and traditional verse alike have line-breaks, and in both cases the fact that the line ends at a certain point and no other means that the words around that break are highlighted in a way that words in the middle of the line are not (although a poem with very short lines minimises this effect). In breaking the line with 'of it' and 'over it', the poem draws rhythmical attention to phrases that are not syntactically the most important in the sentence: if H. D. had closed the poem 'And over it the great waves / Break', it would be more conventional and more portentous, but also less deliberately flat-footed. In her original, the effect is one of blankness: the pattern tells us the last words should be significant, and yet syntactically they are subordinate. But in confronting its readership with the words' nakedness, the poem has changed its ground. Rather than communicate their import directly, it is communicating the feeling of its own directness, its own status as a direct poem. An utterly direct, accurate transmission of the poet's sensibility would not be noticeable as a poem at all, as Hulme realised in a self-defeating moment: 'if we could come into direct contact with sense and consciousness, art would be useless and unnecessary'.[105] The problem is manifest in May Sinclair's reply to Monro's assertion that Imagism was not the only direct mode of poetry around:

The Image is not a substitute; it does not stand for anything but itself. Presentation not Representation is the watchword of the school. The Image, I take it, is Form. But it is not pure form. It is form and substance.

It may be either the form of a thing – you will get Imagist poems which are as near as possible to the naked presentation of the thing, with nothing, not so much as a temperament or a mood, between you and it . . . or the Image may be in the form of a passion or emotion or mood . . . The point is that the passion, emotion or mood is never given as an abstraction. And in no case is the Image a symbol of reality (the object); it is reality (the object) itself. You cannot distinguish between a thing and its image.[106]

In which case, one is entitled to wonder, how does one know one is looking at an image at all? Or to put it the other way round, if it is the 'form of a thing' directly presented, why do we need to know this if we could never tell the difference between a thing and its image anyway? For if the thing and the image were indistinguishable, any criterion of directness and immediacy is presupposed, since we couldn't know the thing any other way. 'What the Imagists are "out for" is direct naked contact with reality', continued Sinclair, which is either trivial (all poems are real) or pointless: if the real is only knowable through the image, then the image cannot but be direct, and if it *is* knowable outside the image, why bother with the image? By claiming to be a more direct transmission of 'the object' than any other sort of poetry, Imagist verse was trapped in a contradiction, that the more successfully it demonstrated the directness of its language, the more it had to point to the mental experience of this directness rather than the object it was transmitting, in order to have anything to say.

But as the Poetry Bookshop publications demonstrate, directness was equally the goal of the Georgian poets, and this contradictory demand for the poem to be visibly transparent, the sentimental constructing the naïve, means they are prone to exactly the same difficulty with a directness that self-consciously presents itself, rather than its material. Lawrence made a typically acute complaint to the Georgian editor Edward Marsh in 1915, when he noted that despite promising emotional directness, Ralph Hodgson's work had a subtext: '"oh I do want to give you this emotion", cries Hodgson, "I do"', and hence the poem is full of Hodgson, not the emotion.[107] Masefield made his reputation with a rough-and-ready verse whose frequent manglings of grammar and syntax for the rhyme were ostensibly justified by the direct passion of his unlettered speakers. For all his pouring forth, though, a self-conscious directness is evident in the drunken reprobate Saul Kane, hero of *The Everlasting Mercy*:

> And looking round I felt a spite
> At all who'd come to see me fight;
> The five and forty human faces
> Inflamed by drink and going to races,
> Faces of men who'd never been
> Merry or true or live or clean;
> Who'd never felt the boxer's trim
> Of brain divinely knit to limb,
> Nor felt the whole live body go
> One tingling health from top to toe.[108]

The false innocence of 'merry or true or live or clean' reveals Masefield presenting his character in the act of being simple, not actually being simple. These are descriptions of simplicity by someone complex, and their admiration is consequently detached; 'merry', 'true', 'live' and 'clean' are not virtue but feelings of virtuousness, as the bodily self-admiration then proposed is not health but the remoter feeling of healthiness. Here Masefield resembles W. W. Gibson, a writer whose working-class speakers frequently stop to admire themselves or check how they are feeling:

> When, my heart answering to the call,
> I followed down the seaward stream
> By silent pool and singing fall,
> Till with a quiet, keen content
> I watched the sun, a crimson ball,
> Shoot through grey seas, a fiery gleam
> Then sink in opal deeps from sight.
> ('Devil's Edge')

> Out of the sparkling sea
> I drew my tingling body clear and lay
> On a low ledge the livelong summer day . . .
> ('Hit')

> By the lamplit stall I loitered, feasting my eyes
> On colours ripe and rich for the heart's desire . . .
> And as I lingered lost in divine delight,
> My heart thanked God for the goodly gift of sight
> And all youth's lively senses keen and quick . . .
> ('Sight')[109]

Gibson's verse, like Masefield's, aims at directness through the thoughts and attitudes of working-class life, using deliberately ordinary language and jog-trot rhythms. 'Hit', above, comes from a volume which has a good claim to be the first volume of blunt, prosaic, unillusioned war poetry, and having survived the carnage at Loos a month earlier, Robert Graves wrote to Marsh from the front to say how good it was, especially compared to the wretched verses of stay-at-home armchair poets.[110] Yet Gibson, confined by poor eyesight to menial work in England, had written the whole thing up there from newspaper reports, an irony that testifies to the way 'realism' is a genre like any other, but which is also symptomatic of the second-hand innocence of his poetry. In being honest or simple, Gibson's speakers might justify their clichés and hand-me-down phrases – 'divine delight' or 'goodly gift' – because the conventionality is expressive of the simple sensibility of the person saying them. Yet in talking about themselves with 'quiet, keen content', feeling their 'tingling' and 'lively' sensations, they display a detached, judicious enjoyment of their own directness, and it was this self-conscious admiration of sensation that Edward Thomas found he intensely disliked, in both Gibson and Masefield:

Both write as 'working men', and make use of words or actions which are supposed to look odd in poetry. Yet neither of them is exactly a 'working man', or seems to write of 'working men' except in complete detachment, however admiring. Both, perhaps in consequence, have to make up for some lack of reality in the whole by intense and often violent reality in detail . . . they are both spectators, to some extent connoisseurs.[111]

The quotation-marks around 'working man' are deadly, for they mimic the Pateresque, self-congratulatory delicacy of admiration with which Gibson and Masefield approach their topic, and as Thomas remarked about Pater himself, 'literature is not for connoisseurs'.[112] The self-consciousness endemic in trying for pure experience was the downfall of Pater and all who followed him, Georgian or Imagist, and Thomas privately considered it the problem of Rupert Brooke's poetry as well. Like Hulme's definition in 'Romanticism and Classicism', Brooke once explained that 'the point of Art is to present events, emotions, moods, for their own sake as ends', and amplified this comment in a review:

'I saw – *I* saw', the artist says, 'a tree against the sky, or a blank wall in the sunlight, and it was so thrilling, so arresting, so particularly itself, that – well really, I *must* show you! . . . There!' Or the writer explains, 'Just so and just so it happened, or might happen, and thus the heart shook, and thus . . .' And suddenly, deliciously, with them you see and feel.[113]

But for all his insistence that the object is 'particularly itself', what leaps out is the state of the artist's mind ('*I* saw') in treating the object as itself, and the enjoyable sensations of such a thing ('deliciously'). Brooke, like several of his Bloomsbury colleagues, derived much of the official portion of his aesthetics from reading G. E. Moore's *Principia Ethica*, where 'the beautiful should be defined as that of which the admiring contemplation is good in itself'; in Brooke's work, the thing itself is witness to the admiring contemplation which has seen it so.'[14] In 'Dining-Room Tea', for example:

> I watched the quivering lamplight fall
> On plate and flowers and pouring tea
> And cup and cloth; and they and we
> Flung all the dancing moments by
> With jest and glitter. Lip and eye
> Flashed on the glory, shone and cried,
> Improvident, unmemoried. . .

Improvident perhaps, unmemoried never. Brooke's vision of tea is a Pateresque moment of connoisseurship, savouring the 'dancing moments' precisely because they are dancing and momentary, not for what happened in them. Lips and eyes are detached from their owners because what they say or see is not as important as their surface of saying and seeing. Seeing things 'in themselves' means self-consciously spectating them; like the blank wall in the sunlight, this intense, immediate experience is exactly the opposite because it is simultaneously being admired as an intense, immediate experience. Brooke 'was a rhetorician', wrote Thomas to Frost, for 'he couldn't mix his thought or the result of it with his feeling. He could only think about his feeling'.'[15]

### 4

Thomas's complaints about the self-conscious innocence of Georgian poetry were picked up a year or two later by Eliot's 'Reflections on Contemporary Poetry' in *The Egoist*, a series which marks one of the first determined barrages of the poetry wars. But Eliot also had some of the Imagists in his sights for their espousal of an aesthetic based on spontaneous non-reflection, and so his strategy was premised on bracketing Georgian and Imagist poets together as sufferers from the same problem. By trying so conspicuously to avoid the 'rhetorical, the abstract, the moralizing', Eliot remarked, both groups ended up with rhetoric just the same, because the struggle to sound direct had overwhelmed any personal expression. To ensure it does not abstract from the thing, for example, American free verse focuses on the accidental object to the exclusion of all emotion, and is therefore prone to blankness. Georgian poetry, on the other hand, follows Wordsworth by focusing on the trivial (animals, flowers), and therefore denies itself the opportunity to express serious emotions. In Wordsworth, apparently, 'the emotion is of the object' not of specifically human associations, and 'such emotions must be vague (as in Wordsworth), or if more definite, pleasing'.[116] Lacking even Wordsworth's limited grasp on philosophy because he fears rhetoric, abstraction and morals, the Georgian poet thus either apes Wordsworth's sensibility or, if he departs from Wordsworthian topics, 'is subject to lapses of rhetoric from which Wordsworth, with his complete innocence of other emotions than those in which he specialized, is comparatively free' (119). Georgian poetry is rhetorical, in other words, because it has no emotions except those unconsciously borrowed from Wordsworth, and because its blind patriotism 'has borrowed little from foreign sources', it lacks any possibility of stepping outside this tradition and expressing something truly personal (118). As Eliot put it a little later, 'because we have never learned to criticize Keats, Shelley and Wordsworth (poets of assured though modest merit), Keats, Shelley and Wordsworth punish us from their graves with the annual scourge of the Georgian Anthology'.[117]

Eliot's attack continued in the third of the 'Reflections', where he again noted that the editors of an anthology called *The New Poetry* (which included Georgians, Imagists and Eliot himself) had bracketed their contributors under a common goal. Opposed to 'all the rhetorical excesses' of the previous generation, the new poetry would be 'a concrete and immediate realisation of life; it would discard the theory, the abstraction, the remoteness, found in all classics not of the first order. . . it has set before itself an idea of absolute simplicity and sincerity – an ideal which implies an individual, unstereotyped diction, and an individual unstereotyped rhythm'.[118]

Eliot recognised the aim 'to wring the neck of rhetoric', as Verlaine had demanded, but he doubted whether many had pressed hard enough:

But as for the escape from rhetoric – there is a great push at the door, and some cases of suffocation. But what is rhetoric? The test seems unsatisfactory. There is rhetoric even among the new poets. Furthermore, I am inclined to believe that Tennyson's verse is a 'cry from the heart' – only it is the heart of Tennyson, Latitudinarian, Whig, Laureate . . . The writers in *The New Poetry* who have avoided rhetoric . . . have done so chiefly by the exercise, in greater or less degree, of intelligence, of which an important function is the discernment of exactly what, and how much, we feel in any given situation.'[119]

In other words, Georgian and Imagist poetry is bad when it is insufficiently aware of its own emotions, and thus always has *borrowed* elements in it; Georgian formulae, convention, vagueness and insularity are both causes and symptoms of this basic lack of self-awareness. Eliot's remedy, though, was not suggested until the fourth and final 'Reflection' of 1919, that in order to change 'from a bundle of second-hand sentiments into a person', it is necessary to have a feeling of 'profound kinship, or rather of a peculiar personal intimacy, with another, probably a dead author'. In discovering this intimacy with another, the writer discovers himself, but the poem that results is not a purer distillation of the writer's private self. Rather, it will contain the other author and continue him for the present time: 'we have not borrowed, we have been quickened, and we become bearers of a tradition'.[120] These reflections were reworked a few months later into 'Tradition and the Individual Talent', where the individual author must now surrender himself 'as he is at the moment to something which is more valuable', the tradition of the 'mind of Europe'.[121] It is this famous essay, with its suspicion of the 'metaphysical theory of the substantial unity of the soul' (19), that sets the stage for the fragmented polyvocality of *The Waste Land*. And yet at first it seems that Eliot has swung round 180 degrees over the transition from the first of these 'Reflections' to 'Tradition and the Individual Talent'. In 1917, the poet is urged to discern what he or she really feels. In 1919, the poet is a 'medium' for the tradition, and hence 'emotions which he has never experienced will serve his turn as well as those familiar to him' (21). What connects them both, however, is the same underlying commitment to Coleridge's ideal for the work of art, the elimination of exteriority.

The 'Reflections' series began as part of Eliot's attempt to separate his and Pound's work from the burgeoning Imagist movement, which in Pound's words had become 'the dilutation of *vers libre*, Amygism, Lee Masterism, general floppiness'.[122] Free verse was becoming nothing but an expression of the undisciplined whim of the individual poet, rather than the ruthless pruning of the Imagist poem, as the preface to Amy Lowell's rival Imagist anthology made clear in a borrowing from Pound's favourite critic, Rémy de Gourmont: 'Individualism in literature, liberty of art, abandonment of existing forms ... the sole excuse which a man can have for writing is to write down himself ... He should create his own aesthetics and we should admit there are as many aesthetics as there are original minds.'[123]

But although Pound's political individualism remained as forthright as ever in his *New Age* series 'Studies in Contemporary Mentality' and 'Provincialism the Enemy', he insisted with Eliot on discipline in poetry. 'Remedy prescribed "Emaux et Camées" (or the Bay State Hymn Book). Rhyme and regular strophes'.[124] Or, as Eliot had put it to a lecture class in 1916: 'The beginning of the twentieth century has witnessed a return to the ideals of classicism. These may roughly be characterised as *form* and *restraint* in art, *discipline* and *authority* in religion, centralization in government (either as socialism or monarchy).'[125] For such a famous monarchist to admit that socialism might also be a form of classicism only underlines the vehemence of his anti-individualism.

The results of this form-as-restraint, according to Pound, were his own 'Mauberley' and Eliot's ultra-regular quatrains of 1920, designed to eliminate any possibility of Romantic self-indulgence, since in Eliot's recollection, 'the form gave the impetus to the content'.[126] As he insisted at the time: 'To create a form is not merely to invent a shape, a rhyme or rhythm. It is also the realization of the whole appropriate content of this rhyme or rhythm. The sonnet of Shakespeare is not merely such and such a pattern, but a precise way of thinking and feeling.'[127]

Nevertheless this classicism of form is not the authority it seems, for it tacitly maintains de Gourmont's programme (a few years later, Eliot was to anoint him one of his two perfect critics). In his earlier essay, 'On Style or Writing', de Gourmont had anticipated Eliot by arguing that if form really is inseparable from content, then it is not only the case that content should match form exactly: it also follows that 'to change the form is to change the idea'.[128] Three pages later, in a discussion of the style of Prosper Merimée, de Gourmont worked out the implication; if changing the form alters the meaning, then 'Merimée's surplusage expresses the very subtle observations made by a man who. . .' and so forth.[129] Yet surplusage was the very thing modernism was supposed to be expelling; the word itself occurs in Walter Pater's essay on 'Style', a foundational text for Imagism, where 'in truth all art does but consist in the removal of surplusage'.[130] But according to de Gourmont's logic, there can be no such thing as surplusage. If form creates content, and vice versa, then all form is coterminous with content, and there is no possibility for any excess or rhetoric to exist. Merimée's work says what it says, and that surplusage is as expressive as anything else. If form always realises content, then no poem, or person, can be rhetorical, sentimental or generalised at all. Although asserting the priority of form seems to attack Romantic freedoms, Eliot's formulation actually maintains the perfect unity of form and content which was the original artistic expression of that freedom.

The purported classicism of 'Tradition and the Individual Talent' performs the same trick, for at the same time as it demands submission of the poem to a prior standard of judgement, it actually adapts the tradition which provides that standard to the work:

The necessity that he shall conform, that he shall cohere, is not onesided; what happens when a new work of art is created is something that happens simultaneously to all the works of art which preceded it. The existing monuments form an ideal order amongst themselves, which is modified by the introduction of the new (the really new) work of art among them. The existing order is complete before the new work arrives; for order to persist after the supervention of novelty, the whole existing order must be, if ever so slightly, altered; and so the relations, proportions, values of each work of art towards the whole are readjusted; and this is conformity between the old and the new. Whoever has approved this idea of order, of the form of European, of English literature will not find it preposterous that the past should be altered by the present as much as the present is directed by the past.[131]

On this reckoning, it is difficult to see what work would not cohere. Anything new will have been found to have its antecedents in the past, because the entire past is altered by it, and the past 'abandons nothing *en route*' (16). And this has repercussions for the notion of 'impersonality', for if impersonality means giving up the pretence to unique self-expression for the sake of being a medium for the voices of the tradition, then every form, word or rhythm in the poem can have its justification by reference to that all-embracing tradition, rather than to some interior quality of the poet. The radical strategy of 'Tradition and the Individual Talent' to attack the 'metaphysical theory of the substantial unity of the soul' (19) means that any attempt to say where the voice of one poet ends and another begins is a fiction, just as for the Eliot of the Ph.D. on Bradley, there is no *a priori* distinction between the self and the world that surrounds it, and the necessary attempts at division we make are pragmatic rather than metaphysical:

The self, we find, seems to depend on a world which in turn depends on it; and nowhere, I repeat, can we find anything original or ultimate. And the self depends as well on other selves; it is not given as direct experience, but is an interpretation of experience by interaction with other selves. The self is a construction.[132]

But if poetry is a matter of the inseparable dependency of tradition and the individual talent, then no poetry whatsoever can be rhetorical. For there can be nothing foreign to the poet's self-expression, because by making the meaning of the poem dependent on the ahistorical Tradition, there is no original internal reality to traduce by convention. 'Tradition and the Individual Talent' is both a parody and a culmination of the Romantic drive for sincerity, for inner, private expression and other people's words have become indissolubly one.

The strangeness of 'Tradition and the Individual Talent', in fact, is that it rejects Romantic poetry to present in its place a classicism which recapitulates some of the chief characteristics of Romantic poetry suggested by the original definer of those terms, Friedrich Schlegel. Schlegel's definitions were conceived as part-development and part-criticism of Schiller's opposition between naïve and sentimental; both began with the principle that poetry was the incarnation of freedom, but where Schiller wanted a reunification, Schlegel thought that such freedom could more truly be realised by a Romantic takeover. 'All the classical poetical genres have now become ridiculous in their strict purity', he declared, whereas Romantic poetry

alone is infinite, just as it alone is free; and it recognises as its first commandment that the will of the poet can tolerate no law above itself. The romantic kind of poetry is the only one that is more than a kind, that is, as it were, poetry itself: for in a certain sense all poetry is, or should be, romantic.[133]

Romantic freedom exceeds not only generic classification, however, but the limits of every individual poem. Building on Schiller's idea of the sentimental poet as one whose inner reflections allow him a new kind of freedom, Schlegel claimed that poetry itself manifests this infinite, reflective freedom in the relation *between* poems, and hence to retain the contingent form and expression of any particular one would place a limit on this freedom. Instead, poetry models infinite freedom by the transcendence of any determined perspective, an endless moving-beyond which Schlegel baptised *irony*. 'Internally, the mood that surveys everything and rises infinitely above all limitations, even above its own art, virtue or genius; externally, in its execution: the mimic style of an averagely gifted Italian *buffo*.'[134] The role of the *buffo* was as an ironic framing device, mixing comic and tragic genres by stepping in between the acts of a play and commenting on or parodying what had just happened – just as Eliot's most famous poem never settles into one voice or perspective, but mixes tragedy with sonnets, or nursery rhymes with ornithological handbooks. If this constant irony ensures that the poet or poem is constantly moving beyond any fixed position in a perpetual alternation of points of view, it also means that no moment stands on its own account: 'no idea is isolated, but is what it is only in combination with all other ideas' explained Schlegel, 'all the classical poems of the ancients are coherent, inseparable; they form an organic whole, they constitute, properly viewed, only a single poem, the only one in which poetry itself appears in its perfection . . . an eternally developing book'.[135] Or, as Eliot put it, 'no poet, no artist of any art, has his complete meaning alone'; his complete meaning is to be found in his relation to the 'organic whole' of the Tradition, which is eternally developing since it is always open to revision by the really new work of art.[136] And for Schlegel, the only appropriate literary form for this expression of perpetual interlinking irony was the fragment or fragments. Only a 'motley heap of sudden ideas' (or what *The Waste Land* calls its 'heap of broken images') rather than a centrally organised poem could manifest such freedom, since the fragment's incompletion would testify to its resistance to all *external* genres, unities, totals and wholes that would encompass it, while simultaneously making infinite freedom potentially visible in its ironic, democratic relation to all the other fragments in 'an *endless* succession of mirrors'.[137] In other words, because all limited perspectives are transcended by irony, the fragments would resist any individual completion for the promise of an infinitely diverse relation of irony; but that which is infinite is that which has nothing outside it and which nothing could complete, and therefore this ironic in-finitude becomes another sort of unconditioned absolute. Despite their admiration for each other, among commentators on Schlegel's theory there is a division between those who see the fragmented form actually encompassing this infinite absoluteness (Benjamin, Lacoue-Labarthe and Nancy) and those who stress that since irony is endless it thus never attains the synthesis of an absolute (Blanchot, de Man, Gasché).[138] This division roughly follows their respective revisions of Romanticism itself as a movement which eliminates discontinuity or promotes it; nevertheless, Eliot's insistence that the Tradition is a *simultaneous* present puts his version of modernism closer to the realisation of this absolute, a plural version of the singular Bergsonian absolute he had rejected in the Imagist poem.[139] If the famous *Athenaeum Fragment* 206 – 'a fragment, like a miniature work of art, has to be entirely isolated from the surrounding world and be complete in itself like a porcupine' – sounds like a description of the ideal Imagist poem, then such self-completion would be truly realised by the Tradition.[140] For where the meaning of a poet's experience is only in its relation to the Tradition, this meaning would be both 'extended and completed' (Eliot's words) and hence become *unconditioned* by any private history or experience, for that Tradition ironises all contingent points of view.[141] M. A. R. Habib has drawn attention to the similarity between Hegel and Bradley's philosophical Absolute and Eliot's ideas about literary form: the 'Tradition' is, in the words of Lacoue-Labarthe and Nancy's book on Jena Romanticism, a literary absolute.[142]

The 'Reflections on Contemporary Poetry' and their culmination in 'Tradition and the Individual Talent' present themselves as an attack on Wordsworthian notions of the individual poet. Rather than poetry being words that depend on the poet's internal emotions, poetry is the unconscious 'concentration' of the Tradition, involving the thoughts and feelings of persons far removed from the individual who makes it. But 'Tradition and the Individual Talent' was not Eliot's last word on Wordsworth or the Georgians. In 1933, in a memorial essay for Harold Monro (with whom he had remained friends), Eliot tried to wrest Monro's poetry from the Georgian context that Monro had helped create:

> With Georgian poetry he had little in common . . . I supposed long ago, that Harold Monro's poetry belonged in this category – with the poetry of writers not unfairly representable in anthologies; and in those days I was interested only in the sort of thing I wanted to do myself, and took no interest in what diverged from my own direction. But his poetry differs from Georgian verse proper in important respects. The majority of those writers occupied themselves with subject matter which is – and not in the best sense – impersonal; which belongs to the sensibility of the ordinary sensitive person, not primarily only to the sensitive poet.[143]

The admission that there might be a worse sense of impersonality – the work that might have been written by anybody sensitive enough – implies that the best sense of impersonality, Eliot's own, actually depends on not taking his philosophical scepticism about personality as an experienced truth, since its whole force actually depends on a fairly vigorous conception of the individual poet. For in a sense, the case of the Georgians reveals why Eliot's argument for impersonality is too strong. If the whole of literature really does form a simultaneous order, why should Wordsworth's presence embarrass the Georgians, if poetry is not the expression of personality but the voice of the Tradition in the poet? Unless Wordsworth is not part of the Tradition at all (and sometimes Eliot writes as if the Tradition skipped straight from Marvell to modernism), the problem can only be that the Georgians are not conscious enough of Wordsworth's influence to sacrifice themselves to it, and what this underlines is the way that being impersonal actually depends upon the persistent conscious submission of the individual artist, with all that it implies about a difference between internal and external, one person and another. 'The progress of an artist is a continual self-sacrifice, a continual extinction of personality', runs the famous phrase, but a continual self-sacrifice is one with the wit to keep crawling off the altar.[144] And it is important that some notion of private, conscientious struggle is preserved, if we are to defend Eliot's metaphor against the charge that 'self-sacrifice', for an exhausted post-war London, smacked less of religious duty and more of the official propaganda that had sanctified the recent slaughter of six million soldiers. Eliot's analogy was to see the poet's mind as a catalyst, which 'may partly or exclusively operate on the experience of the man himself; but, the more perfect the artist, the more completely separate in him will be the man who suffers and the mind which creates' (18). But if the mind which creates really is nothing but a shred of platinum, seizing and combining images in a purely chemical process, then there is no reason to attribute the kind of spiritual victory to the dispassionate use of one's feelings in the service of art that 'self-sacrifice' actually implies. For all its attack on Wordsworthian notions of poetic creation, ultimately Eliot's alternations between an 'unconscious' (21) necessary process and a conscious deliberate act – neatly conflated in the chemical and mental semantics of his word 'concentration' (21) – reflect Wordsworth's own alternation between spontaneous overflow and recollection in tranquillity, and require some continuity of the person between them. Perhaps fearing that his account of the unconscious process of creation has strayed too closely into Romantic territory, Eliot recoups himself at the end of part II: 'only those with personality and emotions know what it is to want to escape from these things' (21). But this sneer costs his argument dear, for it effectively means that impersonality in poetry is in the final analysis always a sign for personality in abeyance, and the focus of the argument is firmly back on the individual artist again. The conspicuous presence of Tradition in 'Tradition and the Individual Talent' would covertly testify to the emotions whose private limitations it was supposed to overcome; its autonomy, in other words, would itself turn out to be contingent.

5

Modernism's arguments to justify its own verse and diminish that of its Georgian rivals were made in the name of denouncing rhetoric, the presence of words and forms externally influencing the poem's heart. There are various names for the remedy – Imagism, Classicism, the

Tradition – but all share the Romantic desire for poetry at one with itself, free from exterior determination, 'acting creatively under laws of its own origination', as Coleridge put it.[145] Although modernist critics often denied this Romantic heritage because it linked them to the dominant poetic tradition of their enemies, it is Romanticism's desire to eliminate the extraneous which provides the common ground between the excisions of Imagism, defending a free inner subjectivity from exterior determinations of formal pattern or generic words, and the poetics of plurality and fragmentation in Eliot, separating off the poem from the contingencies of personality and history, dissolving the possibility of externality in Tradition's perpetual irony, as Yeats would analogously recuperate private loss into the cosmic syntheses of *A Vision*. And it is unfinished business within Romanticism about the possibility of this autonomy – of the aesthetic and of the poetic subject – that relates the modernists to their non-modernist contemporaries. For by writing poetry with a detectable exteriority of form to content, non-modernist poetry witnesses to a lack of perfect unity, and the presence of forces alienating the speaker from him- or herself. In formulating the aesthetics designed to eliminate the possibility of that exteriority, de Gourmont had argued that 'substance engenders form as the tortoise and oyster engender their shells'.[146] Picking up de Gourmont's metaphor, Pound's point was more political: 'The shell-fish grows its own shell, the genius creates its own milieu . . . there is no misanthropy in a thorough contempt for the mob. There is no respect for mankind save in respect for detached individuals.'[147] It is exactly because Hardy, Thomas, de la Mare and Owen did not find themselves solely creators of their own milieu, but also determined by it, that their form is not just an outgrowth of their substance, but is actively and sometimes awkwardly directing it. For Hardy, such exterior determination reflects the implacable indifference of events to human desires; for de la Mare, the echoes of verse-form are part of the self-displacement of the uncanny. It is the subtle, almost-invisibility of his poetic patterns that allows Thomas to explore the relations of chance and choice in enlisting; for Owen, the extraordinary discrepancy between his ultra-patterned formal structure and the shattered content testifies to the unbearable strains of trench life itself.

As with Wordsworth, though, the presence of a form which is palpably out of kilter with its material does not mean that the poem is purely derivative, a poetry-by-numbers whose meaning would already be supplied in advance (although Hardy grimly gestures in this direction, he does so in protest). Such a reversal would simply maintain the absolute antithesis of inside and outside, an antithesis whose origins are visible in Coleridge's binary opposition between poetry which is *either* organic *or* mechanical, from within or from without – a gesture whose anti-industrial logic is also basic to Eliot's complaint about the generalised character of *Georgian Poetry* whose middle-class readership 'rejects with contumely the independent man, the free man, all the individuals who do not conform to a world of mass-production'.[148] Pound and Eliot were fixing the greatest of gulfs between the pure exteriority of the mob and the interiority of the free individual for polemical reasons, of course, but their antipathy left no room to consider those complications of human agency where the private self is always being acted upon by outside forces and yet also alters and adapts them creatively – namely, the situation in which most of us live. For in the last analysis, the possibility of 'rhetoric' is also the possibility of any kind of interaction between collective and individual, outside and inside, a relation without which there would be neither poetry nor politics.

For the Romantic, Symbolist and modernist tradition which bases its legitimacy on organic autonomy, formal externality reveals a heteronomic compulsion inimical to the freedom and self-direction of the aesthetic, and alien to the unique and individual person or situation it describes. In the chapters that follow, however, I aim to show that poems where this perceptible exteriority of form becomes relevant but not wholly reconciled to the interior content can register exactly the difficulties of compromise, mediation, determination and contingency that are excluded by the ideal of perfect freedom. Criticising the self-enclosure of this ideal freedom, however, does not mean abandoning the possibilities of free verse. For despite appearances, free verse is equally unthinkable without some tension between its structure and its material, since it has at the very minimum line-endings, and with them, the possibility of enjambment, 'the opposition of a metrical limit to a syntactical limit, of a prosodic pause to a semantic pause'.[149] A line-break means that there is always a possibility of the rhythmic sound of the line bisecting the sense of it, and they allow the rhythm of a free-verse poem to make links across the syntactic sense, or across the natural pattern of stresses and unstresses inherent in every word and phrase. Once it is admitted that free verse is not solely 'a gapless and unforced unity of form and the formed', in Adorno's words, though, there can also be no objection to more regularly patterned verse as necessarily traducing its content.[150] All poems, in fact, involve the possibility of a difference between semantics and semiotics, formal structure and poetic content: even poems in prose maintain that tension in their very title, because it still opposes the *idea* of poetic content to the prosaic absence of sound-pattern, since there would be no point in prose poetry if the audience didn't know they were poems. To think about the moments when the sounds and rhythms of a poem's structure run, if ever so gently, counter to its ostensible content is to think through the formal inside-outside dynamic of poetry itself – and with it, the problems of freedom and determination manifest in the situations the poem creates, and its paradoxical status as an aesthetic object, contingent upon social and historical forces, its vaunted autonomy a social relation in denial, but an object whose meanings are not finally reducible to those forces and relations either.

If this sounds like having one's cake and eating it, the possibility of such a formal structure was recognised in a backhanded manner by Eliot himself in his preface to Pound's *Selected Poems* of 1928:

People may think they like the form because they like the content, or think they like the content because they like the form. In a perfect poet they fit and are the same thing; and in another sense they *always* are the same thing. So it is always true to say that form and content are the same thing, and always true to say they are different things.[51]

The fact that they 'fit and are the same thing' indicates that they are not the same thing, of course, and Eliot's ineffable last sentence smudges the fact that form and content are the same thing in a way that is necessarily true (all poems would mean something different with a different form) and is therefore useless for critical purposes, but form and content are different things in a way that alters – that there are degrees of fit, in other words. It is the presence of this difference between form and content, no matter how small, that makes Eliot's desire for their unification meaningful; the perfect poet actually relies on the possibility of the difference he or she has overcome, as it were. And the presence of this difference in the most 'perfect' verse is important, because by countenancing a non-identical relation between form and content, it allows for a dynamic between them which is somewhere between autonomous and compulsory, and hence suggests a more nuanced account of social agency than the Romantic binaries of either organic or mechanical, interior or exterior, would allow. In a sense, it is these complications and negotiations between self-presence and the force of the other that also stand for Thomas, Hardy or Owen's relationship with modernism as a whole, as poets neither inside its boundaries nor wholly alien to its aims, and as such, tacit indicators of modernism's difficulties with its own autonomous literary status.

Yet perhaps some of this same internal externality has been residually present in the organic tradition all along, tucked inside the original Romantic metaphors for the ideal poem. As Derrida noted of Schlegel's metaphor for the self-contained fragment, the '*Igel*' (porcupine or hedgehog) only curls up on itself when threatened, as when a hedgehog crosses the road and is almost mown down by the traffic: its perfect self-enclosure, that is, is actually a sign of a highly defensive relation to a mechanical outside.[152] And de Gourmont's perfect shell is, of course, another version of Schlegel and Coleridge's organic tree, the form of which symbolises aesthetic autonomy because it 'is innate, it shapes as it developes itself from within'.[153] Whatever its poetic merits, this definition of tree growth is not very good gardening. The form of a plant is not wholly determined by its unfolding from within: it needs water, wind, sunlight, gravity and many other environmental factors to make it the shape it is. Certain plants prefer specific amounts of light and shade, soil pH, wind or salt, and will simply grow differently, or not at all, without them. Hence organic form is not only 'innate': plant form is determined by its external context and situation as well as from within.[154] The following chapters will trace the influence of that situation on the forms of the poets outside modernism.

# CHAPTER 2

# Edward Thomas in ecstasy

The list of poets who might have been published in *Georgian Poetry* crosses some interesting boundaries of literary history. A. E. Housman refused as he felt himself too old; Ezra Pound was asked but since *Georgian Poetry* wanted only recent work and Pound was reluctant to excerpt anything from his forthcoming *Ripostes*, he was left out.[1] As *Georgian Poetry* gained more of a reputation, its admissions became more selective, and so despite the enthusiasm of their Georgian backers, Robert Frost was considered too American, Charlotte Mew too unusual, and Edward Thomas too posthumous.[2] But the fact that Thomas, of all people, never appeared in *Georgian Poetry* might not be the flagrant injustice it seemed at the time to his supporters, for his opinion of it was, at best, ambiguous. On the one hand, Leavis was wrong to think that 'only a very superficial classification could associate Edward Thomas . . . with the Georgians at all', since many of them were his friends and companions.[3] Always close (or as close as the prickly Thomas ever got) to de la Mare, he also spent holidays with the Gibsons and Abercrombies, had Rupert Brooke to stay, and had actually shared a writing cottage with W. H. Davies, whose work he promoted generously. He had faintly hoped to be in the second Georgian volume himself, and when his reviews summarised the Georgian ethos as the 'modern love of the simple and primitive, as seen in children, peasants, savages, early men, animals, and Nature in general', the gentle mockery is being turned on his own prose work too.[4] On the other hand, he was consistently critical of the poetry that actually appeared in the Georgian anthologies. 'The only things I really much like were de la Mare's and perhaps Davies's', he commented to Frost about the second volume, just as he had singled out their work as the only complete achievement in the first.[5] He was scathing about the 1915 Georgian spin-off called *New Numbers*: Abercrombie 'applies the lash', Drinkwater is 'hopeless' and Gibson 'for me, almost equally so'.[6]

Yet the one other Georgian poet whom Thomas was very interested in was the one poet who was a Georgian and by all accounts shouldn't have been: D. H. Lawrence. Or rather, by all accounts except Thomas's, because in a review of the first volume of *Georgian Poetry*, Thomas crowned Lawrence one of the three poets at the 'core of the group' (the others were Rupert Brooke and the long-forgotten E. B. Sargant), and explained his judgement a month or so later:

Ten years ago the surviving *Yellow Book* men would have been pleased with Mr D. H. Lawrence's subjects, enraged with his indifference to their execution. Nor would they alone have been enraged, and not only Mr Lawrence would have given offence. They would have contracted a chill from so much eagerness both to come at truth and to avoid the appearance of insincerity, the fidelity to crudest fact in Messrs Abercrombie, Gibson and Masefield, the fidelity to airiest fancy in Mr de la Mare, and to remotest intuition or guessing in Mr Brooke, the mixture everywhere of what they would have called realism and extravagance.[7]

Lawrence's eagerness for truth and sincerity places him at the head of this list of Georgians, and not because Thomas was basing his judgement on anthologised poems or ignoring Lawrence's brand of free verse. Rather, it was exactly his verse-form that made him so utterly sincere:

It is obvious at once that the poems would be impossible in 'In Memoriam' stanzas, for example. Their metrical changes, like their broken or hesitating rhythms, are part of a personality that will sink nothing of itself in what is common. They have the effect which Whitman only got now and then after a thousand efforts of rhymeless lawlessness. Mr. Lawrence never runs loose. You can call him immoral or even incontinent, but not licentious. He is no more licentious than a dervish. Moreover, his senses are too wakeful and proud. He sacrifices everything to a certain mood, emotion or frame of mind, but nothing to fine lines, or to false emphasis. There are no 'fine' verses or lines of the usual sort, and the whole of the poem is intense and unchangeable like some of the beautiful single lines of old, when poets were still rhetoricians . . . so honest and patently vivid are they that no man can regard them as foreign to him.[8]

Thomas here makes the same link between free-verse form, total concentration on the object and personal sincerity that Pound and Hulme were in the process of theorising. It was exactly these qualities that he admired in the Imagist F. S. Flint, whose poems in *Des Imagistes* he called 'a sincere and sensitive attempt to write poetry without admitting any commonplaces of verse, in form, language, or sentiment'.[9] When Thomas concluded another review of Lawrence, then, with the comment that Lawrence's free-verse form is 'as near as possible natural poetry', his adjective is striking.[10] For a 'natural poetry' would be what Thomas himself had been seeking for so long, combining his desire to 'wring the necks of all my rhetoric', as he described it to Frost, with his lifelong and consuming relationship with the natural world. The comment about rhetoric was written within days of the Flint review, in a letter that asks Frost teasingly 'whether you can imagine me turning to verse?'; if free verse were sincere, sensitive and natural, it is a fair question to ask why Thomas did not write it.[11]

In fact, he did, but Thomas's free verse is mostly of a kind that is not usually recognised as such, because of the preponderance of other patterns in it, and in general most of Thomas's verse is carefully formal – as, for example, a poem on the topic of natural poetry itself:

> I never saw that land before,
> And now can never see it again;
> Yet, as if by acquaintance hoar
> Endeared, by gladness and by pain,
> Great was the affection that I bore
>
> To the valley and the river small,
> The cattle, the grass, the bare ash trees,
> The chickens from the farmsteads, all
> Elm-hidden, and the tributaries
> Descending at equal interval;
>
> The blackthorns down along the brook
> With wounds as yellow as crocuses
> Where yesterday the labourer's hook
> Had sliced them cleanly; and the breeze
> That hinted all and nothing spoke.
>
> I never expected anything
> Nor yet remembered: but some goal
> I touched then; and if I could sing
> What would not even whisper my soul
> As I went on my journeying,
>
> I should use, as the trees and birds did,
> A language not to be betrayed;
> And what was hid should still be hid
> Excepting from those like me made
> Who answer when such whispers bid.[12]

The poem celebrates, as so many of Thomas's poems do, an unforeseen and vanishing instant of rapture, but in a verse that, like its speaker, is all too aware of the before and after in its regular rhymes and rhythms. It would be a remarkable declaration of Thomas's poetic alienation from the language of trees and birds, were it not for what Thomas actually says a language not to be betrayed is like: that it comes in 'whispers', like the 'breeze / That hinted all and nothing spoke', a phrase whose off-rhymes with 'crocuses' and 'hook' are making his point about indirection in another way. 'Some goal / I touched then'; unidentified, the goal must be unpredicted and only found *en route*, and it is exactly the regular form that makes such distracted satisfaction possible. 'I never expected anything / Nor yet remembered', for example; the usual stress of 'ánything' moves quickly across the line-ending onto 'nor' and cuts short the verse's demand for a full stress on 'thing' – as if the reader were not expecting the end of the line – so that the rhyme with 'sing' two lines later refers back to a sound which has gone by without being fully noticed, and yet, like the unidentified goal, must always have been there. This movement is characteristic of the poem as a whole, its two easy, almost natural sentences winding down across line-breaks and between stanzas, so that its rhythmic boundaries and unstressed or half-rhymes seem to happen only in passing.

The paradoxical demands of this self-evasive goal seeking underlie not only Thomas's verse-form, but his entire poetic career, from its beginnings in his nature writings and criticism to its end in the war. It was a suspicion of too determined an approach to poetic goals that caused him to distance himself from both Georgian and Poundian verse, a suspicion which has left its traces above when Thomas gently reminds Lawrence's potential readers that this ultra-modern direct poetry is not more 'intense' (i.e. concentrated) or unchangeable (i.e. its form is inseparable from its content) than poetry written in eras less obsessed with the elimination of rhetoric. If poetry is poetry whatever its author set out for it to be, then it will not come of deliberation. This welcome of the unsought and dispossessing power of poetry was part of his own desire to eliminate a rhetorical self-awareness, but escaping from such awareness, and the outdoor life Thomas associated with that escape, was also part of his subsequent attitude towards enlisting and the probability of death in France. When asked what he was fighting for, he reportedly picked up a handful of earth and let it crumble between his finger and thumb, saying 'literally, for this', which is usually thought of as a nature-lover's patriotism.[13] But the gesture's bivalence between a love of the earth and the funeral rites that accompany the words 'dust to dust' is telling; in 'The Signpost', it is a 'mouthful of earth' that will 'remedy all' the speaker's regrets and wishes. Nevertheless, this desire for self-avoidance meant that while death is always present, Thomas did not make his own the central focus of his poetry; indeed, he fictionalised his own suicide attempt as 'vanity', its self-importance inimical to the way he thought poetry worked.[14] Rather, his distinctive poetic explores a mode of agency in which self-expression would become inseparable from self-dispossession. It was while he was reviewing Lawrence and reading Frost, the Imagists and the Georgians that Thomas began to write an essay on the topic which gives an name to this contrary condition: ecstasy.

ECSTASY

It began in 1913 when its shy author suddenly found courage in a 'fit of curiosity and daring' to ask a publisher to give him a contract for a book he felt would really say what he wanted, unlike his usual drudgery, and perhaps belonging to the poetic impulse that his correspondent Eleanor Farjeon had assured him he possessed:

Now perhaps the strong warm tide which you tell me of is beginning to reach me. I wish it would – I was going to say with all my heart, but that is or was the difficulty. If it were not I should not hesitate to do so much about Ecstasy. However I am really quartering the ground now. (28 July)[15]

This hope that he would be able finally to write something from the heart did not last. Struggling with deadlines (Thomas published four books that year alone), he was overcome by another wave of grey depression, and when came back to it the topic seemed ironically remote:

I feel cured of the ambition to do Ecstasy & must seek for something more profane & more suitable for a material if insubstantial pen.  (18 September)

Today I began writing about Ecstasy and very badly and the only thing to do for my peace is to go on and on writing and see what happens. Now a great deal might happen in a few days. (undated, mid-October)[16]

Nothing did happen: Thomas abandoned the essay, considering it 'mostly muck & so ill-arranged that it could not be re-written'. But 'Ecstasy' is important in Thomas's life for two reasons. Firstly, because its impulse represented the beginning of the burst of creativity that culminated in his own poems less than a year later. After abandoning the essay, he tried autobiography (posthumously published as *The Childhood of Edward Thomas*), but remained unsatisfied: 'I want a subject to substitute for Ecstasy', he wrote to Farjeon in January 1914.[17] Over the next two months, he began two prose fictions, the first which explores mystical-natural states of consciousness – a preacher who exhorts the crowd to 'forget yourselves in prayer, forget yourselves in love' – and the second about an orphan boy whose father lived and died as a tramp outdoors, 'buried by robins', and whose meetings with a mysterious girl make him feel that he too is living in the 'eternal present of nature's unconsciousness'. Like most of Thomas's fiction, the story goes nowhere, but the situation and phrases from this manuscript are the genesis of lines in his poems. The mysteriously lovely girl appears in 'The Unknown' and 'Celandine', the boy sees animals hanging from a tree in indifference to weather and time, as in 'The Gallows' and the green stoat of 'Under the Wood', and he hears a fairy story which compares the 'crescent moon' to the 'huntsman's ivory horn', an image which begins 'The Penny Whistle'.[18] Of course, neither of these prose explorations was completed either; the preacher manuscript is marked 'dropped at Ledington April 1914', which is a significant place for it to be dropped, for it was at Ledington over this time that Frost cajoled him into believing what Farjeon had suggested, that his prose work was secretly the work of a poet. Six months later the first poem appeared. Of course, the travel, historical and literary books Thomas had to write contain proto-poetic material as well, but the sequence of writings from 'Ecstasy' is important because Thomas began them all for his own sake, the first lappings of the 'strong warm tide' that turned into the flood of poems, written at the rate of more than one every five days for two years.

Secondly, the 'Ecstasy' essay is important because in it ecstasy is synonymous with the poet's highest goal. The original opening sentence was: 'Where the life of the great known or unknown poet culminates, there is ecstasy: they are exalted out of themselves, out of the street, out of mortality'.[19] The greatest moment in a poet's life is to be lifted out of it; the poet may be famous or obscure because ecstasy makes such consider-ations irrelevant. Poetry's ultimate aim is greater than the poet's private self: the mystics, Thomas continues, thought 'the essence of true ecstasy was self-forgetfulness, and that no delight dependent on personal desire, should be given the holy name'. Ecstasy is 'self-surrender', a word which reappears in Eliot's famous call for the artist's 'continual surrender' of himself to the Tradition.[20] And like 'Tradition and the Individual Talent', the desire for impersonality is related to a strong sense of personal suffering, as Thomas continues:

When we are carried out of the daily humour of consciousness, in the rare, magnificent moments when love is admiration of something outside ourselves, [it] causes us to obliterate our personal tendencies, having at the same time a wonderful sense of humanity and lightness, making us regard our ordinary personality in its dusty stock of little thoughts or feelings with astonishment, even contempt.[21]

The rapidity with which Thomas moves from ecstasy as self-forgetfulness to ecstasy as self-contempt suggests that ecstasy's happiness may be closer to its opposite than one would think. For ecstasy is not a word one would normally associate with Thomas's miserably self-absorbed verse, the relentless self-interrogation of phrases such as 'I cannot bite the day to the core' or the 'avenue, dark, nameless, without end' of his childhood memories. Thomas then confesses his own awareness of this contradiction: 'My chief ground and qualification for making this choice [to write on ecstasy] was my intimate acquaintance with the opposite. I knew so well the grief without a pang, described by Coleridge with some flattery, in "Dejection: An Ode" [quoted] where lack of ecstasy seems to become an ecstasy itself'. Poetry in despair is still a kind of ecstasy, because in both rapture and melancholy, there is a sense of being carried out of one's proper self. Ecstasy is 'the condition of being out of place, being out of the accustomed, or if you like, the proper place . . . the term for alienation or distraction of mind'.

If ecstasy is not the first term that springs to mind in describing Thomas's poetry, alienation or distraction of mind might be closer. His poems are famously thickets of yets, ifs and buts, whose process of perpetual qualification and hesitations defies any settled resolution. Sometimes the speaker's mind seems gripped by a word which it cannot let go, helpless and insistent as the vowel-sound in the last stanza of 'Aspens' suggests:

> We cannot other than an aspen be
> That ceaselessly, unreasonably grieves,
> Or so men think who like a different tree.

The words and sounds, like the grief, return again and again, causeless and inevitable. Mulling over the name of 'Old Man, or Lad's-love' is the verbal equivalent of smelling the plant again and again, and thinking of nothing, for 'in the name there's nothing' either:

> Even to one that knows it well, the names
> Half-decorate, half-perplex, the thing it is:
> At least, what that is clings not to the names
> In spite of time. And yet I like the names.

Here the phrase 'the names' itself becomes what it describes, a name whose repeated turning-over thickens it into a thing itself, shadowing its referent. As Wordsworth says, the repeated words interest the speaker's mind 'not only as symbols of the passion, but as *things*, active and efficient, which are themselves part of the passion'.[22] Yet 'name' is only the most obvious of the many repetitions in the poem: as well as the herb, 'garden', 'sniff', 'think', 'feather', 'tree', 'bush', 'shrivel', 'bitter', 'scent' 'perhaps' and 'nothing' all return at shorter or wider intervals, as if the mind in talking to itself is being brought up against its own terms, terms which reveal nothing further other than the effort to remember ('try / Once more to think what it is I am remembering, / Always in vain'). But like the scent, these words are also something to cling to, as if they held firm while the speaker drifts. They are repetitions without an original memory to ground them, and this sense of displacement is amplified by the simultaneous question of the poem:

> And I can only wonder how much hereafter
> She will remember, with that bitter scent,
> Of garden rows, and ancient damson trees
> Topping a hedge, a bent path to a door,
> A low thick bush beside the door, and me
> Forbidding her to pick.

The present-tense clauses make the poem's voice blend into what *will* be the words of the child probing and recalling the scene in her own future. In other words, the poem's present is not just about failing to remember but simultaneously becoming somebody else's history; its own narration does not belong to itself either. Perhaps most subtle are the fleeting suggestions of rhymes buried within the blank verse: the 'tree / Growing with rosemary', 'snipping the tips . . . so well she clips it', 'a low thick bush beside the door, and me / Forbidding her to pick', 'I have mislaid the key . . . I see and I hear'. These are rhymes that, without rhythmic prominence, might be coincidences; heard only in passing, they echo like a memory that cannot place when or where, or know whether it is significant or not.

These processes of self-distraction and alienation are exemplified in one of Thomas's most famously despairing poems, 'Rain'. As the six stresses of the first line weigh its rhythm down, the poem seems melancholically unable to lift away from the title word, turning it over and over:

> Rain, midnight rain, nothing but the wild rain
> On this bleak hut, and solitude, and me
> Remembering again that I shall die
> And neither hear the rain nor give it thanks
> For washing me cleaner than I have been
> Since I was born into this solitude.
> Blessed are the dead that the rain rains upon:

The repetition of 'rain' (and its rhyme in 'again' and later, 'pain') is like the monotonous drumming of the rain itself, a weary reiteration of word in a thought which is itself not new ('remembering again'). The poem has only two sentences, and although the second begins with an attempt to break away from his self-absorption ('but here I pray'), it winds on with two similes which drift away from this wish back to the speaker's self:

> But here I pray that none whom once I loved
> Is dying tonight or lying still awake
> Solitary, listening to the rain,
> Either in pain or thus in sympathy
> Helpless among the living and the dead,
> Like a cold water among broken reeds,
> Myriads of broken reeds all still and stiff,
> Like me who have no love which this wild rain
> Has not dissolved except the love of death,
> If love it be towards what is perfect and
> Cannot, the tempest tells me, disappoint.

The verbless clauses from 'either' to 'like me' lie almost paratactically suspended, succeeding one another in a 'helpless' drift back to the original thought of being dissolved by the rain. Like 'rain', phrases and words such as 'solitude' / 'solitary', 'still', 'love' and 'broken reed' come back; the latter as if the speaker's mind were fastening onto the phrase to find some further meaning in it, but the former sufficiently far apart to make Wordsworth's idea that repetition arises from a 'craving' or 'luxuriation' in the mind sound rather too dynamic.[23] The craving in the speaker's mind here is beneath conscious enunciation; the words indicate the irresistible gravitation of the voice back to its own situation 'remembering again', for love of others returns to 'love of death', and their 'lying still' becomes the 'still and stiff' reeds 'like me'. It is as if these words no longer belonged entirely to the speaker's active will, but mark the helpless drift of his thoughts back to misery.

Yet the ending is not wholly abandoned to its own abandonment. In doubting whether the perfection and reliability of death is really lovable,

Thomas was picking up a theme of the poem 'Liberty' written a few weeks beforehand:

> And yet I still am half in love with pain,
> With what is imperfect, with both tears and mirth,
> With things that have an end, with life and earth
> And this moon that leaves me dark within the door.

What Thomas is not half in love with is Keats's easeful death which would 'cease upon the midnight with no pain': although he had loved the Nightingale Ode since boyhood, he once compared the 'morbidity' of its tone to the Ode on Melancholy's 'connoisseurship' of misery where 'he flatters life and the bitterness of it'.[24] Such unexpected venom indicates Thomas's strength of feeling about deliberately cultivating emotion: he loathed the connoisseur's tacit security which collects things to admire them at a distance, just as he was convinced that 'happiness become conscious has deteriorated to pleasure, that life is not worth living for the sake of its pleasures, that ecstasy sought and bought, as the mystics have said, is impious'.[25] 'Rain' is a poem whose mental distraction finally evades single-minded impulses towards death as well as life, for ecstasy is inimical to any kind of self-determination. And it was this unwitting connoisseurship of ecstasy that Thomas felt was the problem with large swathes of Georgian and Imagist poetry, a problem inherited directly from ecstasy's proto-modernist prophet, Walter Pater.

## THOMAS AND PATER

Thomas had been thinking about Pater all through the year previous to writing the 'Ecstasy' essay, because he had been writing Pater's critical biography on commission. Most of its chapters are as padded-out and rushed as Thomas's other bread-and-butter prose, but the reason why Thomas took it on is evident in the care he takes in certain chapters to exact revenge on Pater's model of thinking, feeling and writing. This was the aesthetic doctrine he felt had strangled his own youthful prose and consequently his own chances of artistic expression, and hence was partly responsible for his enslavement to writing oversized biographies of subjects such as, well, Walter Pater. But in thinking out what was wrong with Pater's approach to style, art and subsequently ecstasy, Thomas was also working out what he felt was wrong with his Georgian and modernist contemporaries, and unconsciously preparing his own future turn to poetry. There is thus a good deal of contemporary art at stake in

Thomas's criticism of Pater's ideas, which homes in on the latter's insistence that art is a matter of self-conscious selection. In his preface to *The Renaissance*, Pater described the task of the aesthetic critic to 'distinguish, to analyse, and separate from its adjuncts, the virtue by picture, a landscape, a fair personality in life or in a book, produces this special impression of beauty or pleasure . . . His end is reached when he has disengaged that virtue, and noted it'[26]. Its 'virtue' was its inner core of individuality, and Pound used the same word when he described the poetic quality 'which is in some peculiar and intense way the quality or *virtù* of the individual; in no two souls is this the same'.[27] The idea of a poem's individual *virtù* is the basis of Imagism's demand for precision and the *mot juste*, and sponsors Pound's condemnation of Wordsworth, who buried the Imagist he sometimes was 'in a desert of bleatings'.[28] This critical opinion was also borrowed from Pater's remark in the preface that 'in that great mass of [Wordsworth's] verse there is much that might well be forgotten', so the task of the aesthetic critic is to locate in Wordsworth despite himself, 'the action of his unique, incommunicable faculty, that strange mystical sense of a life in natural things. . . the *virtue*, the active principle in Wordsworth's poetry' (xi). The Imagist poet, in other words, is the heir of the aesthetic critic of Wordsworth, cutting down the poems to their essential and unique core. The great enemy of such an art was redundancy, as Thomas describes:

It is not surprising that one thus in search of the exquisite, of what has been cleansed of the impurity, irrelevancy and repetition of ordinary life, should arrive at the opinion that music is the typical art, and that all art constantly aspires towards the condition of music, because in music it is impossible to distinguish matter from form. . . [he] denied formulas 'less living and flexible than life itself', and saw poetry cultivating in us those 'finer appreciations' on which true justice in this subtle and complex world depends.[29]

But Thomas's description of Pater's 'virtue' as 'the exquisite' contains the essence of his complaint. For Pater's criticism combined two things that Thomas thought self-contradictory. In order to be faithful to the experience's uniqueness, the aesthetic critic must do away with prescriptive categories, means–end rationality and moralising: beauty must simply be experienced as it is experienced. As the infamous 'Conclusion' to *The Renaissance* has it:

Not the fruit of experience, but experience itself, is the end. A counted number of pulses only is given to us of a variegated, dramatic life. How may we see in them all that is to be seen in them by the finest senses? . . . To burn always with this hard, gemlike flame, to maintain this ecstasy, is success in life. Failure is to form habits; for habit is relative to a stereotyped world. (236)

Yet in order to arrive at the purely ecstatic flame, Thomas complained in *Walter Pater*, Pater has had to consciously refine away the superfluous in the most intellectual, conscious manner possible, discriminating his way through the collected Wordsworth:

He spoke of the 'splendour of our experience' and its 'awful brevity', and the lack of time for theories about the objects of it. And yet one had to be sure that the passion . . . really was passion, and really did yield the full number of pulsations, which meant a considerable wisdom and a 'looking before and after'. (75)

A neat example of the self-contradiction this involves is Pater's summary of his views on 'Style': 'say what you have to say, what you have a will to say, in the simplest, the most direct and exact manner possible, with no surplusage'.[30] This is a sentence whose second and fourth clauses are pure surplusage, because the consciously displayed act of testing and refining his words to find the simplest and most direct manner has utterly overridden any simplicity at all. In short, Pater manifests the old problem of the naïve that turns out to depend on the sentimental. All his simple and direct experiences are intellectualised, shaped and formed as exquisitely pure experiences. And for all Pater's insistence on the unique, and by extension against the mass-produced in life or literature, Thomas tartly notes that this 'conscious conquest of sensation' (94) makes Pater an efficiency expert, 'the aesthetic spectator with a stop-watch', professionally eliminating the 'wasteful', and making sure ecstasy 'pays for itself by "this fruit of a quickened, multiplied consciousness"'. (95)

Hence despite placing ecstasy at the core of his aesthetics, Pater's perfect self-control has eliminated its possibility. The aesthetic critic's 'connoisseurship' means events 'appear only at his desire, rarely taking us by surprise as they do in Nature and in poetry' (96). When Thomas turns to the relation of ecstasy and poetry in the 'Ecstasy' essay, then, it is Pater that he homes in on.

His writing is one of the attempts, one of the failures to make literature all of one even – and mechanical – intensity. It is no more a proof of the possibility of 'burning always with a hard flame' than is ragtime music. . . or the lives which are all sunflowers, peacock feathers and crème de menthe and aesthetic poetry and pseudo-Bergsonism. The mystic knows that ecstasy and notable days are not marked out in advance on the calendar: above all he knows that the other days are far less humbled in comparison with the great and notable days than exalted by their influence: he does not question the possibility of long poems, or of poets where lives no poems tho' without great scent or audible music [*sic*]. Rather is the mystic to be found among those who would wring the neck of rhetorical attempts at imitating the poetry in life as in literature.

If this passage conflates the interior décor of the 1890s with the Bergson cult of the 1910s, it is because Thomas wants to make that link between a Pateresque aestheticism and the Imagists, whose Bergson-inspired fidelity to the unanalysable absolute will always turn out to have been very thoroughly and self-consciously analysed indeed. It was the Imagists who, like Pater, demanded 'maximum efficiency of expression' from a poetic that nevertheless 'washes its hands of theories', a self-betraying denial nicely confirmed by the connotations of Pilate's guilt.[31] 'Modern poets have seen ecstasy, and they have seen the lack of it', remarks the 'Ecstasy' essay, and the result has been the doctrines of Pater and Poe that long poems 'do not exist', in the sense that they are a contradiction in terms. But for Thomas, the concentration they believed essential to poetry is inimical to ecstasy; crucially, the implication of his rejection of an 'even intensity' is that an ecstatic poetics must include moments not 'of the first intensity', the Wordsworthian repetitions and redundancies that Pater sought to eliminate from his prose as from his life. For ecstasy means standing outside oneself – a certain exteriority to oneself—and hence will not align neatly with the perfect *interiority* of form which the Imagists followed Pater in desiring. The refinement that utterly eliminates the superfluous and the common (two of Thomas's favourite words) in the interests of perfect integrity with the uniqueness of 'life itself' leaves no opportunity for that life to go outside itself. For Thomas, Pater's aesthetic philosophy stemmed from his intense desire for self-detachment:

> The isolation of the individual among the terrible inharmonious multitudes impressed him and made it seem certain to him that art should become 'an end in itself, unrelated, un-associated'. He himself is one who continuously writes of all things as a 'spectacle'. . . . Nothing whatever is alien to such a one, for everything is indifferent. (*Walter Pater*, 185)

There is no otherness in Pater, and as Thomas's sly adaptation of Terence's tag indicates, no common humanity either. Pater's aesthetic autonomy, with its correlative organic unity of form and content, is here explicitly translated into social isolation, the elimination of any voice but Pater's own. For although his self-conscious style tries to eliminate everything but the desired meaning, actually 'no man can decree the value of one word, unless it is his own invention; the value which it will have in his hands has been decreed by his own past, by the past of his race' (215).

Words are public things with meanings beyond the power of the private individual. But Pater distrusted anything beyond himself:

The most and greatest of man's powers are as yet little known to him, and are scarcely more under his control than the weather: he cannot keep a shop without trusting somewhat to his unknown powers, nor can he write books except such as are no books. It appears to have been Pater's chief fault, or the cause of his faults, that he trusted these powers too little. (213)

And it was for just this Pateresque excess of self-awareness that Thomas criticised the Imagists – not, as subsequent battle-lines in twentieth-century poetry would suggest, because he held a general contempt for modernist innovation. In fact, his review of *Des Imagistes* declares that Flint's poems 'will interest readers as theorists, and touch them as men', and the same piece notes that 'Mr Pound has seldom done better than here under the restraint imposed by Chinese originals or models': since Pound's best earlier work had, according to Thomas, a 'directness and simplicity', a lack of rhetoric and a 'beauty of passion, sincerity and intensity' that did not depend on verbal pyrotechnics, then it is real praise being offered here.[32] But Thomas had also always been uncomfortable with the intensity of Pound's self-awareness. He is 'so possessed by his own strong conceptions, that he not only cannot think of wrapping them up in a conventional form, but he must ever show his disdain for it a little', remarked a generally positive review of *Personae*. This was also the fault of *Exultations* (his 'verses show us only such things as the writer's effort to imagine'), and turns into the substance of his review of the Imagists. Their writing is 'in the manner of translations' but the foreign-ness of influence and effect they seek is overridden by such self-conscious-ness adoption of otherness: 'There are in this book sixty-three pages, many of them only half-filled; yet it sticks out of the crowd like a tall marble monument. Whether it is real marble is unimportant except to posterity; the point is that it is conspicuous'.[33]

Such self-conscious conquest was equally what he disliked in *Georgian Poetry*, though. Always 'fervently and loudly pursuing some form of magic, rapture or beauty', the contributors always ended up trying too hard:

All in some way adore Aphrodite, Mr Sturge Moore's 'Goddess of Ruin' or one of her priestesses, 'gay, invulnerable setters-at-naught of will and virtue'. Nearly all would give anything to be beyond good and evil. Messrs Davies and de la Mare alone have penetrated far into the desired kingdom, and that without having been certain of their goal or of their way.[34]

'Some goal / I touched then'; Davies and de la Mare have attained poetry precisely because they resist such Nietzschean self-assertions.

This equation of the poetic with the self-transcending of ecstasy also suggests why Thomas's own turn to poetry did not adopt a Lawrencian free verse, however much he admired Lawrence's bravery in doing so. For like Pater, Lawrence's verse 'sacrifices everything to intensity', but as Thomas remarked in the essay, ecstasy cannot happen if there is nothing but intensity since it needs the unnotable and common moments as much as the great ones. Lawrence's 'metrical changes are part of a personality that will sink nothing of itself in what is common', but the common metrical grounding of regular verse, with its necessary lack of intensity at certain points, may be less a hindrance than part of self-dispossession he hoped for.[35] Or to put it another way, a certain exteriority of form to content may be necessary for the 'ec-', the 'outside' of ecstasy. Thomas's paraphrase of ecstasy as 'distraction' contains the same etymological point: distraction means being drawn in two directions at once, whereas free verse and the whole Romantic–Symbolist tradition behind it try to find a form which frees the word, line or self to be itself alone, to follow its own rhythm. As Clive Scott has remarked, 'free verse acted as a release of the present from its assimilation by the past and the future, and into its own changing instantaneousness', for in free verse 'the measure can become a self-sustaining entity'.[36] Thomas's formal rhythms and rhymes mean that words and lines are never self-sustaining, but are always being traversed by patterns and forces beyond themselves, where, in the prayer of 'Words', Thomas's poem about writing poetry, they become both 'fixed and free':

> Let me sometimes dance
> With you,
> Or climb
> Or stand perchance
> In ecstasy,
> Fixed and free
> In a rhyme,
> As poets do.

For Thomas, ecstasy is a state which can be manifest in poetic structures as much as personal experiences, and tracing its *modus operandi* provides a way into understanding the distinctive character of Thomas's own poetry – a poetry that as here, is always in the process of disowning itself.

ECSTASY IN POETRY

'Words' ends 'as poets do', which might be glossed as 'as we poets do', or 'as I do when being a poet', or equally, 'as I would do if I were a real poet'. Six words after 'ecstasy', such delicate shades of self-criticism might seem to poison it. They are so characteristic of Thomas's poetry, with its yets and buts and perhapses and almosts on which so much of his nuanced uncertainty turns. But the poem's point is that poetry, like ecstasy, is never certain, because being a poet is not something the poet can be wholly in charge of:

> Out of us all
> That make rhymes,
> Will you choose
> Sometimes –
> As the winds use
> A crack in the wall
> Or a drain,
> Their joy or their pain
> To whistle through –
> Choose me,
> You English words?

It is not that poets do not work at their writing: they 'make rhymes', and Thomas knew that 'most writers are elaborate; and those certainly not the least whose style is furthest removed from ornament, being simple and natural'.[37] But words are more powerful than the poet, and Thomas is careful to make sure that the self does not secretly reassert itself in making this denial. Lest the Romantic associations of inspiration sound too self-exalting, he gently deflates them by making the poet into a drain rather than Coleridge's Aeolian harp, and asks for ecstasy only 'sometimes', in case it should become as predictable as Pater's. It is this unpredictability that then becomes the crucial factor in the 'ecstasy' of rhyme the poem develops. 'Words' is free verse, in the sense that there is no pattern to the number of beats per line, which range from one to three. However, it does not sound like free verse, because of the frequency of rhymes – in fact, every line has its companion, but those rhymes are often missed because they come so far apart. In the passage above, 'choose' and 'use', 'rhymes' and 'sometimes' come with only a line between them, but 'words' does not find its companion until line 18 and 'me' until line 26. This gives two entirely different reading experiences: as it is being read through or heard, the lines appear to come as free verse does, without overt reference to what has gone before or suggesting what will come. When the poem is perceived as a whole, however, outside the flow of words, each ending can be seen to have its counterpart, so that the rhymes are both 'fixed and free'. This is the condition of the ecstatic, Thomas explains in the essay, because when the mystic is removed from his time-bound private self he or she is thereby enabled to see the true interconnection of the world:

'A touch in one place sets up movement at the other end of the earth'. That is to say that a robin redbreast in a cage sets all heaven in a rage. Here is surely the essence of ecstasy. The man who speaks so has stepped out of self into some boundless world in which most men are isolated as in a diving bell without a window. He has come clear of what belongs merely to the family, to the state, clear as he thinks of all that is finite, space and time.

The poem emulates such mystic harmony: everything has its connection but in the limited time of its enunciation, those connections can't be foreseen or appropriated. It is a state 'out of self', and its ecstasy depends on its formal pattern. Rhymes that are 'fixed and free' in 'Over the Hills' allow another ecstatic memory to reveal itself:

> Often and often it came back again
> To mind, the day I passed the horizon ridge
> To a new country, the path I had to find
> By half-gaps that were stiles once in the hedge,
> The pack of scarlet clouds running across
> The harvest of evening that seemed endless then
> And after, and the inn where all were kind,
> All were strangers. I did not know my loss
> Till one day twelve months later suddenly
> I leaned upon my spade and saw it all,
> Though far beyond the sky-line.

In coming long after the ear has forgotten the first line-ending, the unobtrusive rhymes (again/then, ridge/hedge, and so on) act like a Proustian exploration of memory, where events in the present suddenly and involuntarily recover an unexpected harmony with the past. But as the poem continues with a disappointed admission that 'recall was vain', the rhymes close up as well:

>                              It became
> Almost a habit through the year for me
> To lean and see it and think to do the same
> Again for two days and a night. Recall

Was vain: no more could the restless brook
Ever turn back and climb the waterfall
To the lake that rests and stirs not in its nook,
As in the hollow of the collar-bone
Under the mountain's head of rush and stone.

Not only do the end-rhymes become much more obvious, but the internal chimes between 'again' and 'vain', 'hollow' and 'collar', 'restless' and 'rest' suggest that the past is no longer suddenly and captivatingly reappearing: rather, in demanding to get back to this country of lost content so much, the satisfactions of rhyme are also demanded more often. Yet they are thereby more predictable; it is the mysterious grace of the happenstantial rhymes at the poem's beginning that confirm that the speaker is out of his place, and on condition that he cannot get back there. Ecstasy is not satisfaction or completion, but rather self-displacement, which is why Thomas includes depression and happiness in the 'Ecstasy' essay, and in his poems, more often both at once:

When we two walked in Lent
We imagined that happiness
Was something different
And this was something less.

But happy were we to hide
Our happiness, not as they were
Who acted in their pride
Juno and Jupiter:

For the gods in their jealousy
Murdered that wife and man,
And we that were wise live free
To recall our happiness then.

Happiness cannot be consciously held, just as to stress the word 'happiness' here in accordance with the verse-structure would be to force it artificially, and it is not coincidental that the only full rhyme in this poem is with 'pride'. Yet to leave 'happiness', 'different' or 'jealousy' with their third syllables unstressed ensures that the rhyme will never be full, and happiness is always somewhere else than now. These unstressed / stressed rhymes are simultaneously a recognition that happiness is unexpected, glancing like a by-product of the sentence's turn, and ungraspable. In 'Beauty', the moment when happiness unexpectedly interrupts him comes with this unmarked harmony, which to stress for the rhyme would be to ruin:

This heart, some fraction of me, happily
Floats through the window even now to a tree

'The Wasp Trap' is also about such unintended beauty in a jam-jar left
on a tree overnight. Intended for the unlovely task of killing wasps, in the
moonlight it is transformed:

Nothing on earth,
And in the heavens no star,
For pure brightness is worth
More than that jar,

For wasps meant, now
A star – long may it swing
From the dead apple-bough
So glistening.

The spoken sentence of the poem moves across the line divisions
quickly, varying between two and three stresses per line and eliding the
expected pause at the end of lines like 'For wasps meant, now / A star' and
'For pure brightness is worth / More than that jar'. This makes it run
slightly contrary to the structure of the lines; if one reads that last stanza as
four clear lines of poetry, there is an accent on 'worth'; as a sentence
naturally spoken, there is not. This mismatch between the poem's own
rhyme and rhythm captures the glancing, accidental beauty of the jar, as
the rhyme doesn't fall on the beat in the first stanza's 'lovelier' / 'meadows
were', or only on one half of the rhyme in the second and fourth stanzas,
'more / Lovely [. . .] before' and 'swing' / 'glistening'. This beautiful
moment can only appear in passing, for to expect it might spoil it: as he
says in 'The Ash Grove', 'I had what most I desired, without search or
desert or cost', in a moment which itself is always elsewhere:

Scarce a hundred paces under the trees was the interval –
Paces each sweeter than sweetest miles – but nothing at all,
Not even the spirits of memory and fear with restless wing,
Could climb down in to molest me over the wall

That I passed through at either end without noticing.
And now an ash grove far from those hills can bring
The same tranquillity in which I wander a ghost
With a ghostly gladness, as if I heard a girl sing

The song of the Ash Grove soft as love uncrossed,
And then in a crowd or in distance it were lost,
But the moment unveiled something unwilling to die
And I had what most I desired, without search or desert or cost.

All happiness is a state of suspension in this poem. Grammatically, the last stanza might be a statement of what happened, but equally a conditional dependent on the 'as if' of the girl singing (and the word 'sing' itself is suspended between full and a half-stress running over according to whether the line is hexameter or pentameter: the poem gives no help). And the original moment of happiness seems never firmly there either: it was an 'interval' whose walls the speaker passed through without noticing (as the poem's sentence passes through the wall of the stanza without noticing) and in passing through walls, as well as being 'something unwilling to die', this moment anticipates the ghost that the speaker becomes in reliving it. It is fitting that 'unwilling to die' itself is a rhyme without completion: the rhyme scheme of aaba, bbcb and so on means that each third line is picked up in the next stanza except this one, left in expectation for a resolution that the form simultaneously ensures will not come.

## THE SOUND OF SENSE

Understanding how Thomas's formal poetic structures are part of his ideas about ecstasy distinguishes him from the modernist tradition of Walter Pater. However, it should also be evident that neither is Thomas's poetic one of clear observation reported by a stable subject in simple speech, a version of Thomas that would turn him into a conspicuously ordinary, empirically British Movement poet. Ecstasy is precisely when the normal and everyday fall away: 'all the products of the merely reflective faculties partake of death', remarks the 'Ecstasy' essay. And for Thomas, plain speaking was not enough, as the form of 'After You Speak' illustrates:

> After you speak
> And what you meant
> Is plain,
> My eyes
> Meet yours that mean –
> With your cheeks and hair –
> Something more wise,
> More dark,
> And far different.
> Even so the lark
> Loves dust
> And nestles in it
> The minute
> Before he must

> Soar in lone flight
> So far,
> Like a black star
> He seems –
> A mote
> Of singing dust
> Afloat
> Above,
> That dreams
> And sheds no light.
> I know your lust
> Is love.

The endlessly enjambed lines isolating each couple of words for inspection would make this poem almost Imagistic, were it not for the fact that each line has an unpredictable rhyme, and so turns out to be linked to something beyond itself. Plain speech in this poem is inseparable from a meaning hidden from its speaker; if lust/dust and love/above are a conventional opposition, the lark who is the 'you' belongs to both worlds at once, a piece of singing dust and black star. Plain speech is only one side of the 'dark' and 'different', and the poem's form is continually bringing the other side out.

This is not to say that Thomas was not interested in speech at all, though. As he wrote to Frost:

You really should start doing a book on speech and literature, or you will find me mistaking your ideas for mine and doing it myself. You can't prevent me from making use of them: I do so daily and want to begin over again with them and wring the necks of all my rhetoric – the geese. However, my Pater would show you I had got on to the scent already.[38]

But in Thomas's book on Pater, speech is not held up as a model of poetry. Pater's problem was that his self-consciousness made him use 'words as bricks', with nothing of the 'sincere expressive style' of speech. Speech and its rhythms indicate a core of emotion that it is beyond the power of the self-conscious writer to alter. Instead of reinstating speech as a literary ideal, though, Thomas then changes the argument. It is not a solution to write as one speaks, either, for the problem is with expression of any kind:

Men now understand the impossibility of speaking aloud all that is in them, and if they do not speak it, they cannot write as they speak. The most they can do is write as they might speak in a less solitary world. . . there would be no poetry if men could speak all that they think and all that they feel. (208–9)

Poetry involves an inevitable difference between words and mind that speech cannot override; indeed, it *depends* on the disparity between inside and outside that it is always trying to cross. Thomas's point is provoked by his discussion of Pater's belief that 'literature finds its specific excellence in the absolute correspondence of the form to its import' (196); making speech such a correspondence would override the unknownness of oneself and other people, and confirm Pater's underlying ideal of literature as militantly self-determining, an ideal that it has been his book's constant mission to attack. It is important to bear this passage in mind when we read Thomas's heartfelt praise of Frost's 'revolutionary' poems, written three months after his review of the Imagists:

With a confidence like genius, he has trusted his conviction that a man will not easily write better than he speaks when some matter has touched him deeply, and he has turned it over until he has no doubt what it means to him, when he has no purpose to serve beyond expressing it, when he has no audience to be bullied or flattered, when he is free, and speech takes one form and no other.[39]

For all his admiration for Frost's theories and his verses, this passage indirectly diagnoses why Thomas's poetry is not the same as Frost's – why his speech is consistently rhymed and patterned in a much more structured way than Frost's favourite laconic blank verse. Thomas thought Frost's speakers knew what they meant and where they were coming from, but Thomas was ever doubting himself; and as an army officer, a sufferer from depression or just a shy Englishman, neither could he fully share Frost's American confidence in his own freedom. The unity of agency and purpose that Thomas saw behind Frost's speech was not his own, for Thomas's patterns suggest forces, restrictions and connections that undercut or overrun the speaking voice's present, and displace its speaker.

In fact, Frost's ideas about speech and literature were important to Thomas in just this respect. Frost did not want a transcript of a conversation, but a poem that had kept the 'sound of sense'. This is the unique rhythmic and tonal curvature of people's sentences, what he called the sound of 'voices behind a door that cuts off words'.[40] The 'sound of sense' is so because it is overheard by someone who is not the speaker, and of whom the speaker is not aware. In this way it concurs with what Thomas had declared a few years earlier: 'Love-poetry, like all other lyric poetry, is in a sense unintentionally overheard, and only by accident and in part understood, since it is written not for anyone, far less for the public, but for the understanding spirit that is in the air roundabout or in the sky or somewhere'.[41]

The truth of speech in poetry is there when it is being overheard by someone else, and so many of Thomas's poems begin as if the speaker suddenly overheard someone, in the manner of 'Up in the Wind' ('I could wring the old thing's neck that put it there!') or 'A Gentleman' ('He has robbed two clubs'). Or we overhear the poet thinking, as in 'The Barn' ('They should never have built a barn there, at all'), interrupting himself, as in 'But these things also are Spring's–' or more generally, just talking to himself. In a beautiful image, Walter de la Mare described Thomas's poetry as a rehearsal: 'We listen to a kind of monologue, like one of his own nightingales softly practising over its song, as though in utmost secrecy we were overhearing a man talking quietly to himself, or to some friend silent and understanding'.[42] Hearing a nightingale is perhaps an over-familiar poetic trope, but de la Mare's image comes from a nature-lesson he had from Thomas (recorded in the poem 'Sotto Voce'), when on an afternoon walk Thomas suddenly hushed him to hear the faint notes of a nightingale practising the song he would use that night. The implication is that it is easy not to hear Thomas's voice not only because it seems to be preparing to say something, but also because the listener is not expecting to hear it at all.

It is this unexpectedness in overhearing that makes de la Mare's metaphor and Frost's sound of sense germane to Thomas's self-evasive agency. A spectator is always on the edge of their visual space, able to perceive it as a whole, and ascertain to some extent what will happen next and to orient him- or herself accordingly, as words such as 'foresee' and 'speculate' suggest. This distancing Thomas associated with self-protect-ing connoisseurship: Pater 'has no sense but vision' and consequently always 'admires at a distance'.[43] Even when a sight is unexpected, one comes upon it; it occurs in the direction one is already facing, so to speak. By contrast, an auditor is in the middle of his or her world, and the ears are involuntarily awake to sounds that may occur around and behind. This state of permeability suggests why sound is so important to Thomas's rare moments of happiness. In 'Home [2]', the sense of home-coming, where suddenly 'it seemed I never could be / And never had been anywhere else' is accompanied by the fading of light and the sounds of animals, the speaker surrounded by them, peacefully able to hear their interruption of silence because he is not involved in doing or expecting anything else. 'The call of children in the unfamiliar streets' with the twilight birdsong 'completes a magic of strange welcome' in 'Good-night'; the 'moments of everlastingness' in 'The Other' are more heard than seen:

And all was earth's, or all was sky's;
No difference endured between
The two. A dog barked on a hidden rise;
A marshbird whistled high unseen;
The latest waking blackbird's cries
Perished upon the silence keen.
The last light filled a narrow firth
Among the clouds. I stood serene,
And with a solemn quiet mirth,
An old inhabitant of earth.

The poems themselves are often meditations on somebody's words, like the old man's 'Happy New Year, and may it come fastish too' in 'The New Year', or the child's exclamation, 'Nobody's been here before' in 'The Brook'. As J. W. Haines recalled, so many of Thomas's poems were composed in trains by talking to himself when it became too dark to read, and were only written down later.[44] This auditory self-evasiveness is also important for suggesting the pull of half-heard memories lying just under the surface of consciousness in a poem such as 'The Unknown Bird', for example, where the notes of the bird themselves have a rhythm that in music would be called three-over-two; that is, there is space in the line for two beats, but the identical phonemes give no clues as to where the stresses should fall. Are they 'Lá-la-lá!', or 'La-lá-lá!', or 'Lá-lá-la!'? Not knowing the bird's cry means there is no reason to prefer any of these choices over another; the most likely outcome is to pronounce the rhythm as if it belonged to all of them at once and none of them entirely, hovering three-over-two in 'La-la-la! he called, seeming far off' and 'As now that La-la-la! was bodiless sweet'. This sweet uncertainty then works its way into the rhythm of the opening three words, as if the delightfully unpronounceable call is subconsciously directing his description:

> *Three lovely notes* he whistled, too soft to be heard

Again, their uncertain weighting can be detected beneath the first sentence of his declaration:

> I never knew a voice,
> *Man, beast or bird,* better than this. I told
> The naturalists; but neither had they heard
> Anything like the notes that did so haunt me
> I had them clear by heart and have them still.

As the bird's own song appeared 'seeming far-off [. . .] as if the bird or I were in a dream', so the rhythm can be traced behind other phrases, as if it were half-present to his consciousness. It is a rhythm that can't be pinned down, that floats within itself and floats through his mind, present behind his memories but never captured. These uncertain beats haunt the poet, of course, because they are the aural equivalent of his own emotional uncertainty, the impossible conjunction of "twas sad only with joy', where mutual exclusives are both true. No more than the bird's rhythm can his state of mind be separated out so that each emotion is in its proper place, or be made finally recoverable for analysis; the poem is like footprints left by a chase after its own out-of-place core. But such displacement by birdsong would also be a definition of ecstasy:

> The poets who could say that in words which can make me nothing but ear and soul, as the Persian did that he was neither Christian nor Jew nor Moslem; that he came not of any country, not of East or West, not of land or sea, not of this world or the next, of Paradise or of Hell; for his place was the Placeless.

### PLACELESSNESS

Thomas's ideas about ecstasy were framed within his critical writings about poetic form. As the quotation above suggests, though, being out of place is equally evident in the content – the geography, theology and social organisation of the world of Thomas's poems. Although he is usually thought of as a rural writer, his prose travel books usually consist of a selection of nature-sketches that might have occurred anywhere in the south of England – as *The South Country* admits, its landscape is 'a kind of home, as I think it is more than any other to those modern people who belong nowhere'.[45] Even when there is a definite route to his books, the reader never knows very much about where Thomas is along it, as he tells us that he used maps to know what to avoid. 'I never go out to see anything. The signboards thus often astonish me.'[46] Although *The South Country, In Pursuit of Spring, The Heart of England* and *The Last Sheaf* all begin with an escape from the rootless jumble of suburbia into the countryside, the journey is more important than the destination:

> The end is in the means – in the sight of that beautiful long straight line of the Downs in which a curve is latent – in the houses we shall never enter, with their dark secret windows and quiet hearth smoke, or the ruins friendly only to elders and nettles – in the people passing whom we shall never know though we may love them.[47]

The road enables him to experience a complete lack of relation with what he passes, a placelessness which ironically resembles the unhappiness of one of the suburb-dwellers whose attitudes he has supposedly left behind: 'He could never take it as a matter of course to pass, to be continually surrounded by, thousands of whom he knew nothing, to whom he was nothing. Well did they keep their secrets, this blank or shamefaced crowd of discreetly dressed people who might be anywhere tomorrow.'[48] Thomas too might be anywhere tomorrow, and so might the country people he most admires. *The South Country*'s tramp, the 'simplest, kindest and perhaps the wisest of men', likewise 'had no country' and 'is still on the road', and is one with the watercress man of *The Heart of England*, Jack Noman in 'May 23', the wandering 'Lob' whose 'home was where he was free', and all the disreputable umbrella-menders, gypsies and travellers whom Thomas encounters as fellow pilgrims throughout his prose.[49] Unlike them, Thomas did have a fixed home to go to, but his restlessness there is particularly evident in the three poems to which R. George Thomas gives the title 'Home': the first declares that 'that land / My home, I have never seen':

> And could I discover it,
> I fear my happiness there,
> Or my pain, might be dreams of return
> Here, to these things that were.

'Home' always means yearning to be somewhere else. A similar contra-diction animates the end of 'Home [3]' where the word 'homesick' is 'playfully' suspended between being sick for home and sick of home: the poem ends with a wish to end his 'captivity', but delicately and self-distrustingly refuses to limit that captivity to the temporary home that was army camp. And where the first stanza of 'Home [2]' promises an experience of settledness, it actually and joyfully delivers the opposite:

> Often I had gone this way before:
> But now it seemed I never could be
> And never had been anywhere else;
> 'Twas home; one nationality
> We had, I and the birds that sang,
> One memory.

He 'had never been anywhere else' although he had 'come back / That eve somehow from somewhere far'. It is April, and the birds are thrushes, which means that they have recently returned from winter in southern Europe, so evidently the one nationality he shares with them is not restricted to a single place. In fact, Thomas's 'Home' is a place of unresolvable contraries: the mist is 'familiar [. . .] and strange / Yet with no bar', the labourer's cottage is 'dark white', he walks 'half with weariness half with ease', and his sound 'rounded all / That silence said'. Thomas's poems are so often situated at transition points – at crossroads, bridges, dawn, twilight, between winter and spring or rain and sun, pausing at doorways – because ecstasy's placelessness belongs neither to one world nor the other. The ecstatic moment in 'The Lane' is described as 'a kind of spring', but then 'for heat it is like summer too', and yet 'this might be winter's quiet'. The dark hollies 'glint', the inaudible harebells 'ring', until 'little I know / Or heed if time be still the same, until / The lane ends and once more all is the same': the repeated 'same' suggesting simultaneously a return to everyday flatness and, grammatically, that the ecstasy is always continuing.

Of course, these situations of betweenness, belonging to neither and both at once, are the counterparts of his contrary emotional situation of 'both tears and mirth' ('Liberty'). The thought occurs in 'The Wind's Song' that

> There could be no old song so sad
> As the wind's song; but later none so glad
> Could I remember as that same wind's song.

Thomas's cross-hatched emotions refuse the either/or that diagnosis demands:

> But if this be not happiness, who knows?
> Some day I shall think this a happy day,
> And this mood by the name of melancholy
> Shall no more blackened and obscured be. ('October')

The philosophic Thomas-double in *The Icknield Way*, the book that immediately preceded 'Ecstasy', cannot decide whether he belongs 'half to happiness and half to melancholy, or [whether] to cross out one or the other of these headings as being in his case tautogical'.[50] His double appears in 'The Chalk-Pit':

> At orts and crosses Pleasure and Pain had played
> On his brown features; – I think both had lost; –
> Mild and yet wild too.

'Whate'er my choice / Vain it must be, I knew', says 'Melancholy', 'yet naught did my despair / But sweeten the strange sweetness'. But place-lessness is not merely an exterior analogue of his emotions. It is intimately bound up with the economic circumstances of Thomas's writing on the country, and its permanent sense of not really belonging there. Although he lived mainly in rural Kent and Hampshire, Thomas could never afford to be very far from a railway-station, because London was where his employers and his literary friends were, not to mention his readership. 'The villa men and ladies were the first "lovers of Nature," the first to talk and write of the country', he wrote ruefully, 'for the villa residents and the more numerous others living "in London and on London" who would be or will be villa residents, all our country literature is written'. Love of the country is a uniquely suburban thing, indulged in by those whose real desire is to remain in the suburbs. Their love of the country is for their own sake, for what it brings them in 'rest, relief, stimulation, a kind of religion, poetry, cash'.[51] These attacks on the motivation of his readership apply equally to Thomas himself, for writing the books he did fed the market in country literature and, equally, helped him rest, write and feed his family. It is the predominantly town-based middle classes whose 'widespread craving for anything that will vividly contrast with the life of this class' means they admire 'peasants . . . children, saints, savages, vagabonds, criminals, flowers, nature'.[52] Hence when Thomas asserts that 'the freedom and simplicity connected by them [the suburbanites] with some forms of country life foster that cultivation of the instinctive and primitive, which is the fine flower of a self-conscious civilisation turning in disgust upon itself', such disgust is precisely being turned upon his own prose writing.[53] London begins by being what Thomas must escape from, but turns out to have scripted the escape all along. This problem is shown particularly well in the contrary attitudes within one of the many Thomas-doubles who appear in his prose, the suburban clerk in *The South Country*, who works in the City during the winter, and harvests in the country in the summer. The clerk's conversion to rurality is occasioned by a mystical experience of utter negativity, a 'yawning pit' opening up beneath him. So horrified is he by this total lack of connection between his suburban life and anything outside him, 'unlike the mystic's trances feeling out with infinite soul to earth and stars and sea,' that he moves to the country to work as a labourer for the summers and experience a unity of being and surroundings. Yet this new life does not connect him either, for the country people do not trust him, as he admits: 'I realise I belong to the suburbs still . . . a muddy confused hesitating mass.'[54]

In this portrait and the comments that precede it, Thomas anticipates Raymond Williams's famous criticism of Georgian ruralism as writing which rhapsodises about the countryside precisely because it does not belong to it, which ignores the specific conditions of history and labour that make the landscape and turns it instead into a pastoral ideal. For Williams, writers like Thomas began with 'real respect', but their prejudices led them on to 'a specific conjunction of the homely and colloquial with a kind of weak-willed fantasy'.[55] Thomas was aware of this fantasy and berated himself for participating in its circulation, but at the same time the double is a warning to himself of the opposite fantasy of leaving the suburbs socially, mentally and economically.

Moreover, being weak-willed and impractical was of some importance to Thomas's own poetics of nature, delighted by the ecstatic, mystical sense of oneness with his surroundings he found in Richard Jefferies's *The Story of my Heart*. In *The Country*, Thomas quoted William James approvingly on the idle hours Jefferies spent communing with nature: 'It is necessary to become worthless as a practical being, if one is to hope to attain to any breadth of insight into the impersonal world of worths as such, to have any perception of life's meaning'.[56] In the essay from which this is taken, James goes on to say that

> only your mystic, your dreamer, your insolvent tramp or loafer can afford so sympathetic an occupation, an occupation which will change the usual standards of human value in the twinkling of an eye, giving to foolishness a place ahead of power, and laying low in a minute the distinctions which it takes a hard-working conventional man a lifetime to build up.[57]

It is this association of the useless vision with the mystical one that makes Thomas's countryside difficult to recuperate for any theory that places an ultimate value on labour, and harder to merge with his mystical poetic. For his great criticism of modern literature was precisely that its writing was too laboured, especially the country writers and Georgian poets who worked so hard to be simple. As a socialist, he certainly did not think history and work irrelevant, and once recommended that all school children should be taught history, geography and economics not from books but by walking in their local areas and understanding the forces that shaped their particular landscape. But Thomas's personal geography celebrates the out of place and useless because they are the counterparts of ecstasy, and the suburban and the mystical coalesce in the twin uses of the word 'superfluous'. When his *South Country* clerk remarks that 'he is one of the helpless, superfluous ones of the earth' (75), this is often taken for Thomas's own rueful confession of his Balham roots, yet 'superfluous' reappears in 1913 in *The Happy-Go-Lucky-Morgans* (a book which begins 'my story is of Balham') as a compliment. It is applied to Mr Aurelius, the gypsy and 'the most lightsome of men,' whose superfluity to civilisation is itself a warning to society that production and consumption are not the point. He is the antithesis of productive work, for as one of Aurelius's masters said before sacking him, 'such people were unnecessary. Nothing could be done with them.' Aurelius evades all fixed points, for between his mysterious birth somewhere 'between the moon and Mercury' and his perpetual disappearances, we learn that he has been an under-gardener, bookseller's assistant, waiter, commercial traveller and a circus trainer, and 'everyone thought him a foreigner'. Mr Aurelius is one of Nature's 'by-products,' created without intention or reason, and it is hinted he writes poetry; in other words, he is a fantasy shaped by the self-displacement that became so important to Thomas's own writing.[58]

### SELF-DISPLACEMENT

It is exactly this desire not to rest in himself, though, that makes Thomas's actual poems refuse to sit too comfortably with Borrovian fantasies about being a brother to tramps and gypsies. We can hear the squeals of rhetoric's neck being wrung in 'The Penny Whistle', which assembles its ecstatic ingredients promisingly in the nomadic poor of the charcoal-burners and a series of dark–light oppositions characteristic of Thomas's neither-nor geography:

> The new moon hangs like an ivory bugle
> In the naked frosty blue;
> And the ghylls of the forest, already blackened
> By Winter, are blackened anew.

Like so many of Thomas's mutually contrary situations, the forest, water and sky are dark against the ivory moon and frosty sparkle. But when he attempts to draw human beings into this opposition, the tone becomes more awkward; the phrasemaking of 'The charcoal-burners are black, but their linen / Blows white on the line' tries to raise the poetry stakes with an echo of Blake's 'Little Black Boy' ('And I am black / But oh, my soul is white'). The rather rhetorical inversions of the next couplet do not help ('And white the letter the girl is reading / Under that crescent fine'), and the last stanza admits the game is up:

> And her brother who hides apart in a thicket,
> Slowly and surely playing
> On a whistle an olden nursery melody,
> Says far more than I am saying.

'Slowly and surely' and 'olden' are pure cliché, 'nursery melody' is a jingle, and the present participle of the last line invites the reader to feel Thomas's dislike with his own poem. This sense of uselessness and disconnection as a middle-class writer are also subtly up for scrutiny in 'The New Year'. It begins as a description of an old man encountered in the woods, but the terms used also suggest an unflattering superiority in the speaker's attitude. The man is bestial and grotesque, 'far less like a man than / His wheelbarrow was in profile like a pig'. He forms a 'strange tripod', with a head 'like a tortoise's' and calls to mind someone bending over for leap-frog. Shabby old men occur like saintly visions throughout Thomas's books, appearing for good luck at the beginning of journeys, or as symbols of life halfway between human and natural, like the Watercress man at the beginning of *The Heart of England*, who is 'in the penultimate stage of a transformation like Dryope's or Daphne's' or the tramp in *The South Country*, who thinks 'only "green thoughts" under the branches of a wood'.[59] But the tone and description here is not so much appreciative or incisive as slightly patronising, for the animal similes declare themselves so definitely with an end-stopped line (as nowhere else in the poem and unusually in Thomas's verse) that it is as if the statements are pausing for audience laughter:

> Thus he rested, far less like a man than
> His wheel-barrow in profile was like a pig.
> But when I saw it was an old man bent,
> At the same moment came into my mind
> The games at which boys bend thus, *High-cockolorum*,
> Or *Fly-the-garter*, and *Leap-frog*. At the sound
> Of footsteps he began to straighten himself;
> His head rolled under his cape like a tortoise's;
> He took an unlit pipe out of his mouth
> Politely ere I wished him 'A Happy New Year',
> And with his head cast upward sideways muttered –
> So far as I could tell through the trees' roar –
> 'Happy New Year, and may it come fastish, too',
> While I strode by and he turned to raking leaves.

This subtle sense of superiority is continued by the italicisation of children's games. In his *Childhood*, Thomas tells us that he loved 'the strangeness of the words as well as things . . . I was arrested by the quaintness of Izaak Walton's spelling' but when he discusses these same games, he does not italicise them.[60] Nor does Thomas ever italicise other pieces of vivid folk-phraseology, such as the flower names 'Traveller's-joy' or 'Live-in-idleness' which he relishes in 'Lob'. Here, it makes their colourful names look like academic specimens, pronounced with digni- fied relish from one who was never a boy himself, pompous as the phrase, 'The games at which boys bend thus'. So when the old man speaks, the grouchy terseness of the words are rather abrupt after the pigs, tripods and tortoises of the speaker's striding-by. This non-event of a reply, however, is the poem's tacit focus, for it exposes the lack of fellow-feeling on both sides. When the speaker notes that the man 'took an unlit pipe out of his mouth / Politely', this 'politely' may imply 'though he needn't have done' or 'as he should have done', but in either the forces of social division are evidently at work before the two men have even met. And there is no need to reply to the old man's comment, for the contrast between the vigour of 'while I strode by' and the old man's monotonous, lonely work is left to speak for itself. Why is the man raking leaves in a wood (surely an unending task?), and why is he working on a holiday? Whether he is a gardener or a casual labourer, he is not well-off, and the speaker is left to taste his comment's unexpected bitterness in the telling. Left unassimil- ated, it functions very like the quotation in another sketch of 'animal tranquillity and decay', Wordsworth's 'Old Man Travelling', where the detached walking writer's discerning critical insights are simply brought up sharp against an old man's unhappiness. Thomas's loftiness in the first part of the poem may then be an ironic echo of Wordsworth's own, which he disliked; as he wrote approvingly, Frost 'sympathizes where Wordsworth merely contemplates'.[61]

Criticising a lack of sympathy, in other words, makes the poems' encounters with the homeless and poor a paradoxical identification with them, a common out-of-place-ness. But it was writing throughout 1915 and 1916 that gave Thomas powerful reasons for such an identification that went beyond a generalised emotional correlation, as one of Thomas's least-understood poems, 'The Gypsy', indicates. It is tempting to dismiss it on account of the conventional romanticism of its subject; being inspired by 'the spark / In the Gypsy boy's black eyes' is a cliché of countless cheap romances of the period, and with it, part of the confident race-typing and animalisation of their subject practised by Thomas's contemporaries in organisations such as the Gypsy Lore Society, whose magazine combined a desire to take gypsy culture seriously with a lurid

Orientalism. The symbolist critic Arthur Symons could write in 'In Praise of Gypsies' that 'The Gypsies are nearer to the animals than any race known to us in Europe. They have the lawlessness, the abandonment, the natural physical grace in form and gesture, of animals; only a stealthy and wary something in their eyes makes them human.'[62] So also Thomas's poem, in which 'not even the kneeling ox had eyes like the Romany', and for comparison, Ralph Hodgson's 'The Gipsy Girl', published in *Georgian Poetry 1916–1917*:

> She fawned and whined 'Sweet gentleman,
> A penny for three tries!'
> – But oh, the den of wild things in
> The darkness of her eyes!

And the uneven balance between gift and gratitude which the poem debates, 'I gave it . . . and I paid nothing then', was held by gypsy-lovers to be part of the gypsies' disdain for quantifiable monetary analysis of goods and services. 'The Gypsy will have no possessions, knowing, as none of us know, that every possession is a fetter', claimed Symons.[63] When they steal, declared another gypsyologist, it is not for gain, but 'as a child . . . taking what he needs when he finds it lying unprotected before him'.[64] But Thomas equally knew that such sentiments, 'wistful or fancifully envious admiration' for gypsies, were 'akin to the sentiment for childhood and the golden age', for 'unromanized *Germani*, or animals who do not fret about their souls', desires only felt by the Wagnerian, Whitmanian middle classes who 'over-eat and over-dress in comfort all the days of their lives'.[65] Borrow, whom he was hoping to defend from this charge, is more often 'almost on an equality' with the gypsies. And it is this doubtful equality that underlies the large amount of self-questioning in the poem, starting with the notebook from which he reminded himself of the original incident: 'All begging. One boy and girl I ran away from.'[66] In the poem that resulted, Thomas is not content to move from the human to the animal and remain there admiringly, but must probe that fear, trying to work out what was really going on in their exchange. 'I should have given more', he considers, but she had gone 'before I could translate to its proper coin / Gratitude for her grace'. What kind of gratitude pays for 'grace', though, an insouciance of speech and attitude that is lucky and free? This doubt underlies the alternate readings of the conversation with the gypsy, where we can hear the possibility that Derek Attridge has noted is common to English hexameter, that of alternating between four and six actual stresses.[67] If four, then the tone is expansive:

A fórtnight before Chrístmas Gypsies were éverywhere:

But no great damage is done to naturalness by reinstating the two lost beats less forcefully, slowing the line down slightly but making the subsquent rhyme with the stressed 'fair' more equal, and smoothing out the very obvious six stresses of the next line:

> A fórtnight befóre Chrístmas Gípsies were éverywhère:
> Váns were dráwn up on wástes, wómen tráiled to the fáir.

The conversation with the gypsy in lines three to six is similarly flexible. It is quite impossible, though, to pronounce his subsequent rejoinder to the girl as a six-stress line and not hear him pompous and afraid:

> Unléss yóu can give chánge for a sóveréign, my dear

The sense demands that the awkward second stress falls heavily on 'you' (making the line sound like sarcasm directed at her lack of money) and lengthens the word 'sovereign', as if relishing the sound of the large coin. The girl's reply, however, is subtly done. The four- or six-stress alternative follows from the same choice in the previous line, like a conversation. If we are to believe in the speaker's good self and allow him four stresses, then she responds in a genuine question with a rising tone at the end of the line:

> Then just hálf a pípeful of tobácco can you spáre?

But if he is pompous, then her question becomes tired, petulant: her interest is elsewhere, bored with having to labour the request to another snooty middle-class passer-by:

> Then júst hálf a pípeful of tobácco cán you spáre?

To stress 'just' and 'half' together changes the words from appeal to scorn, as if she couldn't believe he was being so mean. Moreover, the three stresses falling so heavily on the second half of the line makes it difficult to read as the rising tone of a question, and this leaden fall on 'spare' makes the question less personal, more as if she had said it hundreds of times before, perhaps already looking for someone else to ask. He gives it and 'with that much victory she laughed content', as if the exchange had been a battle, but not a serious one – a mix of light-heartedness and aggression which leaves the speaker still unsure whether he has been charitable ('content'), unchar-itable ('I should have given more'), the loser or the better-off ('and I paid nothing then / As I pay nothing now'). The undecidable scansion of these lines reflects an encounter with someone that cannot be weighed up in terms of duties and obligations. It is an operation of 'grace', as opposed to the profit and loss of the fair's normal business of selling animals for slaughter, weighed down by seven heavy stresses:

> Píg, túrkey, góose, and dúck, Chrístmas Córpses to bé.

The question which lies behind 'Christmas Corpses' is, however, rather more serious than the price of a meal. For the gypsy's tune is 'Over the Hills and Far Away', suitable for someone who will vanish tomorrow, but originally an eighteenth-century army recruiting song:

> Hark! Now the Drums beat up again
> For all true Soldiers Gentlemen
> Then let us list, and march I say
> Over the Hills and far away.
> Over the Hills and o'er the Main
> To Flanders Portugal and Spain
> Queen Ann commands, and we'll obey
> Over the Hills and Far Away.[68]

Underneath the poem's sudden turn from gypsy Bacchanalia to the 'hollow wooded land' of ghosts, then, is the question whether Thomas will enlist and risk being a Christmas Corpse next year.[69] But the appeal of the gypsy's song is not to bravery or patriotism, but to someone already dead, a 'ghost new-arrived' in the underworld. The pre-war notebook source for this passage saw this living death as melancholy solitude, like a ghost 'friendless, vacant hopeless' in the dark.[70] Two years later, the gypsy's tune peoples the underworld, as his eyes light it up, because enlisting means being in step with the gypsies, always 'over the hills and far away'. Becoming a soldier would make Thomas join the ageless continuity of homeless wanderers his prose had always admired from the outside and whose music he had tried to find in the *Pocket Book of Songs of the Open Air*. In Thomas's poetry, tramps, gypsies and vagrants are not just Romantic ideals, but always also what their author was waiting to become, sleeping outdoors like 'A Private', alone in the night and the cold like the 'soldiers and poor, unable to rejoice' of 'The Owl', passing into the dark like the tramp in 'Man and Dog':

> 'Many a man sleeps worse tonight
> Than I shall.' 'In the trenches.' 'Yes, that's right.
> But they'll be out of that – I hope they be –

This weather, marching after the enemy.'
'And so I hope. Good luck.' And there I nodded
'Good-night. You keep straight on.' Stiffly he plodded;
At his heels the crisp leaves scurried fast,
And the leaf-coloured robin watched. They passed,
The robin till next day, the man for good,
Together in the twilight of the wood.

Lob, Thomas's rather overripe English anyman, is also 'one of the lords of No-Man's Land' both because he is a vagrant (no-man's land originally meant the verge of grass by the roadside tramps and gypsies would camp on) and because he is out in the trenches. As his encounter with the gypsy indicates, ecstasy is always to do with the incalculable and unsecured; if it is the *leitmotif* of Thomas's poetic, then it is also characteristic of the way he faced death in the coming war.

### WAR AND ECSTASY

Robert Frost certainly saw Thomas's decision to enlist and his decision to become a poet as inseparable. 'The decision he made in going to the army helped him make the other decision in form' he wrote in 1921, which is both a simple material explanation (a regular wage freed Thomas from hack-work) and also perhaps a piece of soul-searching.[71] For it was Frost himself who did most to help Thomas make the decision 'in form', and the implications give an edge to the very famous poem Frost wrote to tease Thomas gently for his indecision over whether to write poems or stick to prose, 'The Road Not Taken'. The poem's applicability extends far beyond the personal circumstances of Edward Thomas, of course, but when Frost first sent it without comment in 1915, Thomas knew that the sigh in the last verse was meant as his own:

> I shall be telling this with a sigh
> Somewhere ages and ages hence:
> Two roads diverged in a yellow wood, and I –
> I took the road less traveled by,
> And that has made all the difference.[72]

But his reply maintains that Frost has missed the point entirely:

It's all very well for you poets in a yellow wood to say you choose, but you don't. If you do, ergo I am no poet. I didn't choose my sex yet I was simpler then. And so I can't leave off going in after myself tho' some day I may. I didn't know after I left you at Newent I was going to begin to write poetry.[73]

Thomas is not being entirely fair here, for Frost's poem is more than a little complex about choice, and certainly not the hymn to individual self-reliance that patriotic Emersonians have sometimes wished it might be. It presents its life-defining decision as one without particularly good reason ('the passing there / Had worn them both about the same'), which undermines the rationality of the choice, and thus thoroughly ironises the idea that taking the independent, hard-working 'road less traveled' makes all the difference, for the poem's conclusion becomes then a piece of retrospective self-justification.[74] On the poem's logic, taking the road *more* travelled would also have made all the difference. But for Thomas, the issue was not the reasons for choosing, but whether poetry and the life it represented was really anything to do with freedom of choice at all. For if one could choose to be a poet, then Pater would have been a better writer; knowing he was not, 'Words' prays 'Choose me / You English words'. Thomas's perpetual self-qualification makes uncertainty a baffling of the independent self implicit in choosing. 'If there be a flaw in that heaven' remarks the second voice in 'The Signpost', ''Twill be freedom to wish', and the poem presents a bewildering list of alternatives that might be wished for:

> To be here or anywhere talking to me,
> No matter what the weather, on earth
> At any age between death and birth
> To see what day or night can be,
> The sun and the frost, the land and the sea,
> Summer, Autumn, Winter, Spring. . .

The choices are so various as to be indifferent; in *not* deciding between them, though, the situation remains as placeless and timeless as the mystics of 'Ecstasy', particularly in that last line which resembles the ecstatic moment of 'The Lane' where all seasons are present at once. The same point is made in 'Liberty', where the tortuous syntax makes liberty indistinguishable from its opposite:

> If every hour
> Like this one passing that I have spent among
> The wiser others when I have forgot
> To wonder whether I was free or not,
> Were piled before me, and not lost behind,
> And I could take and carry them away
> I should be rich; or if I had the power
> To wipe out every one and not again
> Regret, I should be rich to be so poor.

It is liberty to 'dream what we could do if we were free' (l. 10), but those dreams would be about using the hours spent dreaming of freedom for something more worthwhile, or for not caring about their loss. It is liberty to dream about the freedom of not dreaming about freedom, in other words; the more liberty is insisted upon, the more it becomes mired in self-absorption, regretting its own regrets and all the while freely doing nothing. Hence the conclusion that he is 'half in love with pain, with what is imperfect . . . with things that have an end' is not only a declaration for the earthly limitation his freedom laments, but for the imperfections of that free lamentation. Appropriately enough for a poem which will not divide freedom from constraint, what looks at first like blank verse actually rhymes twenty-four of its lines at varying, unpredictable intervals; appropriately for a poem about imperfection, it leaves three as awkward half- or vowel-rhymes only, 'I', 'grave' and 'away'.

These three words set the tone for the poem written just over a month later that is Thomas's most direct reply to Frost's 'The Road Not Taken'. It amplifies Frost's later comment on the confluence of Thomas's turn to poetry with his becoming a soldier, but its more enigmatic title, 'Roads', elides even the moment of choice on which Frost meditates:

> Now all roads lead to France
> And heavy is the tread
> Of the living; but the dead
> Returning lightly dance.

Exposed in the solitude of the 'loops over the downs' rather than alone in a wood, Thomas's walking has only one road to take, and its interest is not in the conscious act of choosing such a road, but how the road makes an inseparable, interdependent relation with its traveller:

> The hill road wet with rain
> In the sun would not gleam
> Like a winding stream
> If we trod it not again.
>
> They are lonely
> While we sleep, lonelier
> For lack of the traveller
> Who is now a dream only.
>
> From dawn's twilight
> And all the clouds like sheep
> On the mountains of sleep
> They wind into the night.

It is impossible to separate out road and wayfarer as it is day or night-time, perceiver and perceived, interior and exterior: there is no independent self to make sense of these oppositions, but only one carried along the road by the road itself. In *The South Country*, the expansive road has figured as the opposite of ecstasy:

A yawning pit, yet not only beneath me but on every side – infinity, endless time, endless space; it was thrust upon me, I could not grasp it, I only closed my eyes and shuddered . . . How unlike it was to the mystic's trance, feeling out with infinite soul to earth and stars and sea and remote time and recognizing his oneness with them. To me, but later than that, this occasional recurring experience was an intimation of the endless pale road, before and behind, which the soul has to travel; it was a terror that enrolled me as one of the helpless, superfluous ones of the earth. (75)

But as the superfluous man of the prose becomes the ecstatic poet, so this earlier nightmare of helplessness has now become inseparable from mystical happiness. 'I love roads', the poem begins, simply, and it is on the road that Thomas is walking along both utterly in the moment, 'in remote time' with the Roman soldiers into Wales and with the dead back from France, and also with Wordsworth, who loved a public road and met the discharged soldier on it. 'It is always going: it has never gone right away, and no man is too late', and the road's perpetual going makes the certainty that everything will pass away into a kind of continuity:

> Roads go on
> While we forget, and are
> Forgotten like a star
> That shoots and is gone.
>
> On this earth 'tis sure
> We men have not made
> Anything that doth fade
> So soon, so long endure.[75]

'Roads' shuns definite starts and stops: living and dying become continuous, just as Thomas's favourite enjambed rhyme slides 'are' into 'forgotten', like the trace of the star seen always as it is vanishing. The present continuous tense weaves itself into Ariel's song ('Nothing of him that doth fade / But doth suffer a sea-change'), a text about deathly transformation which Thomas, like Eliot, had long wondered at for its lack of a beginning: 'The magic of words is due to their living freely among things, and no man knows how they came together in just that order when a beautiful thing is made like "full fathom five". And so it is that children often make phrases that are poetry.'[76] This endless road is the opposite of roots, completion and everything that is proper to the living self. In his travel books, among the tramps and gypsies or absorbed in the countryside, Thomas was always someone passing through, never someone who belonged. In other words, it would not be a matter of choosing this solitary road, because it was where Thomas had always been.

In by-passing choice, Thomas's road also skirts round consequences. Frost's traveller has a modicum of foreknowledge and circumspection, since 'knowing how way leads on to way / I doubted if I should ever come back'. But Thomas's walker is always gladly caught on the hoof, because the end is already here:

> No one knew I was going away
> I thought myself I should come back some day
> [. . .]
> I'm bound away for ever,
> Away somewhere, away for ever ('Song [3]')

The refrain of 'bound away for ever' suggests simultaneously being tied up like a slave and perpetual journeying, being both 'fixed and free'. It is not meaningless to say that Thomas actually chose to go into the army, but in his subtle meditation on enlisting, 'As the Team's Head Brass', that choice is expressly made part of a much larger network of forces and relations that un-ground that supposedly free decision, and with it the self-centred perspective on which choosing hinges. The speaker sits on a fallen elm and talks about enlisting to a ploughman with a curious mixture of self-preservation, black humour and suicidal interest:

> 'Have you been out?' 'No.' 'And don't want to, perhaps?'
> 'If I could only come back again, I should.
> I could spare an arm. I shouldn't want to lose
> A leg. If I should lose my head, why, so,
> I should want nothing more. . . .

Indeed he would not, but it is not the ploughman's aim to chivvy him into enlisting. It turns out that the elm was knocked over the same night as the ploughman's mate was killed on his second day of active service:

                                              Now if
He had stayed here we should have moved the tree.'
'And I should not have sat here. Everything
Would have been different. For it would have been
Another world.' 'Ay, and a better, though
If we could see all all might seem good.' Then
The lovers came out of the wood again:
The horses started and for the last time
I watched the clods crumble and topple over
After the ploughshare and the stumbling team.

This is a poem about contingency, in all its multiple, paradoxical *OED* senses – 'close connection or affinity', 'chance, fortuitousness', being 'at the mercy of accidents', a 'possible occurrence', and in its philosophical sense, 'dependent . . . *on* or *upon* some prior occurrence'. It is chance and accident that the elm fell and that the speaker chose to sit on it, but that chance, and the conversation it leads to, depend on someone else's death. The present situation is the contingent conjunction of infinite might-be worlds, and realising its uniqueness ('and I should not have sat here') is equally realising the intricacy of everything. This sense of contingent, simultaneous lives is strengthened by the way the lovers reappear oblivious at the end; perhaps a baby has been conceived while the conversation has been going on, but the couple will only realise it in retrospect, the ploughman and walker just figures on the edge of their future memory, as they are on the edge of the speaker's. This contingent sense of universal relation without inevitability is axiomatic of the decision to enlist. If the speaker goes out like the ploughman's mate, then everything will be different. But if he does not, everything will also be different, because of all the thousands of other decisions and accidents that are already making up his life, like the ploughman's death. Contingency evades the binary division of self and world, fate and freedom: any moment of free inward decision turns out to be already implicated in and anticipated by contingent events. The games of chance and fate suffered by trench soldiers are in fact already being played out back in England, and this confluence of the circumstantial and the inevitable is what lends the closing lines their extraordinary ambiguity between neutrality and melan-choly. 'And for the last time' might be simply factual – the ploughman has finished his square of charlock – or it might indicate the speaker's decision to carry on his walk. Or it may be an admission that he is going where he will never see another autumn, seeing himself stumbling in the ploughed-up chaos of Flanders, and perhaps hearing the faint accents of the First World War's most fateful command in the clods that 'crumble and *top*ple *over*'.

It would be possible to allegorise further in this vein – to see in the 'ploughshare' of the last line an ironic inversion of Isaiah's prophecy about turning swords into ploughshares, to see Thomas's miserable self-portrait in the charlock as the useless remainder of what was once fruitful, and so on. But to make the death-laden meaning the only real one would be to miss the poem's point, since contingency means nothing is certain, including death – as when Thomas picks up a phrase from this poem in a letter to Frost from the front eight months later: 'I should like to be a poet, just as I should like to live, but I know about as much as my chances in either case, and I don't really trouble about either. Only I want to come back more or less complete.'[77]

'As the Team's Head Brass' is an ecstatic poem, in the sense that it is being taken out of one's self to see the interconnectedness of all things, but in such a way as to leave them as contingently free as they are. In this sense it is also a poem with a word to say about poetic form, for the word 'verse' comes from the Latin *versus*, the turn of the plough at the edge of a field as a model for the way the line turns and begins again. This turn is the formal marker common to metrical and free verse, and the possibility it allows for enjambment – the tension between a metrical limit and a syntactical limit – allows for tension between form and content, interior and exterior. Here too, the conversation happens on the turn:

> I sat among the boughs of the fallen elm
> That strewed an angle of the fallow, and
> Watched the plough narrowing a yellow square
> Of charlock.

The enjambments' pull and play between the unique sentence of the speaker and the regular timing of the ploughman contain in miniature the poem's meditation on what belongs to interior choice and what to exterior forces beyond his control. 'And / Watched', for example, breaks the line carelessly across the sentence, as if the speaker's words were merely incidental to the ploughman's progress, as if the form were slicing up the sense with the indifference of fate. But it may be read equally as a momentary hesitation, an intake of breath to settle down to watching the ploughman, or run over quickly as if noting the elm and ploughman only in passing, so that the form is part of the interior orientation of the speaker. The turn of the verse works as a perpetual contingency, touching word and rhythm, interior and exterior together in a singular coincidence which is equally a dependent condition. The poem's formal point is to make them divergent and inseparable, for simply opposing exterior, formal duty and interior flexible desire would obliterate the poem's theme, the reflexive, tangled and unpredictable relation between one's own life and other people's. For all Leavis's brilliant remark that in Thomas's verse, 'the outward scene is accessory to an inner theatre', 'accessory' makes the outward both a way in and something ultimately disposable, which for Thomas it is not.[78] In this poem, as with the ecstasy that Thomas always longed for, it is in being outside oneself that matters, for ecstasy is not, finally, a private experience: the essay calls it 'the only harmony, through it alone can we make harmony, through it alone can we recognise harmony'. Unlike Walter Pater's perfect isolation and his corresponding formal individualism that would eliminate exteriority, ecstasy is where the interior self is taken outside itself towards others, and this possibility has recently led the philosopher Jean-Luc Nancy to consider ecstasy a central idea of communal relations. 'Ecstasy: which is to say that such a consciousness is never mine, but to the contrary, I only have it in and through the community.' Such ecstatic consciousness, beyond any self-founding notion of the 'subject', is brought about by the end of what Nancy calls 'immanence', the folly of believing oneself or any organisation the independent arbiter of reality, the producer of itself and its own chief interest: 'Community, which is not a subject, and even less a subject (conscious or unconscious) greater than 'myself,' does not *have* or possess this consciousness: community *is* the ecstatic conscious-ness of the night of immanence, insofar as such a consciousness is the interruption of self-consciousness.'[79]

Such radical reformulations of post-Romantic subjectivity may seem far removed from Thomas's trees and birds, but in fact Thomas had expressed the same link between the community and the ecstatic de-thronement of self-consciousness long before, in the conclusion to his tract on the countryside:

The country relates us all to Eternity. We go to it as would-be poets, or as solitaries, vagbonds, lovers, . . . to escape ourselves; and we do more than escape them. So vastly do we increase the circle of which we are the centre that we become as nothing. The larger the circle the less seems our distance from other men each at his separate centre; and at last that distance is nothing at all in the mighty circle, and all have but one circumference. And thus we truly find ourselves.[80]

The country interrupts self-consciousness to make a community from those who have become 'as nothing' within its breadth. It is the non-place of ecstasy, an ecstasy which makes the self's becoming 'as nothing' part of its self-discovery. But Nancy argues that ecstasy occurs especially when the subject is confronted by death, 'that of which it is precisely impossible to make a work' (15); if he is right, then the poems that explore Thomas's ecstatic disappearance into the outdoor life of the countryside and the trenches would be inseparable from his most heartfelt hope of self-expression. Could we live in true ecstasy, concludes the essay, 'each one of us would express and represent all that we were', for 'our lives would be poems beyond the dreams of Poe and Pater'.

# CHAPTER 3

# *Walter de la Mare's ideal reader*

About six months before Eliot published 'Tradition and the Individual Talent', Walter de la Mare wrote a series of newspaper articles on the business of reading. Intended as a general meditation on the subject from the author's point of view, it came to a conclusion about the author's part in the reading process that, at first glance, would trouble no one – except, perhaps, Eliot: 'A book is a mirror reflecting its author – his thoughts, desires, dreams, illusions, disillusionments. It may be as "impersonal" as was the primeval block of granite from which was hewn the Sphinx, but its very impersonality is an indication of his being and character.'[1]

On a second glance, however, de la Mare's point about impersonality becomes rather more opaque, and rather closer to Eliot's. 'Tradition and the Individual Talent' declares that 'honest and sensitive criticism is directed at the work, rather than its author', and a generation of critics took this to mean that biographical criticism was irrelevant. But coming from the opposite direction, de la Mare had anticipated them, for if a book is a perfect mirror of its author, then any impersonality reflects the impersonality of the author's being and character too, an ambiguity which collapses the most biographical reading possible into the least. By identifying the author so completely with the work, de la Mare was not recommending author-centred reading: rather, his aim was to make biography entirely pointless, because learning about the author tells us nothing at all we did not already know from the book:

A poem is so direct an entry into the secret mind of its writer that there is usually little reason or justification for any desire to explore the precincts. If further knowledge of his history and personality is necessary to a true understanding, it means that he has left us the task of finishing the unfinished. That perhaps is why the beautiful work of the anonymous is so happily complete and so completely happy. It is as quiet and self-contained as a solitary green-crowned islet in the deep.[2]

Yet if the first part of this paragraph sounds like New Criticism *avant la lettre*, the second half has a characteristically de la Marean twist, for it makes the absence of the author's personality less a point of interpretative dogma than a kind of experience to be explored by the reader, so that the anonymous poem's isolation and self-containment become part of its mysterious emotional character. If a poem is the mirror of its author, then reading an anonymous poem is also an experience of the 'being and character' of anonymity, not a biographical fact simply missing from the work but an active person or presence. This fascination with the *experience* of absence and vacancy is central to de la Mare's outlook, with its abiding interest in ghosts, graves and silences. 'Is there anybody there?' runs de la Mare's most famous question in 'The Listeners', and it is answered, precisely, by silence which 'surged softly backwards'; there is no reply, yet that absence is present, prescient and unsettling. In order for his audience to experience the uncanniness of this encounter, rather than simply read about it, however, de la Mare needed to cultivate a certain kind of reading, a way of dealing with words whose ideal practitioners were for him between two and six years old. De la Mare was a children's poet, the role in which he is mostly read today, because he believed children heard poetry in a way that left them open to the uncanny, and that it was part of the work of poetry itself to return its adult readers to the child's state of dependency as the price of that openness.

De la Mare was also a Georgian poet, though, a disciple of Thomas Hardy and a friend of Edward Thomas, and his explorations of authorial absence share Thomas's desire for poetry that would make its author 'step out of self'. And like Thomas, his pursuit of these self-erasing ideals led him to reject a certain sort of modernist poetry, only then to propose an alternative which sounds much more like an anticipation of Eliot's sort. In a 1915 review of an anthology of Japanese poetry, de la Mare wondered whether English verse had any equivalent to the 'brevity and concision' of the *haiku*, its 'little dab of colour upon a canvas one inch square'.[3] But he does not mention the most obvious candidate for the English equivalent, the Imagist poem; Pound had claimed the year before that 'In a Station of the Metro' was composed with the model of a *haiku* in mind, as the next best thing to a language in 'little splotches of colour'.[4] The direction of de la Mare's musing, however, suggests that this oversight may have been deliberate. The triolet and limerick were the 'nearest approach' in formal terms, he pondered, but what makes Japanese form really distinctive is its effect on the author's relation to the work itself: 'Though the presence of personality may be discovered in it by the expert, it exacts a complete self-sacrifice from its maker. And its renowned masterpieces are apt to leave the British Philistine a good deal perplexed, if not aghast.'[5] And in his reviews of Pound hitherto, de la Mare's chief complaint had been that his work was not sufficiently about self-sacrifice. *The Spirit of Romance*, for example, demonstrated Pound's tendency to dominate all he wrote:

The Church was once scandalised by a creed that ran: 'I believe in Lope de Vega the mighty, poet of heaven and earth. . .' Substitute the author's name for the dramatist's, and critic for poet, and, in spite of the scholarly modesty of his subtitle, we have a not entirely exorbitant misrepresentation of Mr. Pound's point of view.[6]

This excess of self-promotion spoilt Pound's pre-Imagist poetry as well, for unexpectedly, it actually resulted in his poems being less individual. 'It is obvious that Mr. Pound, when he forgets to pose and frees himself from a kind of superciliousness, is a poet as well as a curious experimenter . . . [but] there is too much parade . . . too egotistic and not individual enough'.[7] Richard Aldington's Imagist work was, he felt, 'silk flowers under the glass of self-consciousness'.[8] De la Mare's creed, on the other hand, was that 'a poem indeed is a giving and surrender of life, of life in essence, and the man who claims to have "made" it resembles the fig tree that boasts of its figs'.[9] But although this anti-authorial approach seems to gesture towards the further reaches of 'Tradition and the Individual Talent', the tradition that de la Mare was interested in was rather less exotic than Eliot's, for his review of Japanese poetry then suggests an unexpected native equivalent for the *haiku*: 'Our nursery rhymes are uncommonly like the Japanese, and such a form as the *hokku* or the *tanka* might become acclimatized in England, if only the poet were sure that his tiny sign-post would conduct the wayfarer into the appointed paradise.' Japanese poetry (not to mention Imagism) may be unfamiliar, but it turns out that its self-erasing poetics have been part of everyone's upbringing – and still can be, for reading even modern children's poetry is a way to encounter the anonymous:

They spirit us back, not into an irrevocable past, but into the ever-present, ever new, and lovely realm of childhood, where dwells that best of all the Messrs. Anon – the poet who squandered a rare imagination and romance on that supreme doggerel, the Nursery Rhymes – a poet so artless that he never even breathed a word how artful he truly was, and so selfless as to leave himself utterly out of his work.[10]

Nursery rhymes and their anonymous author were de la Mare's poetic ideal. 'I wish I were Mr. Anon', he confessed to his erstwhile lover,

Naomi Royde-Smith, 'unknown, beloved, perennial, ubiquitous, in that wide shady hat of his and dark dwelling eyes'.[11] De la Mare did not try to publish anonymously, though, for his Mr Anon is not just the missing author, the person who might potentially be identified one day by diligent research. Rather, he stands for a particular manner of poetic creation which is indifferent to an individual author's originality and personality, and wholly at odds with the tradition of Pater and the Imagists whose claim to artistic excellence is based upon its form's fidelity to the author's unique experience or emotion. Nursery rhymes are poems that have developed over time rather than poems that have been made by one person, and Mr Anon is the representative of the thousands of anonymous parents and children who have created them by wearing smooth the sounds of what were originally popular satiric songs ('Little Jack Horner'), charms ('Ladybird, Ladybird'), ballads or ditties.[12] 'Hickory Dickory Dock' and 'Eena Meena Mina Mo' are relics of old counting systems. What matters to the formation of the nursery rhyme as a poem is not any original experience or intention, but memorable speech, the pleasurable fort-da of rhymes and rhythms suspended and reinstated which embed themselves unawares into the child's memory, until they are needed for the next generation; they are poetic language whose form and power has arisen independently of any singular origin and meaning. De la Mare shared his fascination in these processes with Edward Thomas, both intrigued by the way flower-names and place-names had become a kind of anonymous 'way-side poetry', and their interest is a rural version of the long Western tradition of Aeolian poetics from classical antiquity to Surrealism.[13] What interests the post-Romantic end of this tradition is not the irrelevance of the author (Surrealism was never for shrinking violets) but the experience of his or her absence; as de la Mare declared in a lecture some years before 'Tradition and the Individual Talent', the magic of poetry is to find that 'the self counts for nothing' compared to the everlasting symbols it uses, of which the real person is but a 'reflex': 'such magics make real; they make unreal. They nibble at the very foundations of life . . . they prove we are the sport, the shrines of ancient memories, and are bound, too, on a long journey.'[14]

It is this interest in a lack of origins and originality that sets de la Mare's focus on children apart from the general Edwardian shift towards writing with a child's-eye view, subsequently important for early modernist writers in their search for a naive, direct and uncompromised perspective.[15] Schiller's prime example of the unified naïve sensibility was the way children think and feel, and so in 1915 *Poetry* magazine published some experimental 'imagistic poems' by the children of its editors, because it felt their direct and uncompromised perspective might be well adapted to the new form. Even *Blast* shrieked its approval for the same reason:

IN THE SAME WAY THAT SAVAGES, ANIMALS AND CHILDREN HAVE A 'RIGHTNESS', SO HAVE OBJECTS COORDINATED BY AN UNCONSCIOUS LIFE AND USEFUL ACTIONS.[16]

But de la Mare would remain unblessed by *Blast* because his work is the opposite of the fresh, unconventional and unbiased. Like the nursery rhymes he admired, everything in it is already familiar: its diction is archaic and its imagery of castles, witches, flowers and graves plainly hand-me-down Romanticism. It has no eye on the object, and its verse-form is extraordinarily precise and regular. Anyone familiar with Romantic poetry and especially Christina G. Rossetti has heard it all before. But for a writer fascinated with the anonymous processes of nursery rhymes, having heard it all before is an advantage, for if the best poetry becomes itself as it is passed on, then author and reader alike will find themselves becoming the 'shrine of ancient memories'. De la Mare uses an unoriginal vocabulary to talk about the experience of dis-origination, in other words, and the way that his vocabulary's fadedness connotes both over-familiarity and a sense of fading away makes this poem from his best-selling collection of 1912, *The Listeners*, a representative of many others:

> The flowers of the field
> Have a sweet smell;
> Meadowsweet, tansy, thyme,
> And faint-heart pimpernel;
> But sweeter even than these,
> The silver of the may
> Wreathed is with incense for
> The Judgement Day.
>
> An apple, a child, dust,
> When falls the evening rain,
> Wild brier's spicèd leaves,
> Breathe memories again;
> With further memory fraught,
> The silver of the may
> Wreathed is with incense for
> The Judgement Day.
>
> ('The Hawthorn Hath
> a Deathly Smell')[17]

Nothing could be more conventional than smelling the flowers of the field, and the archaic title seems to belong to another century, but de la Mare turns the very worn-outness of 'sweet' and 'hath' into a delicate balance of menace and pathos. Hawthorn blossom is traditionally not allowed in the house because its sweetness resembles the odour of decaying flesh, and hence in the poem the sweet scent is 'wreathed' around the branch like smoke, and like a funeral tribute. By combining the sibilance of 'sweet' with 'smell', 'silver' and 'incense', and threading 'hath' into 'hawthorn' and 'deathly', de la Mare also breathes a quiet, threatening hiss through the poem, like a gas-jet left on. And as the poem winds on, the deadly smell of hawthorn becomes a 'memory' of what is to come, as if the scent were a reminder of a future which in some sense one already knows too well. Past and future blur, so that the thought of a death which is already here makes the old-fashionedness of the vocabulary quite sinister. It is this peculiar ability to transform the most intimate and familiar matter into something disturbing – disturbing precisely because it is already familiar – that is central to de la Mare's work, just as he found in the child's nursery rhymes an experience of loss and vacancy, and it was what Eliot himself admired in de la Mare, in his tribute poem:

> When the familiar scene is suddenly strange
> Or the well known is what we have yet to learn
> And two worlds meet, and intersect and change.
> ('To Walter de la Mare')

The difficulty with using the nursery rhyme as an ideal, however, is that there is simply no way for an individual author to reproduce the lengthy, anonymous processes of their formation. Eliot's artist can procure knowledge of the Tradition and let it percolate into his sensibility, but de la Mare could only wish he were Mr Anon. What de la Mare had found in the nursery rhymes were poems whose sounds seemed to come into being in and through people; what he could reproduce in his own verse instead was the reading context of the nursery rhyme, namely, the situation of the child learning to use language, who cannot drown those sounds in a sophisticated comprehension of the meaning, as experienced and prose-hardened readers will. It is reading as a child that enables the adult to re-experience the poem's sounds at work, and him- or herself as their conduit; indeed, it is because his genres and vocabulary are so familiar that de la Mare can distract the adult reader's attention towards the poem's aural texture. And yet hearing the sounds of words as one used to is also what makes them unfamiliar, for to read as a child is also to find oneself a stranger within one's own language. It was the aural cat's-cradle of de la Mare's verse that Eliot singled out in 'To Walter de la Mare' as the source of its disturbing power:

> By those deceptive cadences
> Wherewith the common measure is refined;
> By conscious art practised with natural ease;
> By the delicate, invisible web you wove –
> The inexplicable mystery of sound.

For a poet as precise as Eliot, 'inexplicable mystery' is something of a tautology, yet in fractionally returning to linger over his puzzlement – inexplicable *and* a mystery – he catches the very de la Marean moment of hesitation, suspension or intuition that there is something going on outside the reader's definite awareness which has, again, just been missed. The implication of 'web', though, is that having allowed oneself to hesitate is to find oneself trapped. This situation of finding oneself entangled within something, rather than independently free and outside it, is basic to de la Mare's verse and the way it wants to be read. It underlies his love of the Nursery Rhyme, whose sound-texture evokes the child-like state of absorption in and by language, and also his admiration of its anonymous, un-original authors who are the subjects of poetic language as well as its users. It is also at the heart of his explorations of the uncanny, the intimation that one's innermost self is already being shaped by an intimately alien presence or force. And as such, it implies a poetry for which the exteriority of formal sound-pattern will prove to be entirely integral.

### SOUND POETRY

For de la Mare, an awareness of sound as sound or its relative, silence, is for the adult the nearest approach to reading like the child learning language. 'We may be able in some degree to repeat the process through which *all* our vocabulary has gone from childhood onwards', he suggested, 'if we open, say, a dictionary at random; in search this time not of *meanings*, but merely of verbal sounds – their meanings as yet unknown to us'.[18] His poetry does this, first of all, by its concentration on sound-texture, making familiar words strange simply by requiring its adult readers to hear them again *as sounds*, as de la Mare believed we all must have as children.

Long before we could talk we had begun to attach meanings to the words, the verbal sounds we heard. But we learned those meanings from a mother, a nurse and perhaps sisters and brothers, not from a book. For the most part, we discovered what certain words – sounds – were for, that is, not by being taught them one by one, but from the frame in which they were set – looks and voices – tender, laughing, scolding, anxious, intent, sorrowful . . . is there anything in life to compare with these three achievements – learning as an infant to understand words, learning to talk, learning to read? and to convert what we read into images, thoughts, feelings and such a thing as a story?[19]

And de la Mare felt that that experience of the emotional quality of sound itself was not limited to children, but was always present if we had ears to hear it. '[In] writing . . . if we both repeat and listen to the words of which it is composed, two voices are audible and two meanings are inherent – that of the verbal sounds and that of the verbal symbols', he declared in a lecture to the very grown-up British Academy.[20] The lecture went on to explain the way mundane sentences such as 'Is this the nine-fifteen to London Bridge' or 'Dear Sir, I write re your demand for tax' would leap out at him with alarmingly poetic force, because the inherent rhythmic structure of the words had unexpectedly coalesced into metre.[21] Elsewhere he drew attention to the 'oddly exotic cadence' of everyday phrases, such as '*I*-was-in-a', and 'like-the-*one*-we'.[22] Hence his children's verse returns to that first point of attachment between the two voices of sound and emotional sense. Some of it seems to have been composed partly for the sake of saying and hearing the names it includes, as when de la Mare takes up dialect words because they sound more beautiful, such as 'shoon' as the plural of 'shoe' – only fairy shoes, however – to rhyme with 'moon' in 'Silver' and 'The Ruin', or the first couplet of 'I can't abear':

> I can't abear a Butcher,
> I can't abide his meat.[23]

'Abear' is a nonce-word to chime with 'a Butcher' and 'abide'. Other verse seems designed to show off the sound quality of ordinary names, such as the two lines of 'The Wanderers', which simply list the seven known planets, or the eponymous heroes of 'Chicken', 'Dorking, Spaniard, Cochin China / Bantams sleek and small'. As in much children's verse, onomatopoeic verbs are common, with 'sizzling', 'champing', 'ticking', 'buzz', 'clapping', 'tap', 'whistling' and 'snip' in the first twenty poems of *Peacock Pie* alone. However, this concentration on sound makes the reader aware of the onomatopoeic qualities of other words within the same poem, as in 'The Barber's':

> Gold locks and black locks,
> Red locks and brown,
> Topknot to love-curl
> The hair wisps down;
> Straight above the clear eyes,
> Rounded round the ears,
> Snip-snap and snick-a-snick,
> Clash the Barber's shears.

After 'snip-snap and snick-a-snick', it is impossible not to hear the metallic scything of the blades in 'clash' and 'shears', or the way de la Mare's nonce-verb 'wisps' mimics the tiny currents of air visible when hair floats and twists down to the floor. This acute aural awareness is particularly appropriate to the barber's, since the scissors come so uncomfortably close to a boy's ear during a haircut, but he can only look forward into the mirror and listen to their small scrapings behind him. And so with sharpened ears, adult readers may also begin to hear onomatopoeias in words that, as grown-ups, they would skip over, such as 'moaned', 'snored', 'nibble and sip' and 'flap' (all also in the first section of *Peacock Pie*). 'Can touch be suggested by sound, velvet, slimy, pricking, gash – are they, as we say, good words for what they mean?' asked de la Mare in a 1920 version of the 'Craftsmanship' lecture entitled 'Poetic Technique'.[24] 'Cake and Sack' certainly are:

> Old King Caraway
> Supped on cake,
> And a cup of sack
> His thirst to slake;
> Bird in arras
> And hound in hall
> Watched very softly
> Or not at all.

Making the sequence of 'k' sounds at the end of 'cake', 'sack' and 'slake' recalls the stickiness of tongue and back palate after a mouthful of cake; the same muscular contractions at the back of the mouth are repeated to reverse effect in 'Poor Henry' when the 'k' sounds sympathise with Henry's choking and gagging at the smell of his medicine:

> Thick in its glass
> The physic stands,
> Poor Henry lifts
> Distracted hands;

> His round cheek wans
> In the candlelight [. . .]

This intimation by sound-quality is equally important to his 'adult' verse, too, as in 'The Mountains', whose iterated sibilants in 'still', 'icy', 'frosty ulys' and hard 'c' in 'cold', 'sculptured' and 'secrecy' mimic the effect of the scraping and cutting of the ice-sculptor's chisel:

> Still and blanched and cold and lone
> The icy hills far off from me
> With frosty ulys overgrown
> Stand in their sculptured secrecy.
>
> No path of theirs the chamois fleet
> Treads, with a nostril to the wind;
> O'er their ice-marbled glaciers beat
> No wings of eagles in my mind.

The poem's rhythm also suggests what it says, as the comma and dropped stress after the double force of 'fleet / Treads' makes the reader accentuate them, as if nimbly but carefully picking a way over the words like the chamois on the rocks. As if to compensate, the 'ice-marbled glaciers' have an awkward transition between 'd' and 'gl' and one too many stresses to keep a regular rhythm, forcing the reader to slide hurriedly over the sounds as if slipping and scrambling over an icy glacier.

Such intimations hover on the edge of our everyday, adult experience of reading, but de la Mare felt that the sounds of poetry could bring them back, for in them a moment of our own childhood turns out to be still present:

What laws of phonology and of harmony regulate these sequences [of poetic sound] may not yet have been discovered. We become acquainted with these laws in the nursery, with Rattle blue beads in a blue bottle . . . also with the schoolboy counting out formula Eena deena deina duss . . . or to take a more sublime example . . . 'Full fathom five'.[25]

Hence poetry is less a return to childhood than a realisation that childhood is always here, as the nursery rhyme can 'spirit us back, not into the irrevocable past, but into the ever-present, ever new, and limitless realm of childhood'.[26] By including Shakespeare in his list, of course, de la Mare's point extends beyond the nursery: through its formal patterning of words, all poetry to some extent marks sound (and silence) as constituent elements; it is the very possibility of the disjunction of sound from sense that marks the possibility of line-endings, and consequently of a meaning different from prose, dependent on the semiotics of sound and spacing as well as the semantics of the dictionary.[27] Yet de la Mare's implication is that we do not grow in understanding the laws of sound in poetry from the nursery to Shakespeare: to read poetry as poetry – even the most sophisticated poetry – is to find ourselves reading like the child we thought we had left behind. As Auden remarked of de la Mare, his poetry makes us experience language in the way that the child does, something which is new in itself, not just an 'instrument for interpreting'.[28]

Yet it remains a question as to how much we can ever know about this experience: one can dispute the empirical claims of de la Mare's account of children reading, but there is a more philosophical issue at stake, as indicated by the difficulties of Auden's own argument at this point:

> In all cultures, however, there is one constant difference between children and adults, namely, that, for the former, learning their native tongue is itself one of the most important experiences in their lives, while, for the latter, language has become an instrument for interpreting and communicating experience; to recapture the sense of language as experience, an adult has to visit a foreign country.[29]

But learning a new language is not the same as learning one's first. Learning a foreign language involves translating terms already known, but the experience of learning one's native tongue is not describable, or perhaps even thinkable, until one has already begun to learn it, until one is within it and can use it. As Adam Phillips remarks, learning a language changes everything about the child's self-understanding, for 'it is not simply one life in terms of another, because that other passionate life had no terms'.[30] This sense of language as an all-involving experience – one from which the experiencer cannot be detached – was what de la Mare most valued in the young: 'that quite young children, however, can be completely illusioned, transported, immersed in conditions of mind produced solely by words, cannot be questioned . . . it is probable even that the emotion exceeds even that of the writer of the story involved'.[31] Such fascination made the child the ideal reader of all lyric poetry, for without sophisticated comprehension of the sense, they can hear the sound as meaning in itself:

> Eleven words in inexplicable collusion: 'Brightness falls from the air, Queens have died young and fair. . .' What do they mean, what is the secret implication of them all? – that the imagination of man transcends reason, that in some far solitary quiet his spirit may free itself from the reality which enslaves his senses, that, so enthralled, it may speak in a beauty of rhythm and music beyond the

mere significance of words . . . Here he is really and indeed telling out his heart in a kind of trance that is life at its most intense.[32]

Children interested de la Mare as a conduit to other realms, not as a touchstone of the everyday. As a result his children's verse is less about representing children as they are – his children are never noisy or in a gang, for example, and do very little other than read and dream – than it is the objective correlative of a sort of ideal child-reading experience, entranced precisely because children have much less sense of detached self-awareness to fall back on. For grown-ups, though, this sort of dependency requires a readjustment of normal priorities, as Ezra Pound recognised in a sensitive and generous review:

If you *try* to read De la Mare he simply declines to impress you. If you keep De la Mare on your shelf until the proper time, a time when all books disgust you and when you are feeling slightly pathetic, you may open him querulously. And gradually, your over-modernised intellect being slightly in abeyance – if you are favoured of the gods – it may dawn on your more intelligent self that Mr. De la Mare is to be prized above many blustering egoists.[33]

The *New Freewoman's* forthcoming change of title makes that last word even more significant. De la Mare's children's poetry deals with moments when a normal sense of self-awareness and the critical faculties that go with it are suspended, for drawing attention to sound is also, in part, a measure of how far the poem has removed its (and its reader's) attention from everyday sense-making. In 'The Dunce', for example, the child left dully alone in the corner can suddenly hear the minute sounds excluded by daily living, the 'buzz' of a fly, the sound of the thrush outside, a clock ticking; and in being so distracted, he is enabled to notice the absence of sound itself in the sunlight's 'silent shine'. And the point of 'Someone' is that its first line is never proven at all:

> Some one came knocking
>   At my wee, small door;
> Some one came knocking
>   I'm sure – sure – sure;
> I listened, I opened,
>   I looked to left and right,
> But nought there was a-stirring
>   In the still dark night.
> Only the busy beetle
>   Tap-tapping in the wall,
> Only from the forest
>   The screech-owl's call,

> Only the cricket whistling
>     While the dewdrops fall,
> So I know not who came knocking,
>     At all, at all, at all.

The poem is a collection of tiny noises heard instead of a sound half-heard. Expecting something or someone and not being satisfied, all one's faculties are left straining to hear, so they pick up the perpetual, minute sounds usually drowned by people's busy presence. The whole poem is full of tiny repetitions that mimic the repetition of a door-knock rhythm – 'at all, at all, at all', 'sure – sure – sure', 'tap-tapping' – or sounds that echo one another. 'I listened . . . I looked to left', 'stirring in the still', 'busy beetle', 'whistling while', 'dewdrops' and so on. 'Whistle' mimics the cricket, and 'screech-owl' is a double onomatopoeia. This doubling of sense and sound is not so much poetic reinforcement of a prior message as making the word-choice motivated by the same anxiety that drives the poem, compelled to repeat 'sure-sure-sure' by the hope or fear of the unheard knock, and the heart-in-mouth attention to the sounds of the forest, and in doing so, it only makes the absence of the actual sound more palpable. This scenario of an engrossing absence is one to which de la Mare's poems return obsessively. Watching someone absorbed or asleep ('Old Susan', 'Miss Loo', 'The Tailor', 'Martha', 'The Sleeper', 'All That's Past'), pondering the perpetually absent dead ('Never More, Sailor', 'When the Rose is Faded', 'The Stranger', 'Where?'), or the stillness of an empty house ('Alone', 'The Dark Chateau', 'The Listeners', 'Time Passes'), the poems' speakers, listeners or dreamers are confronted by an absence that is not merely a fact, but seems to await and precede them, so that they are thrown into the situation of 'Silence' itself:

> Unmoved it broods, this all-encompassing hush
>     Of one who stooping near,
>     No smallest stir will make
>         Our fear to wake;
>         But yet intent
>     Upon some mystery bent
> Hearkens the lightest word we say, or hear.

The verse-form allows silence to press in upon its shortened middle lines, and the final, deliberate comma lets it seep in so that readers can hear that what they have been reading about is suddenly present, listening to them – and has been since the poem was begun. Unlike simply not noticing a noise, silence is absorbing; it is an absence which is actively heard, so to speak, as if one were on the receiving end of nothing. De la Mare's poems about empty houses or silent sleepers not only evoke the atmosphere of their situations, but through their soundscapes attune the reader's attention to hear the same silence already present around them, surrounding them. This kind of silence is wholly dependent, though, on the poems' regular form, because its pattern encourages expectations of a sound, which then allows that sound's actual absence to be heard too, tense and alive: silence cannot exist within prose as prose, because it has no formal markers to space the words in time, and becomes correspondingly more elusive the more free verse resists pattern and its expectations and obligations. Organic, fluid rhythms put pauses or breaks between lines and stanzas, but the difference of the formal frame from its experienced content in de la Mare's patterns is what allows silence to be felt *within* the line itself. In 'Music Unheard', for example, silence is a kind of Siren call towards death, and the play of expectations in the lines are witness to the struggle to stop it seeping in:

> Sweet sounds, begone –
> Whose music on my ear
> Stirs foolish discontent
> Of lingering here;
> When, if I crossed
> The crystal verge of death,
> Him I should see
> Who these sounds murmureth.
>
> Sweet sounds, begone –
> Ask not my heart to break
> Its bond of bravery for
> Sweet quiet's sake;
> Lure not my feet
> To leave the path they must
> Tread on, unfaltering,
> Till I sleep in dust.
>
> Sweet sounds, begone!
> Though silence brings apace
> Deadly disquiet
> Of this homeless place;
> And all I love
> In beauty cries to me,
> 'We but vain shadows
> And reflections be.'

The poem moves between two beats and three per line, but the uncertainty of de la Mare's actual stress-patterns means that the silence the poem is trying to resist can be heard creeping into the short lines, or being conspicuously overridden in the long ones, as in the effort of 'múst / Tréad ón', or the uncomfortable rapidity of 'Déadly disqúiet'. This alternation comes together in the refrain itself, 'Sweet sounds, begone', which would have three natural stresses in prose, but which the poem either stretches over three beats (with too few off-beats) or compresses into an over-brisk two, so that the line seems to hurry and linger at once, wrestling with temptation. The tension between both possibilities, though, is the space where the silence is making itself felt, just as the final line closes with a faintly missing stress so that the unheard insinuates itself into the very texture of the verse. It is the *intimacy* of the silence that is threatening; just as de la Mare idealises child-like fascination because it leaves the listener with no alternative, detached sense of self to step back to, so poems such as 'Silence' or 'Music Unheard' open the space of this silence within the 'rhythmised' consciousness of anyone reading them.[34] By dissolving the borders between silence and sound, self and its outside, de la Mare's verse brings its reader towards an experience of what Freud classically defined as the uncanny.

THE UNCANNY

Freud's famous 1919 analysis of this phenomenon seems at first a gift-wrapped explanation for de la Mare's unusual combination of writing about ghosts, death and silence and writing about young children. For the former, the uncanny feelings of the adult have their roots in familiar infantile complexes – primitive beliefs in doubles, narcissism, or the compulsion to repeat.[35] Hence the uncanny is 'nothing new or alien, but something which is familiar and old-established in the mind, and has become alienated from it only through the processes of repression', and its effects are particularly to be felt in literature. Yet although Freud goes into great detail about some aspects of uncanniness, his overall approach is not very sympathetic to de la Mare's, since its aim is to demystify the feeling by finding rational and scientific explanation for it, whereas the latter wants delicately to evoke its mystery. Still, having introduced the topic with his usual disclaimers about being no specialist in aesthetics, Freud then admits that his own sensibilities may not be the right ones for this problem:

The writer of the present contribution, indeed, must himself plead guilty to a special obtuseness in the matter, where extreme delicacy of perception would be more in place. It is long since he has experienced or heard of anything which has given him an uncanny impression, and he must start by translating himself into that state of feeling, by awakening in himself the possibility of experiencing it.[36]

Why might Freud worry that he will misconstrue the uncanny because he is unsusceptible to it, when he has never needed to undergo all the neuroses of his patients? What is it about the uncanny that requires a personal familiarity, where hysteria or melancholia do not?[37] This implication that the uncanny cannot be viewed from the outside, as it were, provokes a further question: what confidence can we have in Freud's objective ascription of the feeling to the return of childhood anxieties: are those anxieties doing their own diagnosing? As Neil Hertz has brilliantly pointed out, when Freud's essay turns towards the compulsion to repeat, it is itself subject to the uncanny. In his lengthy analysis of 'The Sandman', Freud may be repeating himself, retelling Hoffmann's story as a version of his own rivalries, repeating Hoffmann's uncanny veering between the literal and figural in his own description of the compulsion. What was supposed to be an objective representation of the repetition compulsion turns out to have been motivated by the very compulsion it claims to discover – and this ungroundable repetition is the movement of the uncanny itself. However, Hertz concerns himself only with the section on repetition, following Rieff's summary that Freud's speculations about other infantile complexes are a 'relatively pale piece of erudition', but in fact Freud's difficulty with grounding the uncanny is evident right from the beginning of the essay, especially in the inordinately lengthy dictionary definitions of the first part.[38]

It begins when Freud talks about translating himself into a person sensitive to the uncanny, because he then devotes two pages to showing that the uncanny – *unheimlich* – is a word that can't really be translated. For Freud, only in German does the true sense of the word exist: 'We will first turn to other languages. But the dictionaries that we consult tell us nothing new, perhaps only because we ourselves speak a language that is foreign. Indeed, we get an impression that many languages are without a word for this particular shade of what is frightening.'[39] This fruitless search through other languages displays the characteristic pattern of the uncanny itself, because in order to translate himself into this mysterious experience, Freud must return to what he already knows, German: the *heimlich/unheimlich* couple is waiting for him in his mother tongue only.

The impression that this odd appeal to and simultaneous dismissal of foreign languages is motivated (in the Freudian sense) is strengthened by Strachey's modest note that in fact, English has the same couple in a rare *OED*-only sense of 'canny'. Of course, Freud could not have been expected to know this, but, proud of his schoolboy Greek, he might have pricked up his ears at one of the other examples Reik supplied, for the Greek ξένος has a very similar paradox, meaning at once stranger, guest and host. What Freud or Reik did, in fact, was to look up the word *unheimlich* in Rost and Schenkl's German–Greek lexicons, find it translated as ξένος, and leave it at that. Had Freud looked up ξένς in Rost or Schenkl, he would have found it translated as *Fremde* and *Gastfreund* in both: the uncanny essay treats Greek as if it were structured by a German original, whereas a paradox of translation is that because no word translates back perfectly, a faithful translation is slightly foreign to its own language too.[40] Although the concept Freud wants is in fact already there, instead, Freud is determined to surmise that the dictionaries tell him nothing new, for the mysterious reason that 'we ourselves speak a language that is foreign'. But foreign to whom? Again, the uncanny strange/familiar couple is at work in the logic here: the foreign dictionaries are all too familiar ('tell us nothing new') because Freud's own mother tongue is 'foreign'. Freud's investigations, it seems, are already being structured by what they are about to discover.

This damages Freud's point in one way and confirms it another. So much for scientific objectivity, since the conclusion of his investigation can be seen to be structuring the method. But this itself is exactly the *modus operandi* of the uncanny, which is where we sense a hidden force to have been at work all along – as Coppelius in 'The Sandman' turns out to have been lurking there all through Nathaniel's life, as the double or telepathic twin turns out to be as much yourself from birth as you ever have been, as Freud feels that the Italian town's red-light district is always awaiting him no matter where he turns, and so on. To experience the uncanny is to be secondary to its machinations: we might say that the uncanny is not so much 'whatever reminds us of this inner "compulsion to repeat"' as the realisation that one is *already* repeating, even in being reminded.[41] Unlike horror or fear, the uncanny never comes as a complete surprise: to experience it is to be always already entangled with some strangely intimate network of forces. To use Freud's examples, the dead return because they know you'll recognise them, or the number 62 turns up again and again because you've seen it before. The one thing that is fatal to the uncanny is objectivity, as Freud observes about fairy stories, for the listener can never be absorbed in its strangeness and simultaneously view it from a mental distance.

At the end of his essay, Freud dismisses the uncanny effect of solitude, dark and silence as childhood anxieties, which he explains elsewhere are coded fears for losing a parent.[42] But if, as his essay has shown, the experience of the uncanny is not simply an absence which leaves the loser bereft and alone, but a suspicion that one has already been enveloped and absorbed by it, then the uncanny effects of silence and solitude would be inseparable from their very intimacy. The difference between a normal experience of absence and an uncanny one perhaps emerges more clearly in Leavis's misunderstanding of what he called de la Mare's poetic 'spell', 'legerdemain', 'trick' and 'illusion' in *New Bearings in English Poetry*, which argues that while de la Mare recognises the human plight of the universe's silent 'indifference to human desires', his poetry describes the encounter with a relish that tempers and sweetens it, insidiously soothing us into the experience of nothing. This diagnosis enables Leavis to put de la Mare away with the other Georgians as a poetry that refuses to face up to modern 'reality', and by way of contrast he cites Hardy's 'The Voice', which really does evoke 'the emptiness of utter loss'.[43] Granted, loss is a staple of Hardy's work; lost love, the non-appearance of God, the cart that doesn't come to take Jude away all manifest the disappointing absence of an expected presence, but Hardy's work is not in the least uncanny, for all its ghosts and spectres. De la Mare, on the other hand, is more interested in the presence of an absence, the tentative *experience* of nothing, or silence itself. Hardy or Leavis's loss would create a lonely hero, whereas de la Mare is more interested in the absorbing silence than any formation of character. His work is, in a way, the opposite of Leavis's 'indifference'; its uncanniness depends on the suspicion that the indifference of nothingness and absence is actually a reflection of our own insensitivity.

One such intimation occurs in an early, unpublished story called 'The Master', in which a young aesthete is invited to view a gallery of paintings. One of them, entitled *Nothing*, attracts his attention, though it is nothing but an abstract square of vivid blue. Yet when he comes close to it, he realises that this blue is made up of thousands of eyes. Nothing is watching him; and the uncanny alternation between both senses of this sentence – is it? does it? – is the emotional core of poems such as 'The Sleeper', where Ann feels her mother's gaze even though she sees her asleep, or with the donkey 'Nicholas Nye' who by day seems to communicate 'something much better than words', but who at night is left immobile and unresponsive, 'still as a post'. 'All But Blind' reasons that since

I am aware of the blinded mole, bat and owl, I must be blind to 'Some-one' in turn – and of course, any lack of evidence of such a 'Some-one' only supports the suspicion; in the same way a speaker walks round the deserted 'Old Stone House', aware that though there is 'nobody at the window', tiptoe is the only suitable approach in the silence in which 'a friendless face is peering, and a clear still eye / Peeps closely through the casement as my step goes by'. This uncanny alternation between nothing and someone is also the situation in which 'The Little Green Orchard' suspends its reader. 'Some one is always sitting there, / In the little green orchard' it begins, and just what weight to put on 'there' is the question; is the someone always sitting there, or is the someone always sitting *there*, on that spot? In trying to determine how much stress to lay on 'there', the reader could allow either three beats or four:

> Some one in shadow is sitting there,
> In the little green orchard.

The next stanza, however, suggests that four is correct:

> Yes, and when twilight's falling softly
> On the little green orchard.
>
> I have heard voices calling softly
> In the little green orchard.

But however suitable a four-beat line is to avoid the line tailing off into two or three unstressed syllables, it would run against the syntax of the lines in the third and fourth stanzas, since the verbs suggest 'there' should be casual and unstressed, as if trying to make the poem's obsessive refrain seem more normal:

> Not that I am afraid of being there,
> In the little green orchard
> [. . .]
> I've sat there, whispering and listening there,
> In the little green orchard
> [. . .]
> Only it's strange to be feeling there,
> In the little green orchard.

When the last line iterates that 'Some One is waiting and watching there, / In the little green orchard', 'there' has by now become a hinge between 'watching there' and 'there, in the little green orchard' and its grammatical usage and rhythmic weight depend upon which side of the sentence one chooses to hear. This uncanny dilemma of attention is precisely the poem's point, though; how much 'there' is there, exactly?

This unsettling interchange of intuition and doubt might be summed up in de la Mare's most well-loved poem, 'The Listeners', with its tentative opening question, 'Is there anybody there?', whose very rhythm suggests all the uncanny circlings and checks of the mind faced with the presence of something missing. The poem's metre is famously tricky, and it is difficult to know whether to read its odd lines with a long three or a quick four stresses.[44] But such uncertainty may be germane, for the failure of prosodic attempts to resolve it into a consistent overall pattern suggests that its irregularities may be important, as in 'The Linnet', where de la Mare uses a missing beat to simulate the way the bird is encountered by a couple of unexpected half-glimpses and sounds, perceived only as it vanishes:

> Upon this leafy bush
>   With thorns and roses in it,
> Flutters a thing of light,
>   A twittering linnet.

The two beats of the fourth line evade the too-obvious rhyme set up by 'in it', as if the linnet appeared and then was suddenly gone more quickly than the three beats of the previous lines expect. So here, the three-stress lines are also the ones that describe the positive *absence* of the listeners, felt in what doesn't happen: 'But no one descended to the Traveller', 'And he felt in his heart their strangeness', and 'Never the least stir made the listeners'. Inversely, the additional stresses in 'Stood thronging the faint moonbeams on the dark stair' are also appropriate to the crowded stairway, and twice, the metre gives way entirely to sheer verbal effect, as when the flurry of unstressed syllables in 'And a bird flew up out of the turret' mimics the panicky flap and flutter of wings; 'Fell echoing through the shadowiness of the still house' has so many syllables to it one loses the beat altogether for the sheer clatter and echo of the words tumbling after one another, like the Traveller's own words. But there is no particular reason for the first line to be either three or four, and having two possibilities is crucial to it. If the poem begins with '"Is there ánybody thére?" said the Tráveller', it is an honest question. But if the poem starts, '"Ís there ánybody thére?" said the Tráveller', it is a query that suspects the answer already. The listeners have somehow communicated to him their presence, *his* strangeness, before he has even spoken. This is the uncanny moment; where one becomes a stranger to oneself, like Freud speaking his own foreign language, like thinking as a child again, like reading a poem. For the uncanny predicament of understanding that the poem puts us into is, to an extent, one that literature itself puts all its readers in. Once, asked what it meant, de la Mare replied:

Every poem, of course, to its last syllable is its meaning; to attempt any paraphrase of the poem is in some degree to change that meaning and its effect on the imagination . . . whereas a scrap of science is for the time being a self-contained announcement of what is an ascertained fact, universally provable by those intelligent enough to comprehend it. You can't prove a poem: it proves you.[45]

# CHAPTER 4

# The simplicity of W. H. Davies

'He has no idea of proportion', wrote an exasperated Edward Thomas to his friend Gordon Bottomley in 1906.[1] Thomas was frustrated with his poetic discovery, W. H. Davies, a one-legged tramp and professional beggar who had paid for the publication of his own poems from his hostel in Southwark in 1905, and sent copies to leading reviewers. One had found its way to Thomas, who was, at first, stunned:

He can write commonplace or inaccurate English, but it is also natural to him to write, such as Wordsworth wrote, with the clearness, compactness and felicity which make a man think with shame how unworthily, through natural stupidity or uncertainty, he manages his native tongue. In subtlety he abounds, and where else today shall we find simplicity like this?[2]

Finding in Davies the Wordsworthian simplicity and compactness he sought for his own writing, Thomas visited him in the doss-house and offered to co-rent with him a little cottage in Kent where they could both get on with their writing. Davies accepted, and the arrangement worked for a while until Davies found simple living in the country a little dull and gradually went back to writing (and, apparently, begging) in London to make ends meet.[3] It was an amicable parting: Thomas continued to praise Davies's work highly for its simplicity and naturalness, but, as his mention of Davies's occasional 'commonplace' writing and his comment to Bottomley indicate, he also began to worry about the inconsistencies of Davies's 'natural' output. In a 1908 review, for example, he remarks in Davies 'a fresh and unbiased observation' but also a certain naïve egoism, 'always neglecting what is not of first-rate importance to himself', which is scarcely an unbiased viewpoint.[4] In another review of the same book, Thomas felt Davies's outlook purified the reader from the paraphernalia of modern life:

The simple, lucid expression of beauty and joy is a thing to wonder at continually . . . the air they breathe is of such astonishing purity that I could scarcely endure the stale sight of half the things that met my eyes in the street after reading the book. This man is so right that all the dull, the ugly, the unnecessary things, the advertisements at the railway station and so on, disgusted me as so many obstacles to the life which those verses seem to propose for me.[5]

But such simplicity then chafed: 'his range of ideas is limited', wrote Thomas in 1910, 'and he will always be more pleased than his readers with variation upon "God made the country and man made the town"'. Attempting to explain (to himself, perhaps) how Davies can be simultaneously so delightful and so irritating, Thomas then insists that in fact, Davies's weaknesses are ultimately reassuring, because they mean that 'Mr Davies's good things come of just that inexplicable unconscious simplicity which used to be called inspiration'.[6] In other words, Davies's bad moments – his lack of proportion – only confirm the true simplicity of his good poems.

A tacit but important shift of terms has taken place here. Simplicity is no longer seen as an inevitable effect of the purity of the author's personality, because Davies writes bad poetry too. Rather, it depends on the incongruity or disproportion between various elements in Davies's work, and it is more visible to the reader than the poet himself. In other words, Davies is not simple because he writes about sheep and cows, but because his lack of proportion, his blithe mixture of the inappropriate as well as the inspired, indicates that his poetry's beauty comes despite its author's intentions. This redefinition gives Thomas's verdict a much wider relevance than just to Davies, for it touches on one of the chief problems with admiring simplicity, directness and all the other virtues of immediacy, that at the same time they tend to leave the simple poet with nothing to do.[7] Davies fascinated Thomas, the Georgians and the Imagists, because they saw in him a living version of the unified, naïve sensibility they longed for. By associating him with a child's-eye vision, Walter de la Mare paid Davies the highest compliment in his vocabulary: 'His art is simply second nature. He delights and at the same time shames his reader, who never in all his born days, or at any rate since he was a tiny little boy, saw anything quite so sharply and only its beautiful self.'[8] And Ezra Pound also admired Davies's 'fine sense and still finer simplicity'; despite noting his lapses into sentiment and his tendency to 'talk about things quite as often as he presents them' ('presentation' being a key Imagist virtue), he then declared: 'Compare it with verse of its own kind and you will not find much to surpass it. Wordsworth, for instance, would have had a deal of trouble trying to better it . . . there is a resonance and body of sound in these verses of Davies which I think many vers-librists might envy.'[9]

But if Thomas were right, and simplicity an effect of disproportion rather than of purity of origin, then Davies's simplicity would start to resemble its opposite, sophisticated modernist dissonance, since thanks to Davies's simple, unreflective refusal to sort his ideas out, the reader will struggle to find a single unifying point of view lying behind them. For the irony of admiring any poet's naïvely direct capacities is that the lack of distance between the poet and the work means the poet cannot be a point of reference to explain it, as Schiller had commented:

He flees the heart that seeks him, the need that would embrace him . . . The subject matter takes complete possession of him; his heart does not lie like some cheap metal right beneath the surface, but rather wants to be sought, like gold, in the depths. Like the divinity behind the structure of the world, he stands behind his work. The *naïve poet* is the work and the work is the *naïve poet*. You have to be unworthy of the work or not up to it or have already had your fill of it, to ask only about *the poet*.[10]

The naïve lack of any detached, reflective viewpoint, the utter identification of the poet with the poem makes the sheer obviousness of Davies's poems quite impersonal – and not in the best sense, Eliot would say, but in the sense sufficiently close to it to point up the difficulties 'Tradition and the Individual Talent' had in reconciling a poetic designed to overcome rhetoric through self-sacrifice with a poetic which would simply make rhetoric impossible because there was no actual self.[11] In fact, the contradictions of simplicity, whereby the more directly the poet speaks, the more invisible or untraceable he becomes, make Davies's work a kind of test-case for the whole question of sincerity, form and style among modernists and Georgians, because its blankness suggests the price to be paid for achieving complete directness. Whether Davies was quite as naïve as people wanted him to be is another matter: he knew how much his simplicity depended on a sentimental audience, and he found it in the Edwardian tramp-cult which saw in his work a freedom from respectable life, and invited him to society gatherings to discuss it. But after his death in 1940 Davies's poetry was largely forgotten until Philip Larkin drew attention to it in his search for an alternative to the modernist tradition. Setting his work in just that context, though, suggests a much closer involvement of modernist poetics with the Georgian and Wordsworthian ones they resisted so vigorously.

READING DAVIES

In his review of the first anthology of *Georgian Poetry*, Thomas thought that only de la Mare and Davies had penetrated far into the kingdom of 'magic, rapture and beauty' that all the other Georgians were labouring to enter.[12] It is not difficult to see the relevance of those three criteria to de la

Mare's delicate rhythmic probings of the uncanny in his hypersensitively textured verse. But for the modern reader coming to Davies's work for the first time, magic and rapture, at least, seem a long way from Davies's straightforward nature-poems in jog-trot metre, which mostly tell the reader what he likes: green fields, white sheep and happy cows. Given Thomas's own delicate, precise evocation of the natural world, his admiration becomes more mysterious when one considers a typical Davies poem – and the point is precisely that one can identify a 'typical' Davies poem, since what is most likely to strike a reader about his supposedly 'fresh, unbiased observation' is its conventionality and formula.[13] An often-reprinted nature-poem, 'Early Morn', for example:

> Then I arose to take the air –
>     The lovely air that made birds scream;
> Just as green hill launched the ship
> Of gold, to take its first clear dip.
>
> And it began its journey then,
>     As I came forth to take the air;
> The timid Stars had vanished quite,
>     The Moon was dying with a stare;
> Horses, and kine, and sheep were seen
> As still as pictures, in fields green.[14]

The green fields, green hill and gold sun suggest this picture is being painted by numbers, and 'dip' is particularly unfortunate when the sun is actually rising. A sense of distance from any particular landscape is reinforced by the passive tense of 'were seen', as if it were not Davies looking, and the conventions become even clearer when elements of the poem are reassembled in 'The East in Gold':

> Somehow this world is wonderful at times,
> As it has been from early morn in May;
> Since first I heard the cock-a-doodle-do,
> Timekeeper on green farms – at break of day.

The farm may have been red brick, brown timber or grey stone with fields in shades of brown and yellow, but in Davies's poem it is green because that is the accepted code for nature, the 'green world':

> I could not sleep again, for such wild cries,
> And went out early into their green world;
> And then I saw what set their little tongues
> To scream for joy – they saw the East in gold.

Davies's images return with such frequency – the screaming bird occurs a third time in 'A Bird's Anger' – that the innocuous title of his *Collected Poems* unintentionally suggests poems that have been collected and re-assembled from a rather meagrely stocked poetic store-cupboard. A skylark is a singing star in 'April's Charms', 'Day's Black Star', 'The Evening Star' and 'The Two Stars'. Clouds resemble sheep in 'Clouds' and 'The Likeness'. There are numerous poems about birdsong in the rain. It is not that these are bad images, but recycling them makes the poems seem cooked up according to formula rather than experience, where fields are always green, money is almost always 'gold' and girls usually 'maids'.

If Davies is difficult to appreciate at first, perhaps this simply reveals how deeply embedded Romantic categories of heartfelt diction and authorial originality are, yet interwoven with convention are moments of freshness and surprise. 'Early Morn', above, continues:

> It seemed as though I had surprised
> And trespassed in a golden world
> That should have passed while men slept!

'Trespassed' here beguilingly suggests Davies's mystical awe ('forgive us our trespasses') and more earth-bound tramping fears ('trespassers will be prosecuted'). But such precision is reserved for Davies's feelings, not for the landscape. This poem, like all of Davies's nature-poems, is less about nature than William H. Davies, natural, simple poet. As J. C. Squire observed, 'his moon is bright, his sheep are white, his lambs are woolly, his fields green, his horses dumb, and with "pretty", "fair", "sweet", "sad", "hard" and "soft" one is almost half-way through his vocabulary'.[15] But in a sense it does not matter, for Davies's conventions testify to his open *naïveté* as well; what counts in a Davies poem is not so much accurate observation of nature as the construction of Davies's 'simple' observation itself, and the frequent praise his Edwardian reviewers lavished on him for being simple is all directed at his person, not on the intrinsic merits of his poems. 'Davies tells the truth because it does not occur to him to say anything else', typically, for, opined Squire, 'his real business is to look at common things with the child's freshness and to express his delight with simple spontanaity'.[16] What they enjoy is Davies being a poet, not the poems in their own right. After Shaw's preface to the *Autobiography of a Super-Tramp* made mention of Davies's 'delicate and individual' handwriting, his publishers reproduced it in his *Collected Poems* (1916) for the reader to appreciate the poet's good character.[17] This makes Thomas and de la Mare's admiration for him even more puzzling, for such direct self-promotion is at odds with their own attempts at out-manoeuvring their conscious and divided selves. De la Mare's ideal poem was the nursery rhyme because it brought its reader into the 'selfless' world of Mr Anon.[18] Thomas wrote in anguish to Eleanor Farjeon that 'the central evil is self-consciousness' in poetry.[19] But Davies has his place within their pantheon because of the paradox that Davies's simple self, by being the subject of all his work, is simultaneously ubiquitous and invisible: his achievement was to leave an autobiography that tells the reader almost nothing about his own feelings, and poems entirely about himself that leave no idea of the person who made them.

### AUTOBIOGRAPHICAL DISAPPEARANCE

This autobiographical paradox becomes clearer by comparing Davies's hit *Autobiography* with the considerable amount of contemporary writings on, or by vagrants, for Davies was by no means the only tramp-writer of the period. Fuelled by the problems of increasing homelessness amongst large numbers of returning Boer War veterans, Edwardian society held a dual attitude of official distaste and romantic yearning towards tramping. In 1906 Parliament instigated a Departmental Committee Report on the problem, which recommended labour camps and way-tickets (a kind of internal passport) as a solution.[20] Other writers called for indefinite prison sentences and compulsory sterilisation.[21] Against this condemnation was a proliferation of more sympathetic accounts, either Borrovian descriptions of the Open Road, the wind on the heath and the roving heart, or furtive explorations into the foetid underworld of doss-houses, kips and spikes. Davies's *Autobiography* contains both of these, and appeals to readers of either sort eager for information on types of begging technique or the amusing characters to be met on the road, yet its author keeps his distance from his contemporaries' characteristic narrative attitudes. The following sentence, taken from his introduction to an edition of *Moll Flanders*, well describes the *Autobiography*'s technique: 'The personal I, followed by the verb of action, is in every sentence, and we are never allowed to see the author himself behind his creation.'[22] Davies does not tell his tale as an interior history: for all that he undergoes in the book – years of begging, poverty and binges, losing a leg, and then being transported from the lodging-house to the literary élite – we learn surprisingly little of how he felt. This is in marked contrast to the authors plunging into the urban tramp-world, who tend to dwell lovingly not only on every festering wound or sore, but on each corresponding wave of repulsion. Walking round Spitalfields, Jack London catalogued the 'welter of rags and filth, of all manner of loathsome skin diseases, open sores, bruises, grossness, indecency, leering monstrosities and bestial faces' that he finds in the homeless asleep: 'Looking at this agglomeration of misery, you don't think of our sins and shortcomings. You are conscious only of the revolt of your senses, of nausea, and of a wild impulse to kill.'[23] Thankfully restraining himself, London's pity then took over. 'But then . . . disgust gives way to compassion. A longing springs up to wash those sores, to bind up those bruised and swollen feet.' The self-narrating of that sentence reveals that London's new attitude was not basically different from his former; whether he wished to kill or cure, London saw the homeless poor as violent stimuli upon his own sensibility, a kind of experience he must tell rather than lives to understand.

Because the writer feels so very ill-at-ease in these surroundings, description often slides into an implicitly self-referential running commentary, as when Everard Wyrall cast his trip to a doss-house into gothic horror. The place itself was Dracula's castle: 'a grim weird mass of stone loomed up out of the darkness . . . under such conditions one might be forgiven for wanting to die'. An uncomfortable bed became the rack: 'for two hours I writhed in agony'. An unsympathetic warden enabled Wyrall to see 'a cruel light [that] flashed in his steely eyes . . . I wondered what exquisite piece of devilry he had for me'.[24] Why Wyrall should think that the punishment was exclusively for him is not apparent; surely, part of the degrading experience of officialdom is that nothing – not even pain – is designed 'for' you at all, an institutional indifference R. C. K. Ensor's generally balanced article 'Tramping as a Tramp' had earlier stressed. Yet even Ensor was susceptible to taking heartless jobsworths personally. 'I could never have believed the dogged cruelty of the people; for it was patent that I was terribly tired and the rain would be heavy' he wrote of his attempts to get a bed.[25] The slight mismatch between the weary mindlessness of 'dogged' and the purposeful scheming of 'cruelty' is revealing, implying that Ensor felt they were trying to be cruel to him against their instincts, a struggle that would hardly seem worth it and which sits awkwardly with his picture of a system functioning without reference to its inmates. Mary Higgs, a brave clergyman's wife who made several forays into the workhouse (and suffered a haemorrhage as a result of the work she was made to do), framed her experiences as part of a considered statistical and anthropological analysis. She took careful notes of the mistreatment she suffered, the conditions of the inmates and the cruelty of the wardens, but when her analysis describes the dirt, it protests her incompetence ('I can hardly describe the feeling of personal contamination caused by even one night in such surrounds') followed by pages and pages of description. An uncharacteristic fervour also breaks out at the end:

No words could tell the passionate longing that seized me to breathe free breaths. No such inward struggle may come to those inured to hard conditions. Yet for them, also, the summer life is free, and for freedom they sacrifice much . . . It is best to fall into the hands of God, not into the hands of man. The vagrant life is sweetest. That is how tramps are made.[26]

The aphorisms and determined pauses at the end suggest that Mrs Higgs is breathing hard to keep her anarchic emotions under firm control. Davies, on the other hand, has none of these emotional storms and wounded feelings as he goes in and out of the workhouse; he appears not to notice the dirt greatly, although Helen Thomas remembered him to be 'fastidious' in hygiene.[27] At one point he even maintains that tramps are often cleaner than others because they have to wash every night, and in consequence the dirtiest tramp is the 'most honest and respectable', because he will neither beg new clothes nor commit himself to the workhouse.[28] More importantly, where he does talk about his feelings, they are events that happen and disappear again: part of the sequence, not a key to the man's character. Losing a leg is the turning-point of the book's story, but Davies omits to mention the fact that originally he only lost a foot. His biographer tells us that on waking up he thrashed around in so violent a mental agony that he bruised the stump and caused it to begin to rot again, necessitating a second amputation at the knee.[29] The book itself gives no hint of this, indulging only once in then-and-now recriminations:

Soon I reached Montreal. Only two months had elapsed, and what a difference now! Two months ago, and it was winter, snow was on the earth, and the air was cold; but I was then full limbed, full of vitality and good spirits, for summerlike prospects golden and glorious possessed me night and day. It was summer now, the earth was dry and green, and the air warm, but winter was within me; for I felt crushed and staggered on crutches to the danger of myself and the people on my way.

With that uncharacteristically literary metaphor, his unhappiness ends, for the next sentence begins brightly: 'I soon got over this unpleasant feeling, roused by . . . a one legged man, who defied all Neptune's attempts to make him walk unsteady. Seeing this man so merry, I knew that my sensitiveness would soon wear off.'[30]

And so it seems to have done. This is not to say that the book is without emotion, only that emotions are events that happen within it, and they occur with the same discreteness. The wildest display of passion in the book is probably when Davies is rejected by the people to whom he attempts to sell poetry, and 'with the fury of a madman' burns his own copies. The next paragraph begins, 'It was at this time that I came under the influence of Flanagan.' Ah, thinks the reader, Flanagan will have some effect on his problems selling poetry. But Flanagan does not: the fact that he is introduced at this point is simply because it was at the same time that Davies met him. Davies's fury at the indifference of the public to his work has simply stopped at the end of the previous sentence. This lack of continuity is reinforced by the way that emotions often do not appear at the expected moment, either: when a kindly farmer offers to rescue him from tramping and adopt him as his son and heir, Davies refuses in one sentence and without reflection. On the other hand, he spends two-and-a-half pages detailing his humiliation about once being caught cooking a pancake in his lodging-house, although nothing appears to have happened to him or the pancake as a result.[31]

Although their material is similar, this lack of proportion also marks a crucial difference between Davies's work and its Open Road contemporaries. One can never be sure what will be important to the *Autobiography:* indeed, Augustus John once remarked that 'trifles did not exist in connection with W H Davies. Everything that happened to him was significant.'[32] Such inconsequential consequence makes its author difficult to recognise, for the flow of events (and his emotions are part of those events) is not interrupted, subordinated or organised by the pattern of a particular personality. For example, the episodes in chapters 18 to 21 run as follows. Bored at home, he decides to go to the Yukon. His companions on the boat reserve a table for themselves by fighting. He eats in a worthwhile Salvation Army restaurant. He meets an old companion and travels with him. He is under suspicion in jail for a crime he has not committed. He loses a leg. The Canadians are kind to him in hospital. He returns home and determines to go to London and write. The effect is that for all his determination to become a writer, Davies's life appears just to happen to him: the last chapter closes with a series of assertions to the truth of his account, 'these have been my experiences', as if he were merely a witness to the events in his life. Typically, the last of these events is not the expected climax of his fame and literary triumph, but about a disagreement with a landlady a few months after his recognition by the press. The result is that Davies's story ends with an event that could have happened to anyone (and often does), rather than what was unique to Davies. Making no difference between the two means his life is described in the sequence in which it occurred, rather than shaped according to the principal features he feels have moulded his personality.

This lack of balance, proportion or shaping – life-shaping, self-shaping – is quite the opposite of that of the tramp-enthusiasts. Davies's rival in tramp literature was Bart Kennedy, whose books are as amoral in their approach to labour as Davies ('the secret of life – to live healthily without work'), but whose lifestyle was one of loud self-declaration: 'I was glad to be here with my mates. I was glad to talk with them and eat with them and get drunk with them and to fight with them. I was glad to listen to the throb of the engine as it pulled up the cage.'[33]

Such self-dramatisation is appropriate to the Nietzschean subtext of Kennedy's idea of tramping as a kind of physical training for becoming the *Übermensch*. 'This whole civilisation is the sinister fruit of stay-at-home cowardice' he booms, and enthusiastically cheers the rise of 'the primal and consonant laws that lie within' and 'the glorious and beautiful men and women dowered with the magical powers that now lie dormant'.[34] After such a promise, Kennedy's adventures in Birmingham pubs and factories seem a little tame, although his autobiography appears as evidence of squalid vitality in Masterman's *The Condition of England*.[35] A similar heroism informs a magazine called *The Tramp*, which opens with Whitman:

> Afoot and lighthearted I take to the open road.
> Henceforth I whimper no more, postpone no more, need nothing,
> Done with indoor complaints, libraries, querulous criticisms,
> Strong and content I travel the open road.[36]

For *The Tramp* as for Kennedy, vagrancy is a way of self-remaking, with something of Nietzsche's love of inner strength and forgetfulness – in one article Jack London describes the professional young vagrants of America as 'the primordial, noble men, the blond beasts so beloved of Nietzsche'.[37] Its opening piece is rapturous:

The joys of tramping are to the true vagabond practically infinite. The snow of January, the sun of August, and the damp breezes of April, all are equally welcome. The moan of the wind at night, the noises of the wind over grass, the whispering of trees at dawn . . . these are all the company the [amateur] tramp needs . . . it is only the tramp who is able to realise the meaning of Maeterlinck's statement that we all live in the sublime.[38]

Another writer tells us that 'tramps are of a community as superior to as they are distinct from the common tourist tribe' and consequently they rejoice in bad weather because the roads are empty.[39] The renter of a gypsy caravan 'casts aside all conventions' and 'can laugh at rain and storm . . . Not for him are the cares of rates or taxes, coal bills, rent, and the hundred and one minor worries that the unfortunate householder is heir to . . . he can snap his fingers at the trammels of modern life, and like the Arab, can pitch his camp wheresoever it pleases him.'[40] Needless to say, he certainly could not pitch his camp wherever it pleased him, as the continually evicted, rent-paying, coal-buying gypsies of the day knew only too well, but this conflation of physical with social freedom is fairly consistent. Because the journey is everything to the ideal reader of *The Tramp*, its hero is separated from origin and destination, and while suspended is given the chance to become someone else for a while, or to find some Romantic original self set apart from ordinary social life. Arthur Ransome preferred to tramp abroad, for 'at home, he can only half-escape'. If the tramp is a gentleman he can never disguise it, 'and if he is not, the country folk will find him out'. But abroad, 'nothing is expected of him except strangeness'.[41] Another writer complained, 'It is not enough that a man has an empty stomach and two aching legs; he must also have a name and a native town and a province, and a profession, and many other things which he goes on the tramp in order to forget.'[42] Likewise Bart Kennedy: 'The thing is to walk and to forget everything but the walking and the delights of the road.'[43] Such deliberate forgetfulness is also important to the amateur tramp because it allows access to the normally hidden interior life. Lady Margaret Sackville advises the tramp to take few books with him:

They belong to the world of self-consciousness, and are too emphatically links with ordinary life. Even poetry books should be abandoned . . . such poems as are good for him will come bubbling up of their own accord to the surface of the wanderer's mind . . . only such things as are wholly necessary should be taken (and if possible not these even!) so that for once entire freedom may exist from the tyranny of belongings![44]

Although *The Tramp*'s theme might seem a gift to him, Edward Thomas contributed no walking articles, only a sketch of city crowds, dream-stories and parables. (A periodical of the same era called *The Open Road* describes its interests as 'Religion, Psychology, Sociology, Diet and Hygiene', and does not concern itself with travel at all.) Throughout, tramping is far more than walking; it is a kind of social or personal therapy, an updating and expansion of the Wordsworthian *concordia discors* between man and inner landscape, in the footsteps of Stevenson, Leslie Stephen and Belloc.[45] The magazine itself is an alliance of supposed

contraries – Thomas, Davies, Arthur Ransome and John Freeman alongside Wyndham Lewis, F. S. Flint and Douglas Goldring – indicating their
common liking for socially unaligned/unconventional perspectives, be it
children, gypsies or foreigners, as in Lewis's caustic analyses of Spain.
Davies's *Autobiography*, on the other hand, is interested not in how to be a
tramp, but how its author survived when he found himself to be one. Its
contiguous placing of emotionally non-consecutive material – rather as a
doss-house unites essentially isolated men – makes it less *concordia* than
*discors*. It is no wonder that when Davies himself was asked to grace *The
Tramp*'s pages, he complained to Thomas that its contributors were
writing under false pretences: 'What I ought to be paid well for is not a
good literary article, but for being a real tramp contributor, probably the
only one that will ever contribute to that paper.'[46]

### ARTIFICIAL SIMPLICITY

But contribute he did, and to many other magazines as well, from *Country
Life* to Middleton Murry's pioneering modern art magazine, *Rhythm*.
Given the opportunity to be popular, he took it: his bibliography reveals
that twenty-five out of the fifty-seven *Songs of Joy*, twenty-four out of
forty-four poems in *Foliage* and seventeen out of nineteen poems in *Child
Lovers* had already appeared elsewhere. Davies knew his market lay more
with the open-air market than the grim-reality one, and successive edi-
tions of his poems show the number of simple, happy nature-poems
increasing as the poems about life in the doss-house decrease. As he
remarked in the introduction to a further volume of reminiscences:
'Now, although I am going to write about some of the greatest artists
and writers of their day, I feel certain that not one of them would take the
least offence on hearing their names mentioned with the names of those
other great artists – Harlem Baldy and Detroit Fatty.'[47]

Like the champion beggars he mentions, Davies's artistry was that he
knew how to work on people's feelings. If the public wanted simple
poetry, then they got it, and the lack of structure in his *Autobiography*
only helped him to appeal to the supposedly helpless simplicity of tramps,
an explanation often expounded by Edwardian writers struggling to
understand why vagrants carried on the way they did. Mary Higgs saw
tramps as nomads, and following the law of recapitulation, behaving like
children who cannot 'fix their attention' on anything.[48] W. H. Dawson
believed the tramp was a hopeless case after any time on the road: the
'manhood has left him and there remains for the ratepayers an idle,

dissolute remnant'.[49] Thomas Holmes thought the tramp was harking back to 'the life of the idle savage'.[50] The effect of these negative definitions is to invest tramps with a lack of interiority, the savage or child that acts without thought. This view is also implicit in the labour-camp remedy sought by successive Edwardian Poor Law Conferences, one of which remarked: 'The vagrant's laziness is very much a matter of habit, and industry must be made habitual instead.'[51] In other words, the morality of working (which would imply interior conscience) is inculcated as habit, a purely mechanical response because that is what the tramp is.

But by appealing to these ideas, Davies's simplicity showed itself resourceful, both in the manner and variety of his begging techniques and the ability he had to find markets for his work. Ezra Pound described him as having a 'peasant's shrewdness' and Davies's biographer agrees, showing how Davies carefully made maximum publicity from being a society pet.[52] Such canniness might seem to belie notions of simplicity at all, but on the other hand, the testimony we have from his letters and the many stories about his unworldliness is consistent. Although she also noted his shrewdness, Helen Thomas remembered that Davies bought a velvet jacket when he became a published poet because that was what poets wore, and that he would carry his groceries home inside his coat lining because he did not want anyone to know he had to do his own shopping.[53] In keeping with Thomas's assessment of him as having no idea of proportion, Davies counselled Thomas not to worry about public or critical indifference, because the manager of Davies's doss-house in Southwark had read some of Thomas's work and declared that 'that man deserves a civil list pension'. In case this was not impressive enough, Davies added, 'he is getting a great admirer of your work, and his opinion is worth having, for he is well known in South London as a speaker of good verse'.[54] Here, Davies seems quite oblivious of the importance of the right audience.

This difficulty the reader has identifying a single 'real' Davies, a figure who would unite the contrary evidences of simple innocent and skilful artist, has been every reviewer's difficulty with his poetry as well. Which is the real Davies in the ending of 'The Sleepers', say? The poem describes the homeless asleep on a dockside at night:

> That moment, on the waterside
>   A lighted car came at a bound;
> I looked inside, and saw a score
>   Of pale and weary men that frowned;

> Each man sat in a huddled heap,
> Carried to work while fast asleep.
>
> Ten cars rushed down the waterside
>   Like lighted coffins in the dark;
> With twenty dead men in each car,
>   That must be brought alive by work.

Much of this poem seems composed in lumps; 'at a bound', 'pale and weary', 'huddled in a heap' and 'fast asleep' are terrible clichés, but then the hints of the workers' undead automatism ('I had not thought death had undone so many') in describing their trams as 'lighted coffins' is startling, and suggests that the worn-out phrases might be germane to the poem's point. Similarly, 'Charms' opens with a perfect couplet:

> She walks as lightly as the fly
> Skates on the water in July.

The second line's trochee mimes the fly's ability to put its slight weight upon an uncertain or unexpected footing, but such delicacy entirely disappears in the next couplet:

> When I in my Love's shadow sit,
> I do not miss the sun one bit.

Again, is the reader supposed to be charmed by the quality of the verse, or by the *naïveté* of the telling? So often, after yet another rhyme of 'flower' and 'hour', 'boy' and 'joy', Davies will slip in an unexpectedly vivid physical image that lifts the poem from its *ersatz* simplicity. 'The Boy' starts unpromisingly with 'Go, little boy / Fill thee with joy', but the third stanza continues:

> Fear not, like man,
> The kick of wrath,
> That you do lie
> In some one's path.

There is a certain sympathetic humour in the way the King James-era 'Fear not', 'wrath' and 'do lie' are gently ironised by the modern anonymity of 'some one', as inexplicably angry as Jehovah; for a former beggar that 'kick' may not be metaphorical. The antique coyness of the opening couplet of 'The Visitor' could almost have 'April' printed in italics, half-month and half-goddess:

> She brings that breath, and music too,
> That comes when April's days begin.

Such gentility does not prepare the reader for the modern directness of the blousy visitor herself, 'big with laughter at the breasts, / Like netted fish they leap'. His sheep do not bleat, they 'cough', and a mouse heard alone at night 'inside the papered walls / Comes like a tiger crunching through the stones' ('The Hermit'). Or take these lines in 'Traffic' describing snow:

> Yet back to nature I must go –
> To see the thin, mosquito flakes
> Grow into moths of plumper snow.

'Back to nature I must go' is a pompous inversion of a cliché, but then 'mosquito flakes' catches not only the thinness but also the weightlessness of early snow. Heavier snow is 'plump', a word that nicely mixes onomatopoeia with suggestions of snow's pillowing and swelling of hard outlines. And if assessing the poet's integrity through the quality of poetry like this seems an overly evaluative approach, it is at least implicitly Davies's own, for his description of the beggar as a great artist, above, implies that an artist's worth is based on winning an audience for the artist's persona. Yet his poems provoke contrary responses, because it is not always clear what sort of person has written them. It is like the dilemma of dealing with a persuasive beggar, knowing whether to believe the destitution or the skill in telling the story of such destitution. What sort of poet can write the sharp, direct lines that Philip Larkin respected, and also such reams of formulated, often saccharine verse? Larkin remarked that Davies's verse trembled on the edge of 'stodgy unreality', but 'had the power to rise intermittently above this level by piercingly happy moments of description and observation that carry the poems that contain them permanently into our memory'.[55] Still, one might wonder, why must it consistently wander along the edge in the first place?

One solution to this problem of incompatible material has been offered by Michael Cullup, who sees Davies as a poet of realism and irony submerged by the false nature-poems encouraged by Thomas and others.[56] He cites the black humour of 'The Inquest', where Davies updates the prosiness of 'The Thorn' to a contemporary child-abuse inquiry:

> When I went out to see the corpse
> The four months' babe that died so young,
> I judged it was seven pounds in weight,
> And little more than four foot long. [. . .]

> And I could see that child's one eye
> Which seemed to laugh and say with glee:
> 'What caused my death you'll never know –

> Perhaps my mother murdered me.'

This, and the sardonic final 'Next!' in 'The Hospital Waiting-Room' gives the voice of the modern anyone a characteristically knowing disillusionment, partly covert aggression towards the bossiness of the system and partly relief at knowing what's what – a tone which became an important weapon in the war poetry of Davies's fellow Georgians Graves and Sassoon. Like their parodies of patriotic songs, Davies can play delicately with his own folk-song and cheerful poverty image:

> When I had money, money, O!
> My many friends proved all untrue;
> But now I have no money, O!
> My friends are real, though very few.

A poem about the intricacies of feminine coiffure, its 'strange tools' screwing, twisting, turning and shaping, ends with 'Ah, now I see how smooth her brow / And her simplicity of face'. But leafing through the *Collected Poems*, these are exceptions to the rule of quaint jollity in nature: if Davies could be such an ironic realist about bureaucracy, why did he not turn the same eye on his nature-verse? In fact, it was Thomas himself who noted this mixture of insight and 'a charming artificiality probably due to a combination of nature and memory of books'. His solution, however, was not to discover a real insightful Davies submerged or repressed by powerful forces, but subtly to suggest that the paradox is the point itself:

This artificiality is part of Mr Davies's simplicity. For it is of the essence of simplicity that it is without fear. The improbable, the unusual, the hackneyed, the grotesque, are not known to it by their names . . . the slips of grammar and syntax in his work, the formality of words and phrases and apparently bookish phrases adopted and made real. These are trifles. They are the very low price which he has to pay for his freedom of the world visible and invisible.[57]

Davies's simplicity is not revealed by the absence of thought in twee nature-verses. In fact, he teases his audience for getting their nature from his books:

> Cuckoo! Cuckoo! was that a bird,
> Or but a mocking boy you heard?
> You heard the Cuckoo first, 'twas he;
> The second time – Ha, ha! –'twas Me. ('A Merry Hour')

For Thomas, it would lie in his ability to write a poem as skippily vacuous as 'Happy Wind', *and* the ironically disillusioned final couplet of 'Heaven':

The Welshman's heaven is singing airs –
No matter who feels sick and swears.

For if Davies can write with such irony, then in the next poem he is as likely to be embarrassingly unaware of what he has just written. 'She rises like the lark, that hour / He goes half-way to meet a shower' ('Charms') implies the beloved is levitating from her bed. Struggling for eight syllables returns the 'The Happy Child' – who has hitherto spent his day with the flowers, birds, and butterflies – abruptly back to Stepney:

My world this day has lovely been
But not like what the child has seen.

For all the evaluative approach his artist-beggar association invited, Davies's unembarrassed mix of conflicting messages about his simplicity had an unexpected effect on his modernist admirers. It made him critically unassailable, as Pound felt compelled to confess in his review: 'I do not know that I can submit Mr Davies's work to my usual acid test'.[58] His co-Imagist F. S. Flint acknowledged a similar bewilderment, for 'when one approaches an aboriginal poet like Mr W. H. Davies, all one's theories about form fall to the ground'.[59] Pound and Flint were searching for the superfluous, for rhetoric, for formality, and although Pound notes how Davies 'puts his words hind-side to . . . says did go and did sing and so forth', this 'curious traditional dialect' will not allow him to find it. Pound has to admit his criterion for good poetry fails, because identifying the superfluous means identifying the essential, but Davies's lack of proportion means they could never find that essential. Georgian and Imagist lapses into rhetoric, warned Eliot, occurred when they wrote about emotions which they did not really feel: Davies's poetry can never be caught acting, because its blithe mixture of sentiment and insight never allows its reader a perspective of the man which would determine whether those emotions might be spurious or not, as the *Autobiography* never lets you know which events will be significant or not.[60] To take an analogy from painting, his verse resembles the unified-field perspective of naïve art, where the lack of foreground – background distinction makes everything belong together under one horizon. On the one hand, such pictures make present for the artist his or her world and thus revolve entirely around that artist, and yet because they have none of the independent neutrality of the perspectival grid, the viewer has no idea of the artist's own position. As such, naïve art is an important part of the history of twentieth-century experiments in artistic form, as Alfred Wallis belongs with the sophisticated modernism of the St Ives group. Because Davies's work will not subordinate or proportion any of its elements, his own position can never be separated from it, and its utter directness becomes by the same token a position of complete transparency. As Thomas himself commented, Davies's verse had an 'archaic' simplicity, 'far removed from a merely modern simplicity, like Walt Whitman'.[61]

As a unifier of incompatible perspectives, Davies was perhaps an appropriate editor of the Poetry Bookshop's *Shorter Lyrics of the Twentieth Century* (1922), an anthology which printed his own work alongside Georgian, Imagist and war poetry. How much was his own choice and how much a hidden Harold Monro's is unknown, but it does not much matter: if the latter, Monro saw Davies as an appropriate figurehead to unite Pound, H. D., Aldington, Flint and Lawrence with Thomas, de la Mare, Owen, Sassoon, Graves, Gibson and Brooke. Davies was at pains to stress in the introduction that 'this is an anthology of poems, not of poets', a phrase whose caution immediately suggests the opposite, that the anthology is very aware of what it is doing with the artists concerned – as Davies later suggests, 'an artist's friends are his enemies, as far as his work is concerned, and his real enemies are his best friends'.[62] The comment is also apposite to his own work, for in many ways Davies is the original of the Georgian stereotype of simple poetry about trees, birds and flowers, and Eliot cited him as an example of the dangers of poetry without philosophy, 'purely conceited' in its indiscriminate contentment.[63] Yet he did so by aligning Davies's method with the surrealist work of Cocteau and Breton, who also aimed to overthrow any reflective control for a poetry which would be an indivisible unity of instinct and word. Davies's inscrutable combination of mutually incompatible perspectives is in its own way as hostile to perspective as the multiple voices of modernism: it presents its modern reader with the equal disorientation of unity.

# CHAPTER 5

# *Hardy's indifference*

Hardy was always meticulous about observing anniversaries, and in 1916, on the tercentenary of Shakespeare's death, did not fail to write him a poem. It dwells on one of Hardy's favourite themes, the callous indifference of time and circumstance to the unique and precious, which in this case means the heedlessness of the 'borough clocks' which 'but samely tongue the hour' at Shakespeare's passing, and likewise the snobbish indifference of the Stratford burghers:

> ' – Ah, one of the tradesmen's sons, I now recall. . .
> Witty, I've heard. . .
> We did not know him. . . Well, good-day. Death comes to all'.
>
> ('To Shakespeare')[1]

This complaint about the provincialism of seventeenth-century Stratford nevertheless has a strong flavour of twentieth-century Dorchester to it. Despite his recent freedom of the borough, Hardy had long felt that his birth into the tradesman class still counted for more than his London literary honour with many locals, as it had with his late wife, and the poem's irony is a self-protecting one, like the entry in his notebooks which runs, 'Base-born. Homer is said to be base-born: so is Virgil.[2] But the implied parallel between his own unappreciated genius and Shakespeare's is misaligned in one important respect:

> Through human orbits thy discourse to-day,
> Despite thy formal pilgrimage, throbs on
> In harmonies that cow Oblivion,
> And, like the wind, with all-uncared effect
> Maintain a sway
> Not fore-desired, in tracks unchosen and unchecked.

Hardy celebrates the carefree casualness of Shakespeare's writing in a verse whose compressed hyphenations and alliterations show that nothing in his own harmonies seems 'all-uncared', 'not fore-desired', unchosen or unchecked. The idea that Shakespeare's writing is as careless of its effect as the wind owes more to Romantic conceptions of genius than to any theatrical sensitivity, but its accuracy matters less than the fact that Hardy chose here, as elsewhere, to set himself at stylistic odds with the supreme poet and the poetics associated with him. Hardy's poetry is the opposite of the organic and its corollaries of the unity of feeling and thought, manner and moment. His method instead was to work out 'verse skeletons', stanzaic patterns with an arbitrary substance that he would use later as a mould into which to pour his poetic content.[3] An abbreviated note confirms that this is how he approached the topic from the start of his writing career:

*Lyrical Meth*[od] Find a situ[atio]n from exp[erien]ce. Turn to Ly[ri]cs for a form of express[io]n that has been used for a quite diff[eren]t situ[atio]n. Use it (Same sit[uatio]n from experience may be sung in sev[era]l forms.)[4]

The 'Studies, Specimens &c' notebook shows Hardy continually taking a word or grammatical form and practising variations upon it with no surrounding poem or context. Such a detached approach to content then makes the deliberateness of the form more evident; in the stanza above, for example, 'Oblivion' requires a thumpingly full stress on the last syllable to make the rhyme, whereas in normal speech the final stress is much more slight, so that the verse-form makes a mockery of the word's meaning. In this respect, an admission made in passing to a critic who accused Hardy of mixing incompatible genres in *The Dynasts* is telling. In arguing that artistic beauty isn't determined by that art's own 'mechanical, material or methodic necessities', but can contain elements from other arts, Hardy remarked that 'if we turn to poetry we find that rhythm and rhyme are a non-necessitous presentation of language under conditions that in strictness appertain only to music.'[5] That a poem's rhythms and rhymes are 'non-necessitous' implies a detachable content decorated – or calumniated – in poetic form.

Such an approach to poetry is heresy for any poet after Samuel Johnson, never mind Coleridge. Hardy seems to treat poetic form as if it had no relation to its content; yet, at the same time, the notebooks reveal a man teaching himself to write with conspicuous ambition and effort, and no one's form is more knotted or intricate than Hardy's. It is this paradox of caring deeply about not caring that animates not only his poetry, but his philosophy and his unhappy marriage, and it manifests itself in a division between form and content which is not accidental, although it puts him directly at odds with the main current of Romantic aesthetics, and particularly the Symbolist strand of it which leads towards certain versions of modernism. His supporters ever after have had to struggle to reconcile Hardy's manner and matter; although they admired his poetry above that of all other living poets, even de la Mare and Thomas wondered how Hardy could get away with a form so detached and manipulative. Few saw things as honestly as D. H. Lawrence, whose study diagnosed Hardy's problem as a tragic division between Love and an implacable Law (expressed in his ruthless rhythms and rhymes), and made it a policy pledge for his own work to reconcile them.[6] This chapter will explore why Hardy might have had cogent reasons to allow his work to remain unreconciled in itself and to organic and modernist poetics, reasons which are both philosophical justifications of a particular world-view and private symptoms deriving from the most painful parts of his life.

Justifying Hardy's anti-organicism is easier in principle than in practice, however, for the division between manner and matter in his poetry often feels less like a trailblazing rejection of aesthetic unity and more like flat self-contradiction. If his multitude of stanza-forms, coinages, neologisms, archaisms and syntax-bending hyphenations seem only to confirm the labour and design of the writing, such conspicuous artistry is quite at odds with Hardy's constant theme of helplessness, where his characters are victims of circumstance or the immortals, hopelessly in thrall to Time's passing, and always too late to mend a mistake. Such helplessness was something Hardy was keen for his readers to experience for themselves, moreover, since it is not entirely coincidental that so many of his poems begin with a line which suggests a different rhythm to the one that actually turns out to structure the poem. In 'The Voice of the Thorn', for example:

> When the thorn on the down
> Quivers naked and cold,
> And the mid-aged and old
> Pace the path there to town,
> In these words dry and drear
> It seems to them sighing:
> 'O winter is trying
> To sojourners here!'

The innocent reader is tempted to scan the poem with a three-beat line, because this would give an regular balance of stressed and unstressed syllables, and allows the main verb to fall on the beat. Only reading on does it become evident that the poem has two beats per line and that 'quivers', like 'pace' two lines later, is a verb that has a stress but no underlying beat. A chastened re-reading gives the verse a rushed, uncertain feel appropriate to the subject of being only temporary sojourners here, but the poem has also deliberately set its reader off on the wrong foot. 'The Conformers', too, opens with its apparent four-beat affirmative, 'Yes; we'll wed, my little fay', but like the marriage, the beginning is the exception to the rule, for the first line of all the other stanzas ('the formal faced cohue'. . . 'we shall not go in stealth'. . . 'when down to dusk we glide') conform very strictly to three beats. 'In Childbed' starts:

> In the middle of the night
> Mother's spirit came and spoke to me,
> Looking weariful and white –
> As 'twere untimely news she broke to me.

No sensitive reader would give the first line four stresses: the weight on so slight a word as 'In' might be acceptable, but surely not on 'of', as a tetrameter line would require. Only when it becomes clear that this is another false start, that the rest of the poem is a completely regular alternation of tetrameter and pentameter, does the double sense of 'untimely' become clearer. Unwelcome and ghostly, the missing stress in the first line inaudibly marks the untimeliness of a spirit's prophecy that a new child 'but shapes for tears / New thoroughfares in sad humanity'. The same trick occurs in 'Her Dilemma':

> The two were silent in a sunless church,
> Whose mildewed walls, uneven paving-stones,
> And wasted carvings passed antique research;
> And nothing broke the clock's dull monotones.

Once we learn that the poem is pentameter, it gives a further ominousness to the silent, sunless beginning: in retrospect, something turns out not to have been said, as indeed it proves not to be. But the reader only learns the meaning of all these metrical exceptions after the poem has been misconstrued first. As so many of Hardy's poems want to point out, we may have good reasons for thinking as we do, but we will be wrong-footed, for 'experience *un*teaches – (what at first one thinks to be the rule in events)'.[7] Should we ever learn where we went wrong, where we missed the point, the condition of that knowledge is that it must come too late.

But the trouble with such artful illustrations of helplessness is that they are evidently carefully planned, so that the invention and effort required to make them work belies the meaning. The same contradiction is visible in Hardy's novel vocabulary: for example, the current *OED* cites Hardy as the first user of six words or word-senses in *Time's Laughingstocks* and *Satires of Circumstance*, four of which ('blinkered' 'tristful', 'uneagerness' and 'unsight') concern blind or hopeless pain. The way that so much determined creativity had gone into illustrating life's despair must have struck Hardy's original audience with even more contradictory force than a word such as 'tristfulness' does today. Hardy's frequent use of negative prefixes and suffixes to form a nonce-word, too, makes the conscious shaping of 'unminding whither bound and why' and 'void unvisioned listlessness' in a poem such as 'The Two Rosalinds' entirely at odds with the passivity the words purport to describe, like 'untombed' in 'The Dead Man Walking' and 'self-unheed' in 'By the Barrows'. This determined helplessness is best suggested by a phrase in 'Shut Out That Moon', where a disappointed lover forswears the natural attractions of the garden:

> Within the common lamp-lit room
> Prison my eyes and thought;
> Let dingy details crudely loom,
> Mechanic speech be wrought:
> Too fragrant was Life's early bloom,
> Too tart the fruit it brought!

In the poem, 'mechanic speech' is indeed 'wrought', the hyphenations of 'lamp-lit', 'dew-dashed' and 'years-deep' cramming the maximum of stress-words into a given metrical space. But if 'mechanic speech' suggests an effort to reject the blandishments of the garden, it also suggests automatism, as when Wordsworth speaks of producing poetry by 'obeying blindly and mechanically' the habits of association the poet's mind has made between thoughts and feelings.[8] A determinism rigid with effort is the paradox behind Hardy's worked-at style whose subject is helpless knowledge.[9]

Hardy's critics were not slow to seize on the mismatch, but neither were those who admired him most. Michael Millgate has remarked that Hardy tended to see all criticism as implacably, personally hostile, an attack on his style from those pre-committed to maintaining what he saw as a culpable blitheness about Providence. By and around 1916, though, Hardy had become a mentor to a younger generation of admirers such as Edward Thomas and Walter de la Mare, who found his verse inspirational, but who were nevertheless also compelled to wrestle with their mixed feelings about its style.[10] Hardy's relationship with de la Mare was particularly close, having begun when Hardy wrote to thank him for a review, and to compliment him on *The Listeners*, especially 'those delightful sensations of moonlight and forests and haunted houses which I myself seem to have visited curiously enough'.[11] This sense of uncanny familiarity is strengthened by a letter from Florence Hardy after de la Mare's first visit to Max Gate, which told E. M. Forster that 'we have lately made the acquaintance of Walter de la Mare in the flesh – in the spirit we seem to have known him long and well'.[12] De la Mare in return felt that 'your poems are another life to me . . . the poems just know me by heart - if I may say it like that'.[13] Evidently Hardy felt that de la Mare's work knew him intimately too, for he was particularly moved by de la Mare's 'Song of the Mad Prince', seemingly associating it with Emma's death: 'for myself it has a meaning almost too intense to speak of', he confessed, and in his last few days when 'he thought only of poetry' (as his wife described it to T. E. Lawrence), 'The Listeners' was one of the three poems he wished to hear.[14] On his visits, de la Mare felt he was in the presence of a higher power, rhapsodising that 'all the magic of nature is his, as well as all the wisdom and compassion and human nature'.[15] Being with Hardy, he declared, gave him the sensation of being a character in one of Hardy's novels, and when Hardy asked him how he would have put a certain line, 'it was like God asking one to name the emu'.[16] Yet for all this sense of private spiritual kinship, in public de la Mare's criticisms turn on just this sense of Hardy casually playing God with his material. Despite frequent protestations of variety in his poetry, 'all here is his, and all is himself', and such complete presence is manifest in the signs of effort, 'the intensity, less of impulse than of elaboration, with which he constrains it to his will'. De la Mare continues:

The style is often crustacean . . . the thought, too, may be as densely burdened in its expression as the scar of a tree by the healing saps that have enwarted its surface . . . stubborn the medium may be, but with what mastery it is compelled to do this craftsman's bidding. He makes our English so much his own that a single quoted line betrays his workmanship. He forces, hammers poetry into his words; not, like most poets, charms it out of them. Let the practised poet borrow but a score of Mr. Hardy's latinities and vernaculars – and then invoke his Muse. Difficulty, seeming impossibility, is the breath of Mr Hardy's nostrils as an artist.[17]

Not charms, but hammers: the very opposite of de la Mare's magical verses. For his part, Thomas had been one of the first critics to declare that he thought Hardy's poetry not a wrong turn but an improvement on his novels.[18] A letter from his widow to Hardy after Thomas's death confirmed his admiration: 'There is no living man whose interest he would rather have had than yours . . . [and whom] above all he would have felt honoured by. For him you were the master of living poets and he your endless disciple.'[19] Thomas's poetic discipleship emerges in the parallel titles and themes of 'The Thrush' with Hardy's famous darkling thrush, or the similarity of theme and metre between Thomas's 'The Penny Whistle' and Hardy's 'The Night of the Dance'. Yet his reviews show a marked antipathy to Hardy's stylistic totalitarianism, which permits no surprises. 'There is no ecstasy or glory or magic for him to lose, save what is in the things themselves', Thomas complained: 'As a rule Mr Hardy's poems are the sum of their parts, and it would be easy to show what it is that produces their strong calm effect. Seldom does anything creep in from Nature or the spirit of humanity to give his work a something not to be accounted for in what he actually says.'[20] Hardy has understood everything, but this means that he is also much too conscious of what he is doing. 'Other poetry allows great richness and diversity of interpretation; Mr Hardy's allows none . . . we cannot think of any other poetry so tyrannous', wrote Thomas in an earlier review.[21] Like de la Mare, too, Thomas noticed this oppressive control of his material exactly because Hardy's form fits its material so badly. 'It is possible to wonder if he is poking fun at verse by first making it so unwontedly substantial, then adding a considerable amount of rhyme, alliteration, and assonance, as frills', he commented in 1913; the result of this technique is that 'a certain awkwardness is almost as constant in his work as truth is'.[22]

Linking 'awkwardness' to 'truth' and 'mastery' to 'difficulty' show Thomas and de la Mare struggling to find a reason for Hardy's manifest divergence of style and content, and their comments articulate a problem for Hardy readers which has persisted: how to put his poetry back together again. If Hardy meant to write as he did, then he was laying himself open to the charge of writing with stunning insensitivity towards his topic. This is obviously not true, and so one solution was to say that the disparity is unwitting, and hence testimony to Hardy's unconscious capacity to register the awkwardness of life in collision with itself, an option pursued latterly by John Bayley and Samuel Hynes, but first mooted in a backhanded review by Lytton Strachey in 1914:

And he speaks; he does not sing. Or rather, he talks – in the quiet voice of a modern man or woman, who finds it difficult, as modern men and women do, to put into words exactly what is in the mind. He is incorrect; but then how unreal and artificial a thing is correctness! He fumbles; but it is that very fumbling that brings him so near to ourselves . . . And who does not feel the perplexity, the discomfort and the dim agitation in that clumsy collection of vocables – 'And adumbrates too therewith our unexpected troublous case'? What a relief such uncertainties and inexpressivenesses are after the delicate exactitudes of our more polished poets.[23]

But we can infer from unpublished correspondence with Thomas that Hardy, at least, hated this idea. Two years after he wrote the comment above about awkwardness, Thomas was forced to apologise. He wanted to include some of Hardy's lyrics for his anthology *This England*, and his letter is a mixture of embarrassment, modesty and self-justification:

From something I heard last year I have thought that it might seem to you an apology rather than a request for a favour was to be expected from me; but I feel that if at all, the apology is due to having failed, as I suppose I must have done, to show my admiration and affection for your poetry. I am referring to an article by myself in *Poetry and Drama*, which I daresay you have forgotten and I hope you have.[24]

Hardy had in fact written to Edward Garnett about *Poetry and Drama* at the time, saying it was full of 'queer young men whose wrongnesses are interesting' but his actual reply is lost, probably on the great bonfire of letters from his literary past which Thomas made when he enlisted.[25] However, Thomas's next letter tells the story:

I was relieved to think that the article had not left a bad impression. I cannot think that it would seem to misrepresent deliberately . . . The article in the *New Statesman* I have not seen. But the writer who reviews verse there is a clever man too often carried away by a power to score for the moment. I should not have expected him to make such a mistake in your case.[26]

It is striking, though, just how similar Strachey's verdict is to Thomas's, for both agree that Hardy's awkwardness is what testifies to his truthfulness. The crucial difference is that Thomas's article emphasises Hardy's deliberateness, whereas Strachey's implies he does not know what he was doing. Evidently this was an idea that Hardy abhorred, and when he came to ghost-write the *Life* he lamented 'the inevitable ascription to ignorance of what was really choice after full knowledge' in his poetic form (323). This complaint is amplified in an entry for 1918: 'The reviewer so often supposes that where Art is not visible it is unknown to the poet under criticism. Why does he not think of the art of concealing art? There is a good reason why' (414). It is characteristically sly of Hardy, though, to alter the sense of the original Latin tag behind 'the art of concealing art', *ars est celare artem*. The usual meaning is that artistic skill is so unobtrusive as to make its organising principles invisible in the work. For Hardy it seems to mean that the apparent lack of art is a carefully designed effect, and a demonstration of artistic intention. A year after Strachey's review he wrote to a critic, H. C. Duffin, to comment that Duffin's book had speculated on all sorts of biographical details, but omitted the poetry, 'the only part [of his oeuvre] in which self-expression has been quite unfettered'.[27] Such determination to prove his poetic style deliberate is expressed at length in a famous analogy:

Years earlier he had decided that too regular a beat was bad art. He had fortified himself in his opinion by thinking of the analogy of architecture, between which art and that of poetry he had discovered, to use his own words, that there existed a close and curious parallel, each art unlike some others, having to carry a rational content inside its artistic form. He knew that in architecture cunning irregularity is of enormous worth, and it is obvious that he carried on into his verse, perhaps unconsciously, the Gothic art-principle in which he had been trained – the principle of spontaneity, found in mouldings, tracery and suchlike – resulting in the 'unforeseen' (as it has been called) character of his metres and stanzas, that of stress rather than of syllable, poetic texture rather than poetic veneer; the latter kind of thing, under the name of 'constructed ornament', being what he, in common with every Gothic student, had been taught to avoid as the plague.[28]

Peter Robinson has pointed out that the oxymorons here of 'principle of spontaneity' and 'cunning irregularity' imply that very little is unconscious about this process, as indeed the whole comparison of poetry with architecture implies, for an architect is nothing if not a careful planner.[29] The effect of Hardy's insistence on his complete control of his material, though, is to reinforce the division with his form still further. Just as the separation above of 'artistic form' from 'rational content' in architecture would be anathema to any modernist, Bauhaus insistence that form follows function, so there is an analogous anti-organicism in Hardy's reminiscences on the practical problems of his architectural career devoted to restoration. For the architect, the form of the building counts for everything, the actual substance nothing:

It is easy to show that the essence and soul of an architectural monument does not lie in the particular blocks of stone or timber that compose it, but in the mere forms to which those materials have been shaped. We discern in a moment that it is in the boundary of a solid – its insubstantial superficies or mould – and not in the solid itself, that its right lies to exist as art. The whole quality of Gothic or other architecture – let it be a cathedral, a spire, a window, or what not – attached to this, and not to the substantial erection which it appears exclusively to consist in. Those limestones or sandstones have passed into its form; yet it is an idea independent of them – an aesthetic phantom without solidity, which might just as suitably have chosen millions of other stones from a quarry whereon to display its beauties.[30]

But for the architect as restorer the material of the church has existed uniquely through time, and hence cannot be simply replaced. 'No man can make two pieces of matter exactly alike', concedes Hardy, and moreoever, exact form is unreproducible because it has 'an indefinable quality. . . which never reappears in the copy' (251). For the churchgoer, too, the building's actual stones have associations of memory which the form's 'aesthetic phantom' cannot maintain. And hence Hardy concludes dispiritedly that 'in short, the opposing tendencies excited in an architect by the distracting situation can find no satisfactory reconciliation'. Originally he added, 'all he can do is of the nature of compromise', but crossed it out.

### THE IMMANENT WILL

Why, then, might Hardy wish to insist so deliberately on the irreconcilable opposition between the demands of form and substance, if doing so makes him look like the epitome of bad art? One very plausible answer is to argue that the disjunction itself is part of the poem's message. 'Art', an entry in the *Life* muses, 'is a disproportioning – (i.e., distorting, throwing out of proportion) – of realities, to show more clearly the features that matter in those realities, which, if merely copied or reported inventorially, might possibly be observed, but would more probably be overlooked'.[31] The primary reality that needed pointing out was above all for Hardy the Immanent Will, otherwise formulated as the 'Prime Mover', 'Hap', 'Necessity', the 'All-One' and various other guises, which manifested itself as the determining force behind the events of the world:

The Philosophy of *The Dynasts*, under various titles and phrases, is almost as old as civilization. Its fundamental principle, under the name of Predestination, was preached by St. Paul. 'Being predestinated' – says the author of the Epistle to the Ephesians, 'Being predestinated according to the purpose of Him who worketh all things after the counsel of His own Will'; and much more to the same effect, the only difference being that externality is assumed by the Apostle rather than immanence.[32]

Hardy's theology is pointedly inaccurate, since the crucial difference between him and St Paul is not merely over the externality or immanence of God's will in human affairs, but the responsibility of God himself. For Hardy this Will is unconscious – it cannot but do what it does – and unaware of the results of its actions, which include humankind. As a result, 'humanity and other animal life (roughly, though not accurately, definable as puppetry) forms the conscious extremity of a pervading urgence, or will' (200) and hence is helplessly determined by a force to which it owes its very being but to which it is also ethically superior, an idea St Paul would not have countenanced. Hardy would not have called himself a complete determinist, but his concession to 'a modicum of free-will conjecturally possessed' in the 'Apology' to *Late Lyrics* is countered by his own explanatory metaphor:

This theory, too, seems to me to settle the question of Free-will v. Necessity. The will of a man is, according to it, neither wholly free or wholly unfree. When swayed by the Universal Will (as he mostly must be as a subservient part of it) he is not individually free; but whenever it happens that all the rest of the Great Will is in equilibrium the minute portion called one person's will is free, just as a performer's fingers will go on playing the pianoforte of themselves when he talks and thinks of something else & the head does not rule them.[33]

But a distracted pianist's fingers aren't free, in the sense that a head-less chicken isn't free. They will continue to play the piece they were playing beforehand, or something known by heart, or even if we grant some improvisation, finger chords and runs long practised. Without the possibility of choice, their freedom is inseparable from automatism.

It is almost irresistible to see Hardy's predetermined forms as an expression of exactly such a determining Will, which acts without regard for the conscious pain or pleasure of its subjects. No matter what shape the material would take if left to its own devices, the form will have its way, and Hardy's insistent rhythms, the very arbitrariness of his pre-planned verse skeletons, would testify to the casual, blind forces of an Immanent Will in which chance and destiny come to mean the same thing. Everything must happen because the Will makes it so, but since it has no forethought, everything happens without a reason either. Hence events are simultaneously determined and random, and, in James Richardson's acute observation, 'the very artifice of his chains of events calls attention to their arbitrariness'.[34] As Hardy complained: 'The emo-tions have no place in a world of defect, and it is a cruel injustice that they should have developed in it. If Law itself had consciousness, how the aspect of its creatures would terrify it, fill it with remorse!'[35]

And yet the attractiveness of the parallel runs into the difficulty inher-ent in Hardy's insistence that predestination is immanent. If human events are really entirely predestined from within, how could we ever know it? The more Hardy knows about the cruelties of the Will, the less

powerful or the less immanent its determination must be, for there must
be something in his knowledge that lets him know why things might be
otherwise. If his poetic form really represented total predestination, in
other words, no reader would ever be able to tell, and hence Hardy had
to insist that his work was in no way unconscious or unforeseen, for
relinquishing active consciousness would imply the utter domination of
the Will. But by the same token, such consciousness gains a sense of
itself only by being thwarted, so the poem must display the coerciveness
of the form manipulating its material, careless and self-consciously
awkward at the same time. It is as though Hardy the poet both animates
*and* endures the 'reflex', 'unconscious', 'instinctive' Immanent Will he
accuses of wrecking lives, as he describes ship and iceberg in 'The
Convergence of the Twain':

> Alien they seemed to be:
> No mortal eye could see
> The intimate welding of their later history.

'Welding' suggests the recalcitrance of the separate elements: as if to
point out the strain of the join, the third beat of that last line falls firmly
on 'of', which, like the hull of the *Titanic* crumpled by the iceberg, cannot
bear the resulting stress-impetus. The rhyme-scheme is also carefully
arranged so that despite its apparent *aaa* homogeneity, several words
(such as 'history' above) are forced to rhyme on an unstressed syllable:

> In a solitude of the sea
> Deep from human vanity,
> And the Pride of Life that planned her, stilly couches she.
>                    [. . .]
> Over the mirrors meant
> To glass the opulent
> The sea-worm crawls – grotesque, slimed, dumb, indifferent.

The welding of the rhymes is audible in the wrenched double stress on
'indífferént', as if two things were being forced together and made to fit –
and the parallels with Hardy's strained marriage here in the word 'con-
summation' are ominous. But the stress illustrates the poem's paradox
perfectly, that to pronounce it as the poem demands also involves a
certain drawing-out of the word. Simultaneously, the form of the poem
is indifferent to the normal pronunciation of 'indifferent', and yet that
very indifference makes the word all too conscious of what it's doing. The
very indifference of the sea worm is, for the poem, an insult to the dead
lying around those mirrors whose carrion it is presumably feeding on, and

also a grim rebuke to those once opulent. The Immanent Will is indifferent to human desires, and it is exactly because this is so that conscious creatures cannot but feel it cruel. 'I do not expect that much notice will be taken of these poems', Hardy gloomily noted about the publication of *Moments of Vision*, for 'they mortify the human sense of self-importance by showing, or suggesting, that human beings are of no matter or appreciable value in this nonchalant universe'.[36] 'Nonchalant' is no less anthropomorphic for denying it, but if this tone of mournful self-regard seems at odds with the declaration of human irrelevance, that is exactly Hardy's point. His stylistic awkwardness is therefore a protest against the Will's indifference towards human affairs at the same time as it is a demonstration of it.

This diremption in Hardy's aesthetics is all the more striking when compared with his chief philosophical sources for idea of the Will, Schopenhauer and von Hartmann. Although Hardy was a believer in Fate long before he read either of them, their ideas are often transparent in his work; the notion that humans are puppets animated by a force within, for example, is taken directly from Schopenhauer:

If we conceive the human race and its activities *as a whole and universally*, it does not present itself to us, as when we have in view individual actions, like a puppet-show, the dolls of which are pulled by strings in the ordinary way. On the contrary, from this point of view, it presents itself as puppets that are set in motion by an internal clockwork . . . this human race is innumerable through its being constantly renewed; it is incessantly astir, pushes, presses, worries, struggles, and performs the whole tragic-comedy of world history.[37]

But Schopenhauer and von Hartmann's German Idealist heritage is evident in the way their different philosophies both attribute to art a miraculous power to harmonise things that are left manifestly separate in Hardy's poetry. For Schopenhauer, the will must always develop itself without regard to the supposed needs and desires of its conscious subjects, because it belongs to an essentially different order of being. His division is based upon Kant's fundamental split between the unknowable world as it is in itself, and the phenomenal world which we experience in a certain way because our bodies intuit it like that or, in Schopenhauer's terms, the world as will and representation. Like Kant, Schopenhauer's world of phenomena/representation is a determined one where everything has a necessary cause, whereas the realm of the timeless and undetermined will is free. Unlike Kant, though, Schopenhauer thought causality as much as space and time a category of bodily intuition, so that our logic of reasons why is also limited to the phenomenal world, and since the will lies beyond that world, it is groundless, time-less and purposeless, an endless desire without aim or satisfaction. What-ever the world we experience and represent to ourselves indicates, the reality is determined by the perpetually striving will, which animates the laws of physics, biology and human desire equally, so that physical and emotional stasis or satisfaction is impossible. For Schopenhauer, we are products of this restless, aimless will, and so our whole lives are spent hopelessly desiring new things. All life is perpetual wanting, bound in what Schopenhauer called 'the penal servitude of willing' (I: 196). How-ever, art can be a way to escape our jail-term. In contemplating the aesthetic, a 'miracle' takes place (I: 251):

> We forget our individuality, our will, and continue to exist only as pure subject, as clear mirror of the object, so that it is as though the object alone existed without anyone to perceive it, and thus we are no longer able to separate the perceiver from the perception, but the two have become one . . . what is thus known is no longer the individual thing as such, but the *Idea*, the eternal form, the immediate objectivity of the will at this grade. Thus at the same time, the person who is involved in this perception is no longer an individual, for in such perception the individual has lost himself; he is *pure*, will-less, painless, timeless *subject of knowledge.* (I: 178–9)

Losing our individuality and becoming will-less, in the experience of art we gain a release from the ground of being and prepare ourselves for what Schopenhauer thought the ultimate point of his philosophy, to renounce willing altogether. This is why tragedy was such an important art-form for his system, for by revealing the hopelessness of the human situation it would compel the audience to recognise the necessity of resignation. Hardy thought enough of this definition to copy the passage into his literary notebook:

> <u>Tragedy</u>. Only when the intellect rises to the point where the vanity of all effort is manifest, & the will proceeds to an act of self-annulment, is the drama tragic in the true sense.[38]

So far Hardy's art could be thought of as completely faithful to Schopenhauer's programme, for it is nothing but a revelation of the will's workings designed to manifest the hopelessness of the human situation. But the strange thing about Schopenhauer's theory of artistic contem-plation is the way that its supposed release from the will seems to take place exactly as the subject becomes one with the true forms of that will. If the artist or spectator becomes one with the 'immediate objectivity of the will', then no reflection, no sense of separate will-less self should be possible. As commentators have asked, where would the self-consciousness necessary to grasp the self in renunciation come from?[39] Art seems to need us to become one with the will (as Schopenhauer argues happens parti- cularly in the emotional experience of hearing music, which is the expres- sion of 'the will itself' (II: 448)) and simultaneously see the will for what it is. In lyric poetry or song, for example, the singer experiences an alter- nation of 'pure, will-less knowing' and 'willing, desire, and the recol- lection of our own personal aims', and the lyric is the 'expression or copy of this mingled and divided state of mind' (I: 250). Yet the fact that these moods are 'blended with one another' to any degree contradicts what Hardy noted as one of the basic principles of Schopenhauer's system, namely the complete separation of the will and any kind of purposive intellect.[40] Art, in the grand tradition of post-Kantian aesthetics, turns out to be a reconciliation of things separated in all other circumstances. In fact, we are back on the familiar ground of Schiller's naïve genius and all its organic corollaries, for in art we return to a lost unity:

The identity of the subject of knowing with the subject of willing can be called the miracle κατ' ἐξοχήν [*par excellence*], so that the poetical effect of the song really rests on the truth of that principle. In the course of life, these two subjects, or in popular language, head and heart, grow more and more apart; men are always separating more and more their subjective feeling from their objective knowledge. In the child the two are fully blended; it hardly knows how to distinguish itself from its surroundings; it is merged into them. (I: 250–1)

But willing and knowing, heart and head, are matters that Hardy's aesthetic strives to keep firmly apart. What the regular metre suggests as the will's force, the actual stress pattern is always tugging away from. It is especially evident in the ungainliness of the word 'yes', which frequently stands out as an extra stress in a line, as it stands out as a moment of reflection out of step with the poem's onward march. Hardy's own favourite poem, 'A Trampwoman's Tragedy', places the word at the fateful moment when the trampwoman's flirting with another to arouse her lover's jealousy goes awry:

> Then in a voice I had never heard,
>     I had never heard,
> My only Love to me: 'One word,
>     My lady, if you please!
> Whose is the child you are like to bear? –
> *His*? After all my months o' care?'
> God knows 'twas not! But, O despair!
>     I nodded – still to tease.

Then up he sprang, and with his knife –
And with his knife
He let out jeering Johnny's life,
      Yes; there, at set of sun.
The slant ray through the window nigh
Gilded John's blood and glazing eye,
Ere scarcely Mother Lee and I
      Knew that the deed was done.

The punctuation marks 'Yes' as a fourth stress, a moment of under-standing which stands out as metrically unassimilable to the poem's action, as the two lines that follow also slow the pace to a crawl with five stresses in four beats, its hypnotised reflections making the murder scene into a stained-glass window. The metrical disjunction between knowing and willing mocks the speaker in 'The Night of the Dance', whose assertion that 'She will return in Love's low tongue / My vows as we wheel around' is counteracted by the out-of-time 'Yes' that precedes this, as if reflecting on it could not but tread on the magical moment's toes. 'Yes' or 'Aye' is similarly out of step in 'The Dawn after the Dance', 'The Conformers', 'Former Beauties', 'The Christening', 'A Dream or No' and, most famously, 'After a Journey' – precisely because its subject is knowledge out of time with event. Other moments of ghastly realisation often have an extra stress as if time were proverbially standing still for a second – for example, when the peasant of 'The Curate's Kindness' realises he will have to stay with his wife after forty years of unhappi-ness ('Then I sank – knew 'twas quite a foredone thing'), or the mother realises she has poisoned her daughter unnecessarily in the penultimate verse of 'A Sunday Morning Tragedy'. Thirty stanzas of 4.3.4.3 ballad metre hammer home the fatedness of events, but at the moment of truth:

Thére she láy – sílent, bréathless, déad,
Stóne-dèad she láy – wrónged, sínless, shé! –
Ghost-white the cheeks once rosy-red:
Death had took her. Death took not me.

For Hardy, we always know too late, and when Schopenhauer himself makes the parallel between poetic form and predestination, his difference with Hardy is clear:

A happily rhymed verse, through its indescribably emphatic effect, excites the feeling as if the idea expressed in it already lay predestined, or even preformed, in the language, and the poet had only to discover it . . . the easy and unforced nature of his rhymes . . . have occurred automatically as if by divine decree; his ideas come to him already in rhyme. (II: 428–9)

Hardy's verse sounds predestined exactly because it is unhappily rhymed, because it registers fate by persisting remorselessly with double and triple rhyme schemes, of which 'listlessness' / 'wistlessness' in 'The Voice' is only the most infamous example, or repeating the same rhyme to obsession, as in 'she' and 'me' in the stanza above, which is one of thirty-two insistent long 'e' rhymes in the ballad. The fixedness of the schema is then brought out even more by using occasional rhymes such as 'agony' and 'wantonly', which rhyme on an unstressed syllable (like 'The Convergence of the Twain', above), not so much ringing the rhyme as wringing it out of the word.

For von Hartmann too, art is a unifying of elements which, for Hardy, should be kept separate. His influence on Hardy's philosophy of events is well documented, as for example in *The Dynasts* when the Spirit of the Years explains how the Will can be both blind to human consequence and given any kind of cognitive ability:

> In that immense unweeting Mind is shown
> One far above forethinking; processive,
> Rapt, superconscious; a Clairvoyancy
> That knows not what It knows, yet works therewith.[41]

This idea is based on a note Hardy made of a paragraph from von Hartmann, though his 'processive' alters von Hartmann's 'purposive' with its implications of intention:

This unconscious intelligence is anything but blind, rather far-seeing, nay, even clairvoyant, although this seeing can never be aware of its own vision, but only of the world, and without the mirrors of the individual consciousnesses can also not see the seeing eye. Of this unconscious clairvoyant intelligence we have come to perceive that in its infallible purposive activity, embracing out of time all ends and means in one, and always including all necessary data within its ken, it infinitely transcends the halting, stilted gait of the discursive reflection of consciousness, ever limited to a single point, dependent on sense-perception, memory, and inspirations of the Unconscious. We shall thus be compelled to designate this intelligence, which is superior to all consciousness, at once unconscious and *super*-conscious.[42]

Knowing no difference between means and end, though, is one way of describing the perfectly organic poem, and we do not have to note retrospectively what Freud made of von Hartmann's Unconscious to see how close its *modus operandi* is to post-Kantian notions of artistic production. The Unconscious is where aesthetic feeling originates (I: 274), and like the naïve genius, those who act in accordance with it 'live in eternal harmony with themselves, without ever reflecting much what they do, or even experiencing difficulty or toil' (II: 40). It is entirely opposed to the discursive virtues of judgement and reflection, which would imply self-division; rather, like the genius, it works only according to its own inner laws, with 'unity so perfect that it can only be compared to the unity of natural organisms' (I: 279). In fact, Hardy himself made the comparison:

> It works unconsciously, as heretofore,
> Eternal artistries in Circumstance,
> Whose patterns, wrought by rapt aesthetic rote,
> Seem in themselves Its single listless aim,
> And not their consequence.[43]

The Immanent Will here produces events in a mode identical to the genius producing art: it works in an 'aesthetic' fashion, purposively yet without a purpose, acting as if the artistic patterns of circumstance were their own point, as if their form *were* their content. In other words, von Hartmann's unconscious and immanent will acts exactly like the kind of unified, unmediated artist Hardy did not want to be.

MELANCHOLY

Nevertheless, this does not quite solve the difficulty of Hardy's conscious, conspicuous control of his material. For if his awkwardness indicates any kind of resistance to his all-encompassing Will, by the same token he cannot claim utter helplessness. One might suspect that a situation in which the same style collapses heroic resistance to Fate and utter helplessness before it is obeying the logic of the psychoanalytic symptom, a compromise between two quite opposing wishes. Such conspicuous disharmony would allow the author simultaneously to satisfy unconscious sadistic urges towards the human content while consciously blaming them on the powers that be. Or, as Florence Hardy complained in 1920, 'he is now – this afternoon – writing a poem with great spirit: always a sign of well-being with him. Needless to say, it is an intensely dismal poem.'[44] But it may not be necessary to attribute so pathological a split to Hardy's psyche to understand how persistent self-assertion is compatible with a belief in the Immanent Will, for the definition of tragedy that Hardy copied from Schopenhauer has a similar covert yet persistent self-assertion within it. If tragedy is 'the point where the vanity of all effort is manifest, & the will proceeds to an act of self-annulment', then it remains a question how the tragic drama is actually to take place. How can the will desire self-annulment without promoting itself in disguise? Schopenhauer prohibited suicide for this very reason. But if the hero simply follows Schopenhauer's prescriptions to become will-less and profoundly indifferent to his or her earthly fate, there would be no tragedy at all, for it would make no difference if the hero lived or died. Schopenhauer admits that 'rarely in the tragedy of the ancients is this spirit of resignation seen and directly expressed' (II: 434), and one of his sharpest critics, Walter Benjamin, was to seize on this admission to point out exactly why Schopenhauer's notion of tragedy was not tragedy at all, but a drama which has no ending, the play of melancholia. The comparison comes in Benjamin's *Ursprung des Deustschen Trauerspiels*, which disguises in a learned study of seventeenth-century German Baroque drama an analysis of melancholia as a fully modern political condition, not restricted to the Baroque, and Schopenhauer and Nietzsche its unwitting prophets. According to Benjamin, Schopenhauer's definition mistakes the melancholy of these Baroque dramas for real tragedy, because it makes the tragic hero into a martyr and saint, the passive victim of a cruel external force of Fate. Baroque mourning-plays consequently focus on their characters' sufferings, which are lamented volubly and endlessly. 'Again and again', he wrote, 'the *Trauerspiele* of the seventeenth century treat the same subjects, and treat them in such a way as to permit, indeed necessitate repetition.'[45] In ancient tragedy, by contrast, the hero is not concerned with psychology and self-explanation, but a silence 'which neither looks for nor finds any justification, and therefore throws suspicion back onto his persecutors . . . in tragedy pagan man realizes he is better than his gods' (109–10). For Benjamin, ancient tragedy acts like a trial, where the death of the hero is actually the paralegal staging of the overthrow of the old gods of fate for 'the benefit of the, as yet unborn, national community'; the hero's silence, his absorption of his unjust fate, is what gives the tragedy an ending and a sense of fulfilment. By contrast, the melancholic plays in Benjamin's study have no sacrificial mechanism whereby suffering can come to an end; rather, they exist so as to display endless unresolved unhappiness. 'These are not so much plays which cause mourning, as plays through which mournfulness finds satisfaction: plays for the mournful' (119).

Benjamin's overall purposes for the book were manifold; themes include a covert reading of the totalitarian politics of the state of emergency, an early engagement with Heidegger, and an attempt to re-think the idea of the fragment.[46] But the reader emerging from a perusal of all 943 poems may feel such a comment also throws a good deal of light on

Hardy. As de la Mare commented, 'poem after poem reiterates that this poor scene of our earthly life is a "show God ought surely to shut up soon"', and Hardy's ironies are so endlessly hammered home that after a while the effect draws 'a laugh at the perversity', as Edward Thomas noted, rather than compelling assent.[47] However, reducing Hardy's poems to a psychological study of their author's unhappiness would be to miss Benjamin's point, since the laws that govern it are not 'concerned with the emotional condition of the poet or his public, but with a feeling which is released from any empirical subject and is intimately bound to the fullness of an object' (139). Benjamin's interest in melancholia lies instead in its distinctive way of relating to objects, characterised by a belief that the world is illusory, has no shaping reality of its own, and is instead fundamentally controlled by destiny's machinations. Hence in the world of the mourning plays, nothing is left to chance, for 'everything intentional or accidental is so intensified that the complexities . . . betray, by their paradoxical vehemence, that the action of the play has been inspired by fate' (130).

This way of thinking is visible in Hardy's insistence on seeing the machinations of destiny at work in the tiniest affairs. His friend Gosse noted his way of making poems about the eternal from the trivial – flotsam, a dropped pencil, a rotted sunshade or half a Bible – and the attitude emerges even more clearly in this unintentionally comic passage from the *Life*: 'Hurt my tooth at breakfast-time. I looked in the glass. Am conscious of the humiliating sorriness of my earthly tabernacle, and of the sad fact that the best of parents could do no better for me.'[48] Toothache makes Hardy mourn his mortal situation, not think about going to the dentist. But this ability to see in the minute a cosmic despair does not mean that the minute is actually important; its meaning lies rather in the weight of attention paid to it which it cannot bear. In the melancholic perspective, everything becomes equally artificial and stagey ('images are displayed in order to be seen, arranged in the way they want them to be seen' (119)) because such artificiality manifests the essential emptiness of the world itself. Benjamin remarks on the melancholic's 'self-absorption, to which these great dramas of worldly life seem but a game' (140); Hardy, too, had copied down Arthur Symons's summary of Nietzsche's *Birth of Tragedy*, where 'the object of the tragic myth is precisely to convince us that even the horrible & the monstrous are no more than an aesthetic game, played with itself by the Will'.[49] As Benjamin elegantly says, it is 'the state of mind which revives the empty world in the form of a mask and derives an enigmatic satisfaction in contemplating it' (139). This unreality of appearances is a *leitmotif* of Hardy's: an out-of-season flower is 'but one mask of many worn / By the Great Face behind' in 'The Last Chrysan-themum', and the *Complete Poems* are chock-full of metaphors comparing things to the stage: life is a 'masquerade' in 'She, to Him [II]', the world is 'that show of things' in 'While Drawing in a Churchyard', 'some dim-coloured scene' on which 'my briefly raised curtain' lowers ('In Tenebris III'). The world of *The Dynasts* is variously a 'diorama', 'puppet-show', a 'magic-lantern show', 'phantasmagoric show' and 'galanty-show'. In fact, the magic-lantern show provides the central visual message behind *The Dynasts*, for every so often a new light will shine on the participants to reveal the underlying Immanent Will: 'A new and penetrating light descends on the spectacle, enduing men and things with a seeming transparency, and exhibiting as one organism the anatomy of life and movement in all humanity and vitalized matter included in the display.'[50] This kind of effect – from face to skeleton and back – was indeed achieved by magic-lantern shows using dissolving slides. For Benjamin's melan-cholic, this sense of the transparency of things 'can increase the distance between self and surrounding world to the point of alienation from the body' (140), a sense of utter disjunction well expressed in a famous passage from the *Life*:

For my part, if there is any way of getting a melancholy satisfaction out of life it lies in dying, so to speak, before one is out of the flesh; by which I mean putting on the manners of ghosts, wandering in their haunts and taking their views of surrounding things. To think of life passing away is a sadness; to think of it as past is at least tolerable. Hence even when I enter into a room to pay a simple morning call I have unconsciously the habit of regarding the scene as if I were a spectre not solid enough to influence my environment, only fit to behold and say, as another spectre said: 'Peace be unto you'.[51]

Nevertheless, so casual a slander on orthodox faith at the end sheds doubt on Hardy's claim that he regards the world as a ghost 'uncon-sciously': feeling like the resurrected Christ would be more likely to induce a marked self-consciousness, and indeed without the possibility of absorption into practical affairs, anything the ghost is aware of can do nothing but reveal its isolation. Hardy's melancholy spectatorship is *consciously* self-removed, and such conspicuous detachment is equally the essence of Hardy's style. Like Baroque *Trauerspiel* which has 'artifice as its god' (82), his unlyrical forms emphasise themselves as the stage-machinery of his fate-driven world because they display a melancholy awareness of the loss of the real one, so that the more contrived and

workmanlike his exoskeletally 'crustacean' style is, the more it would
display the loss of very world it describes. Hardy's hyphenations, nonce-
words, and burstings of metrical boundaries are a kind of melancholy
compensation for the absence of the object, marking its loss by their
display of attention to it. The extraordinary gravity with which he treats
his material in 'In Front of the Landscape', for example, only emphasises its evanescence. The poem bursts with alliteration ('dolorous and
dear', 'waste waters', 'coppice-crowned', 'ghost-like gauze', 'meadow or
mound' in the first two stanzas alone), hyphenated phrases ('re-creations',
'halo-bedecked', 'sea-swell') and Latinate circumlocution, in which
walking is 'paced advancement' or 'perambulates' and the dead are 'with
the earth's crust / Now corporate'. Yet the effort that has gone into the
language 'labouring on' seems at odds with the passive content, where
Hardy is always the recipient: 'there would breast me sights', 'later images
too did the day unfurl me', 'so did beset me scenes'. What the poem
reveals is that these visions are of events and people he missed at the time,
which come back 'as they were ghosts avenging their slights by my bypast
/ Body-borne eyes':

> For, their lost revisiting manifestations
>     In their live time
> Much had I slighted, caring not for their purport,
>     Seeing behind
> Things more coveted, reckoned the better worth calling
>     Sweet, sad, sublime.

The extra stress in that last line emphasises Hardy's deliberate covet-
ings, but also that they were placed on the wrong objects and at the wrong
time, and he is paying for it now. There is a kind of desperation in the
labour and attention of the language, a striving to memorialise which only
reveals how the object is already missing. In a passage that might be
commentary on a number of Hardy's poems, Benjamin writes of the style
of Baroque *gravitas*:

The relationship between mourning and ostentation, which is so brilliantly
displayed in the language of the baroque, has one of its sources here; so too does
the self-absorption, to which these great constellations of the worldly chronicle
seem but a game, which may, it is true, be worthy of attention for the meaning
which can reliably be deciphered from it, but whose never-ending repetition
secures the bleak rule of a melancholic distaste for life. (140)

And Benjamin suggests a name for this elaborately self-conscious wrapping up of objects in unsuitable forms: allegory. With Coleridge and

Goethe, Schopenhauer had denounced allegory because it violated the Kantian idea that art must not be a translation of pre-existing concepts into artistic shape, for the true artistic symbol 'expresses itself immediately and completely, and does not require the medium of another thing through which it is outlined or suggested' (I: 237). Allegories separate their appearance from their true meaning, unlike what Benjamin calls the 'organic, plant-like . . . disinterested self-sufficiency' (165) of the symbol. But Benjamin's melancholic will have no self-sufficiency, for 'any person, any object, any relationship can mean absolutely anything else' (175), which means that 'awkward heavy-handedness, which has been attributed either to lack of talent on the part of the artist or lack of insight on the part of the patron, is essential to allegory' (187). In a world inspired by fate, all styles must be extraneous, for there is no intrinsic content. 'Its language was heavy with material display. Never has poetry been less winged', writes Benjamin of a typical play, because in allegory content has to be revealed in its emptiness: 'Written language and sound confront each other in tense polarity. The relationship between them gives rise to a dialectic, in the light of which "bombast" is justified as a consistently purposeful and constructive linguistic gesture.'(200–1).

Unlike symbolism, unlike the modernist aesthetics that grew out of it, Hardy's poetics refuse the union of thing and word in the symbol for the externality of Benjamin's 'allegory', and its fascination with the idea of the ruin, the intervention of time and death between the thing and its meaning; after all, no one was more interested than Hardy in the agony of being always too late. Most ironically, though, one of Benjamin's aims in thinking of art as a ruin was to wrest the idea of the fragment away from Schlegel's hedgehog-like self-completion for a properly modern form of brokenness and non-closure.[52] But if Eliot's notion of tradition maps directly onto Schlegel's fragment-system, as I have argued, then Hardy's melancholy commitment to poetic externality begins to look less like rural clumsiness, and rather more like the principled opposition to Romantic aesthetic unity that post-modern criticism has tended to reserve for the summits of high modernism.

### HARDY'S INDIFFERENCE

Hardy's form and philosophy come together in the aesthetics of melancholy. His consistent stylistic detachment from the poem's material testifies to that material's pure manipulability, and hence its inner emptiness, yet this very emptiness is fascinating, because it is witness to the

emptiness of the world controlled by Fate. The form's indifference to its
content, what Thomas called his 'sonnets . . . so unlike sonnets in spirit'
demonstrates the true vanity of things exactly as it manipulates them
most consciously.[53] And behind this notion of form which is both indifferent and meaningful lies the paradox that has animated Hardy's complaints against the Immanent Will from the beginning: his inability to
accept indifference as simply indifferent. The Will is something that is
both unconscious of human misery and yet always guilty for exactly that
lack of awareness. Everything is predestined, and yet at the same time
everything is random because the Will is unconscious. At the core of a
poem that sets out to prove the opposite to everything I have said so far,
'He Never Expected Much', the world speaks:

> 'I do not promise overmuch,
> Child; overmuch;
> Just neutral-tinted haps and such,'
> You said to minds like mine.
> Wise warning for your credit's sake!
> Which I for one failed not to take,
> And hence could stem such strain and ache
> As each year might assign.

That Hardy claims he was not disappointed only underscores the fact
that he believes the world owed him anything in the first place. 'Neutral-
tinted haps' makes the point, for if neutral is a 'tint' it is anything but
neutral for the painter, for whom its neither-nor character is full of
promise. In Hardy's world, there *are* no 'Neutral Tones', which is that
famous poem's point; the neutral-tinted colours of winter are exactly the
analogue of the emotional situation described, an indifference which is
frozen hatred. He is just a 'tedious riddle', something she can't be
bothered to solve; their parting argument is also merely word-play, her
smile hovering indifferently between dead and alive. The pointed antagonism of neutrality is revealed in the last verse:

> Since then, keen lessons that love deceives
> And wrings with wrong, have shaped to me
> Your face, and the God-curst sun, and a tree,
> And a pond edged with grayish leaves.

The anaphoric 'and . . . and . . . and' is explicitly neutral about the
relation between sun, tree and pond, as if they were being recalled with no
sense of connection between them. But the powerful emotions behind
this sense of detachment are hinted at by the way the neutral-toned

whiteness of the sun has here become evidence of divine wrath; the reader can only speculate about the fury of those calmly grayish leaves. The metre of the last line makes the same point, for if one pronounces it according to the three-beat metre of the previous stanzas, there is no stress on 'edged' and the poem stops at a canter. But read according to the natural stresses of the words themselves, the stress on 'edged' makes the pond and its leaves neutral, separate, prosaically noted. The four stresses give the poem some closure, its iambic regularity counteracting the skipping anapaests of the previous verses that almost seem a parody of Swinburne or Byronic passions, 'on which lost the more by our love', 'like an ominous bird a-wing'. But such closing neutrality is, exactly, achieved at the price of the poem's pattern, and thereby carefully loaded.

'The Voice of Things' likewise insists on the significance of indifference. Forty years ago, the waves he heard were 'in the sway of an all-including joy', because the listener was himself happy. Twenty years ago he heard 'a long ironic laughter / At the lot of men, and all the vapoury / Things that be', whose self-consciously manipulated rhyme reinforces his point about the ironic insubstantiality of the speaker's life. The poem closes in the present day:

> Wheeling change has set me again standing where
>> Once I heard the waves huzza at Lammas-tide;
> But they supplicate now – like a congregation there
>> Who murmur the Confession – I outside,
>>> Prayer denied.

The stanza itself maintains that waves are occupied with their own business and unaware of him, but the poem's overall argument implies that this, too, is a projection of his own emotional circumstances. The refusal to develop the logic any further thus leaves the reader with two different meanings – that the waves just are, without any voice, and that their being so is an exclusion, that their meaning is in the speaker's irrelevance. Lammas-tide in the *Book of Common Prayer* is the time when the story of the prophet Elijah hearing the still, small voice is read, an event whose significance Hardy recalls in 'Quid Hic Agis?' by seeing himself as the broken, disappointed prophet:

> And spiritless,
> In the wilderness
> I shrink from sight
> And desire the night,
> (Though, as in old wise,

I might still arise,
Go forth, and stand
And prophesy in the land),
I feel the shake
Of wind and earthquake
And consuming fire
Nigher and nigher,
And the voice catch clear,
'What doest thou here?'

The question's ambiguity resonates for 'The Voice of Things'; the voice of God was asking Elijah what he thought he was doing in a cave, in order to interrupt his faithless despair and command him to get back to work. Hardy's prophetic task, on the other hand, was to proclaim the impossibility of just that conscious, moral God, and his translation of the divine command makes it sound like a death-sentence, 'a small voice anon / Bade him up and be gone'. On this reading, 'what doest thou here?' is both the voice of God and an ironic assertion of his pointlessness.

This awareness of the intensity of indifference is more than a theological matter, though, since it becomes the emotional crux of Hardy's most famous poems, the 1912–13 series that followed the death of his wife. No commentator has ever doubted that Emma's passing and his own reaction to it came as a shock to Hardy, but in one sense his poems about her death sharpen the same problem that had always underlain his form and his philosophy. Just as he and Emma froze one another out when alive, so in death her utter unresponsiveness to him cannot but be felt as another insult in their struggles, and so poems that are ostensibly about grief at the loss of the beloved actually become a continuation of domestic arguments. There is anger behind the opening question of 'The Going', as well as regret:

Why did you give no hint that night
That quickly after the morrow's dawn
And calmly, as if indifferent quite
You would close your term here, up and be gone

The plaintiveness makes Emma sound like a student or lodger who had irresponsibly slipped away, her headstrong flightiness the only concession to her actions not being entirely, hurtfully deliberate. What follows is an extraordinarily honest mixture of the self-pity and aggression often buried in grief:

Where I could not follow
With wing of swallow
To gain one glimpse of you ever anon!

'Anon' may be shorthand for 'henceforth', or it may mean 'shortly', which hints at self-mourning (I cannot see you again soon, but I will in a while). But the word also suggests its old meaning of 'unity in one body, mind state', as if in glimpsing her they might be together again, and simultaneously flickers with the mournful-angry meaning of 'anonymous', which makes the last three words utter the baffled reality of her disappearance: you, ever, anon. 'In spite of his often deterministic views', comments Ramazani, 'Hardy represents his wife not as the passive victim of circumstance but as an active agent', which is true, except that it is his deterministic views that also make him unable to believe in the indifference of circumstances.[54] For instance, in the next stanza, it is ambiguous whether it is the morning that is 'unmoved, unknowing', or he himself, which suggests the same double emphasis on indifference again: the morning could not have known, but its indifference is frequently a cause of grief for Hardy elsewhere in the poems ('Rain on a Grave', 'A Death-Day Recalled', 'Beeny Cliff'). He, by contrast, might have known, and yet by not doing so resembles the indifference of the morning light, hardening where his wife's longed-for cry is the 'softest'. The irony is that this mutual ignorance is the one thing that he and she actually shared at that great moment, both being 'unmoved, unknowing', and as always in Hardy's ghost-ridden world, the dead seem simply a continuation of the living. And so the dispute continues: in stanza three, 'why do you make me leave the house' implies that *she* is guilty for making him believe that he sees her, and if the syntax is followed through the stanza, guilty for not actually being there. But even as he realises her absence, the 'yawning blankness / Of the perspective' describes her sickening disappearance as if it were someone bored and tired with his constant seeking. Death and non-being have become just another move in the argument, as 'days long dead' are in the fifth stanza:

Why, then, latterly, did we not speak,
Did we not think of those days long dead,
And ere your vanishing strive to seek
That time's renewal? We might have said,
'In this bright spring weather
We'll visit together
Those places that once we visited.'

The comma at the first line-break suggests that perhaps they not only did not speak of the past, but were not speaking at all. The awkwardness of stressing the last syllable of 'visited' to make the rhyme hints at the strenuous brightness of the conversation required to break that silence, and calling the days 'long dead' hints that the present question is hopelessly, tragically rhetorical, for neither then nor now is there an answer, nor can he raise the dead again. Exactly as the last stanza promises to give up the argument because it is pointless, it immediately flares up again:

> Well, well! All's past amend,
> Unchangeable. It must go.
> I seem but a dead man held on end
> To sink down soon . . . O you could not know
> That such swift fleeing
> No soul foreseeing –
> Not even I – would undo me so!

'Well, well' is sadly resigned, but its exclamation mark makes it equally hurtfully brisk, as if washing its hands of her death in two words, or even accepting this novel turn of events with some fortitude. Pretending to accept loss faster than one actually can is common among those deeply hurt, but at the same time its impoliteness marks the way the poem turns to mourning himself as if she were still within earshot. Even as the final sentence alters the tenor of the whole poem by acknowledging that her unwitting participation in his tragedy may not have been intended, there is a sudden irruption of domestic antagonism. 'Not even I' could know how quick your death would be; 'not even I', the wicked husband whom you believe has long plotted your death like Dr Crippen; 'not even I', the poet whose verse you hated because it foresees death for everything.[55] Emma's death occurs in the middle of things, not at the end of them, and the self-defensiveness of this outburst opens up again the question of her not knowing. Could she not know that her death would hurt him so, because not even he could know how much it would hurt? Or could she not know this because she was too insensitive to imagine it?

In 'Your Last Drive', too, her unawareness then that this was her last view of the lights or that she was passing her grave is not just a reminder of the unexpectedness of death. Rather, her heedlessness and lack of discernment parallels her heedlessness now, as if death had changed nothing for her. As her face already tells of her death, so her countenance has 'a flickering sheen', as if its expression were a pre-recorded film and she already gone. This sense of continuous unawareness between life and death is strengthened when it becomes the point of another argument.

'You may miss me then', she says, alternating between possibility and a rather bossy permission:

> But I shall not know
> How may times you visit me there
> Or what your thoughts are, or if you go
> There never at all. And I shall not care.

In an ironic re-working of Christina G. Rossetti's measured unhappiness in 'When I am dead, my dearest' ('I shall not see the shadows / I shall not feel the rain'), Emma's indifference is both bald factual truth and a haughty argument, the ambiguity of which Hardy's reply picks up exactly:

> True: never you'll know. And you will not mind.
> But shall I then slight you because of such?
> Dear ghost, in the past did you ever find
> The thought, 'What profit,' move me much?
> Yet abides the fact, indeed the same, –
> You are past love, praise, indifference, blame.

The extra stress on 'True', like his 'Yes' elsewhere, marks a slowed-down moment, as if stepping out of the argument to mull over the emotions that emerge in the ambiguous possibilities of stress in the line. If it reads 'and *you* will not mind', the implication is, 'but I will', making him sound hurt and aggressive. If it is read 'and you *will* not mind' the stress on that vital word for Hardy indicates volition as well as futurity, that her indifference is a calculated one, that her desire and her fate have conspired to mean the same thing. But the overt meaning of 'what profit', a promise that he will visit regardless, contains a sting: if he doesn't mind performing the profitless task, then he will not mind profitlessly arguing with her either. If something like this thought spurs the resignation of the last lines, then just as he seems to acknowledge that his indifference has been motivated, the extra stresses of the last line say the opposite. The line has four beats, but to say it with only four stresses makes the three introductory unstressed syllables sound liltingly off-handed:

> You are past lóve, práise, indífference, bláme.

A more prosaic stress-pattern of the words would demand a weight on 'Past', which by slowing the line down gives it a twist: in an address that may or may not be to her, Emma is indeed a past love. The line's metrical ambiguity allows indifference and vindictiveness to be as undecidable and simultaneous as they have been throughout the poem.

Perhaps 'The Walk', one of Hardy's most beautiful and painful poems, puts this state of mind most clearly:

> You did not walk with me
> Of late to the hill-top tree
>     By the gated ways
>     As in earlier days;
>     You were weak and lame,
>     So you never came,
> And I went alone, and I did not mind
> Not thinking of you as left behind.

After the strict neutrality of the opening lines, 'You were weak and lame' might be pitying, or it might have an undercurrent of suppressed anger at her weak and lame excuses, a suggestion bolstered by the stress possibilities of 'So you never came'. If on 'you', it simply emphasises that you didn't come and I did; but if on 'never', it makes her action irritatingly perpetual in the manner typical of long-term domestic irritation ('you *never* do the washing-up'), especially as he has previously said that she did come in the past. With this in mind, saying that 'I did not mind' might be protesting a bit much, for as the poem progresses, not minding or caring come to mean something quite the opposite. If he did not think of her as left behind, the implication of the second stanza is that nothing has changed:

> I walked up there to-day
> Just in the former way:
>     Surveyed around
>     The familiar ground
>     By myself again:
>     What difference, then?
> Only that underlying sense
> Of the look of a room on returning thence.

The understated sensitivity of this last line must have inspired one of Larkin's best openings, 'Home is so Sad':

> Home is so sad. It stays as it was left,
> Shaped to the comfort of the last to go
> As if to win them back.

Rooms look the same on returning to them, which is how we know that we have changed. By insisting that nothing externally has altered between then and now, the poem makes its point backhandedly, for noticing the unexpected continuity is testimony that something has happened. The very indifference of gate, hill or tree is noticeable because it should not be so, and the same charge is tacitly being made against his own 'not thinking' and not minding.

The poems of 1912–13 feelingly trace such indifference again and again; Nature's lack of respect in 'A Death-Day Recalled' and 'Rain on a Grave', the world's in 'Places' and 'A Circular', and his own necessary ignorance in 'The Haunter' and 'His Visitor'. Its dual aspect appears especially when her indifference in death is seen as all of a piece with her married life, as in 'Without Circumstance' or 'I Found Her Out There', where her passing was that life's chief event:

> I found her out there
> On a slope few see
> That falls westwardly
> To the salt-edged air
> [. . .]
> I brought her here
> And have laid her to rest
> In a noiseless nest
> No sea beats near.

The life they shared for forty years is skipped over: she was an *objet trouvé*, as inactive when picked up as laid down. Yet by linking 'out there' with passion, romance and anger (the smiting Atlantic, flailing hair and sobbing, throbbing sea), the poem also quietly admits the emotional burial of her life 'here' in Dorset. With its rocking, lullaby rhythm, the poem seems to be singing her to sleep like a baby (her grave is a 'nest', she has the 'heart of a child'), a gesture which simultaneously offers an explanation for her childish lack of understanding while alive and a consolation that her death is a return to what she always was, as in 'Rain on a Grave':

> Soon will be growing
> Green blades from her mound
> And daisies be showing
> Like stars on the ground
> Till she form part of them
> Ay – the sweet heart of them
> Loved beyond measure
> With a child's pleasure
> All her life's round.

The pun on 'sweet heart' adds to the hurt behind 'a child's pleasure' – she loved the daisies with the measurelessness more appropriate to the lifelong commitment of marriage – but making her life a 'round' means her grave is continuous with that childhood, and nothing has really changed. 'A Dream or No' wonders about the reality of 'the woman I thought a long housemate with me', quietly picking up on Ecclesiastes' description of the grave as man's 'long home' (12:5) to imply their marriage and her death were very much of a piece. Such an uninterrupted transition between the two smoothes over the shock of parting, but at the price of making her unresponsiveness in death always part of the life they shared.

But revealing the emotional charge within such indifference has an impact on the awkwardness of the poems' form as well, for the more the diction feels inappropriate or the rhythm clumsy, the more it would testify to the strain between the couple while alive, and the estrangement that continues afterwards. Sometimes the complex alliterations and re-petitive rhymes seem too willingly to enforce a shape on loss, as in 'Lament':

> But
> She is shut, she is shut
> From friendship's spell
> In the jailing shell
> Of her tiny cell.

The triple rhymes and two-beat line determinedly make the stanza's end something of a tiny cell itself, but then, what choice do mourners have but to lavish attention on the heedless? This manipulated, unavoidable superfluity is also audible in 'After a Journey':

> Hereto I come to view a voiceless ghost;
> Whither, O whither will its whim now draw me?

Its repetitions and echoes are conspicuously noisy in the ghost's silence, as extrinsic as the stanza pattern proves to be. It is very difficult to tell, for example, if the penultimate line of each stanza has two or three beats; 'With your nut-coloured hair' might be either; 'with us twain, you tell' is very awkward if it is not two; 'I am just the same as when' is difficult to squeeze into two without gabbling. The effect is an odd combination of formal coerciveness and uncertainty which mirrors the way the speaker alternates between being led on by the ghost and holding her to account; indeed, the metre itself keeps changing gear between iambic and trochaic/dactylic, spurring itself on and then lapsing as if not sure whether to lead or be led, a question which reappears in the argument itself:

What have you now found to say of our past –
Scanned across the dark space wherein I have lacked you?

It is angry, but in every way one tries to scan the second line, hopelessly awkward as well, and if the metrical meaning of scanning is here equated with a kind of judgement on the past, then the form's inadequacy implies there is no easy way to apportion due weight without either forcing or being forced. The formal extraneousness, in other words, registers not only the unresponsiveness of its object, but the uselessness of trying to settle scores:

Trust me, I mind not, though Life lours,
The bringing me here; nay, bring me here again!
I am just the same as when
Our days were a joy, and our paths through flowers.

'I am just the same' promises a return to the happy past at the same time as it is an accusation – it was *you* who changed – and with it, a hopelessness, for if you have changed, then there is no going back.

Talking to someone who isn't there to listen is a situation many mourners have found themselves in; the difference with Hardy is only that in his complaints against Time and the Will he had been doing it for longer than most. But if the intense pain of irrelevance is a continuing concern of Hardy's melancholic form, the poems of 1912–13 are only sharpened by the irony that here his melancholia actually finds a lost object, so that its endlessness is present here and now. 'At Castle Boterel', one of the last of these poems, movingly traces this disjunction in the way it tries to say goodbye while simultaneously knowing that 'goodbye is not worthwhile' ('Without Ceremony'). It oscillates between seeing the past as intensely significant and quite trivial, so that on revisiting a hillside spot of their courtship, the speaker insists that 'what we did as we climbed, and what we talked of / Matters not much, nor to what it led', only to assert immediately that this lack of importance is 'something that life will not be balked of'. Then, with a nod to a familiar Victorian anxiety:

Primeval rocks form the road's steep border,
And much have they faced there, first and last,
Of the transitory in Earth's long order;
But what they record in colour and cast
Is – that we two passed.

The rocks record the transitory moment as a microsecond of geological time, and equally make their passing something written in stone. This

mixture of the evanescent and the enduring comes to a head in the last
stanzas, when the formal design of the poem shows through:

> And to me, though Time's unflinching rigour,
>     In mindless rote, has ruled from sight
> The substance now, one phantom figure
>     Remains on the slope, as when that night
>         Saw us alight.
>
> I look and see it there, shrinking, shrinking,
>     I look back at it amid the rain
> For the very last time; for my sand is sinking,
>     And I shall traverse old love's domain
>         Never again.

Each of the last stanza's longer lines contains a word that in prose use
would be stressed but is passed over by the 'unflinching rigour' of the
metre, a phrase which encapsulates Hardy's complaint that Time is
determined and mindless at the same time. But the ghostly possibility
of stressing 'there', 'look', 'last' and 'old' makes it possible to hear the
time of the last verse being stretched out too, as if the speaker were
deliberately clinging onto the fading vision at the same time as he is
dragged away from it, looking and looking as it (or he) shrinks and
shrinks. It is a *cleaving*, in the sense of a simultaneous clinging and
parting of form and material, or an inseparable separation of husband
and wife. 'Cleave' is a word that Hardy would have heard in his marriage service in its joining sense ('a man shall leave his mother and
father and cleave unto his wife') and during his marriage must have
wished for more of its dividing sense, but it is its possibility of meaning both at once which describes the antagonistic indifference of his
poetic.

Unexpectedly, it was also this cleavage of form and content that proved
a revelation to one of Hardy's most surprising admirers, Ezra Pound.
Pound's respect for Hardy began early and never ceased: in 1914 he had
not quite casually suggested that Hardy's clarity should earn him a place
in an Imagist anthology, and in the late *Confucius to Cummings* he
nominated Hardy his poetic grandfather in the line descending from
Browning.[56] The most intimate contact he made, however, was in 1921,
when he wrote to Hardy privately and very respectfully for advice on
'Homage to Sextus Propertius' after Eliot had given *Quia Pauper Amavi* a
frosty reception. Hardy's reply is lost, but it seems to have come as a
bombshell:

You have really said a good deal and diagnosed the trouble with nearly all the art and literature of the past thirty years.

I ought – precisely – to have written 'Propertius soliloquizes' – turning the reader's attention to the reality of Propertius – but no – what I do is borrow a term – aesthetic – a term of aesthetic *attitude* from a french [*sic*] musician, Debussy . . .

I ought to have concentrated on the subject – (I did so long as I forgot my existence for the sake of the lines) – and I tack on a title relating to the treatment – in a fit of nerves – fearing the reader won't sufficiently see the super-position[,] the doubling of me and Propertius, England to-day and Rome under Augustus.[57]

Or as one of Pound's letters to a young poet later yelled, Hardy's success came from his single-minded focus on 'CONTENT, the INSIDES, the SUBJECT-MATTER'.[58] It is perhaps only another version of his insistence on direct treatment of the thing, of directing all one's mental faculties onto the 'what' rather than the 'how'. But by allowing a separation of the poem's content from the *deliberate* 'concentrated' mental treatment of it, Pound unwittingly diagnoses the problem with the aestheticist and symbolist doctrines which justified their art by identifying exactly those two things, and whose insistence that the mental impression was being directly transcribed had underwritten so much modernist formal innovation, and so much criticism of everybody else's 'rhetoric'.[59] By admitting Hardy's un-Paterian division between treatment and subject, Pound has effectively hamstrung a good deal of his own earlier criticism. Or perhaps this is what is being tacitly acknowledged in the single sentence at the top of the first page, apparently disconnected from the rest of the letter: '"Good," "Bon," "Bonto," or very probably "Uugh" as Jacob said when the angel finally blessed him.'

# CHAPTER 6

# Going over the top: the passions of Wilfred Owen

What did Wilfred Owen feel about the First World War? If this sounds like an easy question, the answer is not always as obvious as it might be:

> So the church Christ was hit and buried
> Under its rubbish and its rubble.
> In cellars, packed-up saints lie serried,
> Well out of hearing of our trouble.
>
> One Virgin still immaculate
> Smiles on for war to flatter her.
> She's halo'd with an old tin hat,
> But a piece of hell will batter her. ('Le Christianisme')[1]

Is the poem happy about such destruction, or not? Of course not: the war has buried Christ, the gates of Hell are prevailing, and in flattering then battering the immaculate Virgin, the war is linked with blasphemy, seduction and rape; Owen was attracted to Catholicism, despite (or because of) his Evangelical upbringing. But then amid the destruction, the Virgin's very untouched nature leaves her looking slightly foolish, out of touch, naïve, as if she couldn't see the suggestion of 'flatten' lurking within 'flatter'. The saints are similarly unworldly, lying 'packed up': safely stored but also not working, as in 'my machine gun's packed up'. And they 'lie serried' – lying down, or merely not telling the truth; serried, as in serried ranks of angels, or serried files of soldiers. In other words, are their close ranks a point of sympathy with the soldiers or an ironic comment? The next line suggests irony, 'well out of hearing of our trouble', but then are the saints too far away, or simply 'well out of it', mercifully spared our whining prayers, or our guns? Is this poem angry at war's destruction, or is it angry at the way religion is so useless in war, and therefore tacitly siding with the destruction? Whose is the 'Christianisme', the church's or Owen's?

Like the ruined church it describes, this poem is a site of conflict between opposing appropriations, and like most contested territory, it thereby gains a peculiar character of its own. Asking what Owen felt about the war he was fighting in is not such a simple question, because Owen's poetry is itself a site of irreconcilable conflicts of feeling, conflicts that were necessarily irreconcilable if Owen's protest were to continue. If tracing what Owen's poems tell us about the conflicts their author experienced feels like a natural approach, however, placing his work in the aesthetic context of modernism brings it up straightaway against the insistence of 'Tradition and the Individual Talent' that the poem's emotion is a new thing and important for itself, rather than as a testimony to the private emotions and situations that provoked it. But in a strange sense, to put Owen's emotions and his aesthetics together is to contextualise the ethos of 'Tradition and the Individual Talent' in return, for so many of its aesthetic ideals were the realities of Owen's personal experience; the impersonal discipline and anonymity of the army, the simultaneous present of the living and the dead, and the real, bloody fragmentations of his front-line experiences. When Eliot remarks that his essay's aim is to attack the metaphysical theory of the substantial unity of the soul, the most biographical reading possible of Owen's poetry will confirm that this attack was a daily reality, in the trenches and among the traumatised and incapacitated at Craiglockhart mental hospital. As Allyson Booth and Trudi Tate have explored, many of the splintered, haunted and traumatised 'perceptual habits' of the First World War soldier are also those of the modernist work of art.[2] But it is because 'continual self-sacrifice' was rather more than a doctrine of artistic progress for Owen that it is possible to trace in his aesthetics a very different set of needs and ideals from Eliot's, because they are part of Owen's active struggle against the war he was fighting, rather than just a cultural adaptation of the war's collective trauma. Jane Goldman has made a neat comparison between the ideals of 'Tradition and the Individual Talent' and the emphasis on anonymous self-sacrifice displayed in the Cenotaph and other war memorials then being established in every village; like the unknown soldier, the writer gives up his personal existence for the sake of the greater good of the whole.[3] But memorials are for the dead, and Owen was not yet one of them; against Eliot's 'surrender' of emotion to a greater order, his extraordinary poems were provoked by his struggle to hold on to his feelings in the face of his contrary and impossible situation. As a soldier he was torn between hatred of the war and embroilment in it; as an artist, between telling the truth and dealing with the unbearable; and as a gay man, between his unlawfully tender feelings for his fellow soldiers and the officially sanctioned killing that always framed the possibility of such intimacy. Above all, such conflicts of feeling are inseparable from Owen's extraordinary style, for the remarkable division between the form of his poems and their content is a protest against and a symptom of his personal divisions, in the psychoanalytic sense; a compromise-formation designed to ensure his psychic survival. It is also a direct challenge to the Romantic and modernist tradition of autonomous aesthetics discussed in chapter 1, for where Pound and Eliot campaigned for the elimination of excess, artificiality and the generic, Owen's poetry displays them flagrantly, as qualities he must hang onto for dear life. In a situation that was the opposite of autonomous, no version of aesthetics derived from that principle would ever allow him to do that situation justice, or better, render its total lack of justice palpable. The very incompatibilities within his poems are less to be lamented, aesthetically or morally, than recognised as somehow necessary, since the force of his protest derives from their split.

## DIVIDED LOYALTIES

Nevertheless, Owen's poetic is not entirely opposed to Eliot's fundamental aim in 'Tradition and the Individual Talent', to shift the question of poetic agency away from the poet's originating self. For although Owen's work is testimony to his own situation, that situation itself involves some intense contradictions of loyalty which make his voice more divided than singular. Owen's poetry is about the war, but it is made by someone within the war and its system, and one of the system's characteristics is to create a disjunction between what the man is and what the soldier does – a disjunction which honour, loyalty and comradeship do their best to overcome. In a war, a soldier will win medals for actions which in peace-time would put him in prison. He is a guilty hero and an innocent murderer, committing terrible acts for which he is, and is not, responsible. The army is therefore what makes him break the most primary social laws, and gives him an alternative society of shared loyalties to substitute for the civilian ones that have been broken. This question of agency was, of course, rendered particularly acute for the First World War because of its felt absence for most soldiers, conscripted and then pinned down in trench warfare.

What Owen felt, then, was dependent not only on what he did, but what he became, or was made to become. Such a question occurs at the heart of his most famous protest, 'Dulce et Decorum Est', where he describes a file of stumbling soldiers who 'limped on, blood-shod'. Their feet are covered with blood because 'many had lost their boots', but the blood may not be all their own: the phrase cannot but recall tyrants treading blood, or the gorier moments of vengeance in the Old Testament (Psalms 58:10, Isaiah 63:2–4) where the feet are those of the righteous but the blood is always the enemy's. And the question of agency resounds for Owen too, who, in being too late to help the dying man, must watch him again and again. The exclamatory punctuation of 'Gas! GAS! Quick, boys – An ecstasy of fumbling' insists the line has seven stresses, one on each of the first four words, making it both ultra-urgent and weirdly suspended from the time-frame of the pentameter, in a temporal *ekstasis*. This dislocation of time in the attack is reproduced in the shift from past tense ('I saw him drowning') to the perpetual present ('he plunges') of the dreams. The agency of 'plunges' is, exactly, both active and passive; the soldier 'plunges' because he is drowning in the green sea of gas, because he is trying to breathe (*OED*: 'of the chest: to expand with falling of the diaphragm'), but also as if he were a kind of missile (*OED* again: 'of artillery: to send shot downwards from a higher level'), and the 'at' gives the man's fall a kind of accusation. Such an accusation is picked up in the couplet about 'smothering dreams', where the dying man is 'guttering', a word which brilliantly combines candles going out and sewage spilling out. For Owen's dreams are also asphyxiating, like the gas, as if his guilty conscience has allied itself with the enemy's poison, smothering *him* for being too late to help the soldier. Whose side is Owen on?

'I came out in order to help these boys – directly by leading them as only an officer can – indirectly by watching their sufferings that I may speak of them as well as a pleader can'.[4] The difficulty is not just that these two aims are in conflict with one another, but that they are done by the same person: the officer leading his men into suffering and the watcher of that suffering are inextricable from one another. Hence one of the tasks in reading Owen's poetry is not only to see what it says about the war, but what it says about its own situation of saying, for the two cannot be separated. Determining that is an altogether trickier affair than reading Owen as simply an anti-war prophet. A letter to his non-combatant cousin Leslie Gunston regrets that 'you are neither in the flesh with us nor in the spirit against War', implying a similar split between body and soul in himself.[5] Owen was an anti-war protester who was awarded the Military Cross for spraying a trenchful of Germans with machine-gun fire.[6] 'All a poet can do today is warn', Owen writes in his famous projected Preface, but then adds: '(If I thought the letter of this book would last, I might have used proper names; but if the spirit of it survives – survives Prussia – my ambition and those names will have achieved fresher fields than Flanders.)' After denouncing all notions of the glory of war, Owen ends his anti-war protest by setting its spirit against Prussia, thus neatly stepping back inside military orthodoxy: it is Prussia that would silence his verses. This may partly be to pre-empt censorship at home, and partly to suggest that it is truly English to hate war, but nevertheless the terms are caught inside the very binary of England/Germany that poems such as 'Strange Meeting' do so much to resist.

Owen's edgy defence of his own poetry, 'Apologia Pro Poemate Meo' is riven with the same difficulty. The first stanza claims that 'War brought more glory to their eyes than blood / And gave their laughs more glee than shakes a child'. What begins as solidarity with the troops becomes entangled straightaway in the militarist message that war brings glory. And the emotional tone is similarly uncertain, for laughing children are a stock piece of sentiment which Owen purports to reject in favour of soldiers' laughs, but in a phrase whose awkwardly monosyllabic solemnity runs against what he's claiming – 'And gave their laughs more glee than shakes a child', full stop. This intermingling of the sentimental, the personal and the portentous continues through the poem, as it is in some respects its theme; the experience of war forces the utterly serious and the trivial up next to one another, in the sense that every cigarette may be one's last, or then again it may just be another cigarette. 'For power was on us as we slashed bones bare' is epic in its Poundian triple stress (sláshed bónes báre), and only slightly undercut by the lurking of the humbler and perhaps more honest 'feel sick' in the line's continuation, 'not to feel sickness or remorse of murder', and using the very words 'slashed' and 'murder' denies at once the remorseless power the speaker is recalling. The bathetic and the epic stand alongside one another, a complication of soldier-hero and soldier-sufferer which continues:

> I, too, have dropped off Fear –
> Behind the barrage, dead as my platoon,
> And sailed my spirit surging light and clear. . .

The dead platoon are sailed over very rapidly, for their officer, but they return very quickly:

> Faces that used to curse me, scowl for scowl,
> Shine and lift up with passion of oblation
> Seraphic for an hour; though they were foul.

Faces become angelic, a gift equated with the lifting up of the sacrament ('oblation' occurs in the Book of Common Prayer's Eucharistic rite) – yet simultaneously, this connotes sacrifice, killing, offering to God, all the things Owen protests against in 'The Parable of the Old Men and the Young' and elsewhere. Similarly, the bathos of 'though they were foul' encompasses possibilities ranging from 'seraphic for an hour, though their owners were revolting' to 'seraphic in their bestiality' to, simply, 'they were muddy'. In this moment of 'exultation', Owen's poetry registers contempt, repulsion, pity, sympathy, blasphemy, orthodoxy, all at once. The emotional onslaught continues in a swipe at Gunston's poem 'L'Amour': love is not the 'binding of fair lips' but:

> Wound with war's hard wire whose stakes are strong
> Bound with the bandage of the arm that drips
> Knit in the webbing of the rifle-thong.

The last line is restrained, but the curious mixture of ballad *naïveté* and gothicism of the 'arm that drips' does not share its balance, deliberately. It is the pun on 'wound' that provokes its disharmony: love is winding together and wounding together, and so the phrase 'arm that drips' is both sincere and knowingly tasteless, deliberately revolting the Gunstons and insisting that the revolting is true. When Merryn Williams complains of the rhyme of 'beauty' and 'duty' in the next stanza, she is missing the point of the whole poem: to align opposites, the earnest and the provocative, the hatred of war and its celebration, disgust for the men and love for them.[7]

### STYLE

Such a conflict of feelings is inseparable from Owen's extraordinary stylistic conflicts. Jon Stallworthy's edition of the poems notes that Owen's 'Apologia' is indebted to Shelley's *Defence of Poetry*, which claims that 'poetry is a mirror which makes beautiful what is distorted . . . it marries exultation and horror'. Evidently it is a marriage made in 'the sorrowful dark of Hell', but the reference is a helpful reminder that Owen is defending his own poetry rather than his own actions or feelings. His tactic to defend his poems' ugliness, however, was not to reject beauty outright, but redefine it. 'I have perceived much beauty / In the hoarse oaths that kept our courage straight', and the question of who is swearing indicates how the question of beauty itself is caught up with Owen's problems with his own agency in the war. It is not only that he finds beauty in ugliness: rather, the beauty of keeping one's courage straight is both comradely solidarity *and* the spine-stiffening resolve demanded by the army in sending its men out to get killed, resolve which it was Owen's job to dispense. Owen's sense of distortion turns out to be within the beauty itself, rather than in opposition to it.

If Owen refused to remove a notion of beauty, however compromised, from his own war poetry, it would be mistaken to assume that his famous statement in the 'Preface' that 'above all I am not concerned with Poetry' implies a wholesale rejection of the aesthetic. Nevertheless, placed alongside 'Dulce et Decorum Est', the Preface has often been read as the moment where Owen rejects his Keatsian and Aestheticist heritage for a poetry that refuses to prettify war, which will tell the raw, direct and uncensored truth.[8] But one of the most obvious, perhaps too obvious, characteristics of Owen's poetry is that it is patently very concerned with poetry as well as war. There has been surprisingly little discussion of the evident mismatch between his incredible sound-texturing, alliteration, internal rhyme, loading every rift with ore, and the raw, bleeding subject matter, loading every rift with gore, as it were. It is not enough to say that Owen's technique simply emphasises the content, since it emphasises itself, too; as Craig A. Hamilton has demonstrated, his complex revisions of 'Strange Meeting' and 'Anthem for Doomed Youth' always choose a new word as much for the tightening of the sound-patterns as for his poetic argument.[9] Hence a line such as 'found peace where shell-storms spouted reddest spate' literally spits out the 'sp' and 'st' of 'storm', 'reddest', 'spout', 'spate', in plosive floods of mud or blood; but also feels deliberate, worked-at, well wrought, as if Owen were calmly but intensely working his effects to the maximum. The strangeness of 'Apologia' is not only in its riot of beauty and horror, the violently incompatible in a phrase, but in the organised, dedicated execution of such a riot. In a war that popularised the notion of the unconscious, Owen's lush, Keatsian horror is *hyper*-conscious, almost every word bound together with another. 'These men are worth / Your tears. You are not worth their merriment' insists the last stanza, and Owen seems to be stabbing at his audience like Sassoon does, but that final 'merriment' describes the soldiers' mood and simultaneously echoes 'these men' and earlier, 'merry it was to laugh there'. The word itself is knit into the poem's sound-texture, and relating merriment to the absurd laughter of 'merry' as the men 'murder' other soldiers cuts against the supposed oppositions of tears/merriment and superior troops/unworthy civilians that the poem has been setting up. Owen's aesthetic relentlessly binds up incompatible feelings, attitudes and emotions, and does so because the binding *in itself* sets up an impossible conflation of aesthetic enjoyment and disgust, the artificial and the direct. 'Insensibility' dramatises the conflict:

> The front line withers.
> But they are troops who fade, not flowers,
> For poets' tearful fooling:
> Men, gaps for filling.

It is as if Owen reacts angrily to his own metaphor of 'withers' – how can you compare or translate suffering into a poem? – but then again, it is the poets' tears that make him not insensible, and the poetry is still fooling around with pararhyme as it berates poets, and moreover is written in free verse so that there *are* no pre-prescribed 'gaps for filling' with men or words about them, and the subject makes its own form. It is a poem equally sincere about writing poetry and not writing 'poetry'.

This sincerity, even a sincerity about irony, is why Owen, for all his multiple voices, cannot be recruited for Eliot's impersonal version of modernism.[10] Eliot delicately plays off voices against one another, and cannot be identified with any of them. Owen writes with an excess of formal patterning which only emphasises his divided allegiances, but he is equally sincere about all of them. Surely the survival of the unconfirmed story that Owen used to go up to people in the street and show them photographs of mangled corpses is precisely because that is what Owen poems do to their readers – thrust corpses in their face, to make them *see*. Yet at the same time, these are, as it were, carefully photographed corpses with maximum lighting effects and perhaps in a studio, rather than snapshots taken on the hoof, with all the post-Romantic virtues of involuntariness, uncomposedness and therefore 'reality'. Owen himself described his reworkings of 'A Terre' as 'retouching a "photographic representation" of an officer dying of wounds'.[11] His work insists simultaneously on the real, the incredibly real, with an aesthetic of touching-up, hyper-composure and excess. He has too many identifications, too much aesthetic interest for any definition of war poetry which defines its distinctiveness in terms of objective 'realism'.

Seamus Heaney has sensitively explored the dilemma this puts the reader of the poems into. He begins by noting the difficulty of paying attention to Owen's aesthetics at all, since 'his poems have the potency of human testimony, of martyr's relics, so that any intrusion of the aesthetic can feel like impropriety'. But nevertheless, Heaney's poetic conscience persists in asking awkward questions about famous poems, albeit guiltily:

'Is Owen over-doing it here?' I would ask. 'Inside five lines we have "devil's sick of sin", "gargling", "froth-corrupted", "bitter as the cud", "vile, incurable sores". Is he not being a bit over-insistent? A bit explicit?' However hangdog I might feel about such intrusions, I also felt that it was right to raise questions.[12]

Heaney does not have an answer to his questions, except perhaps a good deal of his own poetry. Indeed, the question of 'over-doing it' is begged by the war itself; what could possibly count as aesthetic excess, faced with the unimaginable situations of the trenches? But the reply is that given such horror, there is excess in making any sort of poetry at all, since no aesthetic form could be adequate to the situation. This is why no argument that discusses Owen's aesthetics only in terms of realism will ultimately be adequate to them. When Keith V. Comer states that 'Owen's intent is to confront the reader with as much reality as he is able to create . . . in Owen's poem we are supposed to hear as well as see the "blood / Come gargling"', we are entitled to wonder how 'reality' can be 'created': the very unrepresentability of traumatic experience emphasises the general situation of the aesthetic, rather than overriding it.[13] Of course, Comer is right to say that Owen is aiming for vividness, but his aesthetics are not simply a signal booster for his poetic content-transmission. Rather, they bind content together in a form that calls attention to its own intensity as form, as if the very act of unifying drew attention to its own flagrant contradiction, resulting in an aesthetic for which it is vital *not* to harmonise or simply fit with its content.

For a harmony of aesthetics and situation, of experience and treatment of that experience, would imply a harmony of the two things Owen had to keep separate; his fighting self and his writing self, his exterior participation in killing and his interior feeling of sympathy. Owen's conscience demanded he make the readers see the horror, but his conscience also demanded the utter rejection of it, and simply bringing the war to life would suggest some mental accommodation to it. Rather, Owen's artificial intensity simultaneously vivifies war *and* insists on its unimaginability, the impossibility of its assimilation. Given his situation, emotional consistency, harmony, or integrity are Owen's enemies, a conflict which lies behind 'Insensibility'. Owen distinguishes between the soldier who cannot help but be numb and the civilian or general in safety who can ('dullards whom no cannon stuns'). But Owen's irony is the parallel between them, that there is no difference in situation between the blessed and the cursed, and hence it is insensibility that is the necessary sustaining condition of the War itself. It is because soldiers have stopped feeling that they can continue to live with themselves, and because non-combatants are insensible to soldiers' suffering that the war continues. In the trenches, the only internal consistency is that of the insensible soldiers, who can reconcile interior feeling with exterior duty because they have no interiority left at all, not feeling 'even themselves or for themselves'. In reaction, Owen's style maximises its exteriority, its unnatural intensity, in order to insist that no reconciliation can take place; it is an aesthetic which, in the very act of vivifying, calls attention to the emotional necessity of its own failure.

BAD TASTE

Behind Heaney's anxiety lies a question of taste, a worry that Owen might be 'over-doing it' because he doesn't know how much is too much. This question of artistic good taste has its roots in Kant's founding definition of truly aesthetic judgement, whose basic criterion is disinterestedness. For Kant, taste is 'the ability to judge an object, or way of presenting it, by means of a liking or disliking *devoid of all interest*', rather than liking it because it agrees with morality or satisfies our appetites.[14] Both of these would make the aesthetic subservient to some relation of interest (§4), whereas true aesthetic taste is free from such contamination and thus reflects a more universal and less self-interested way of thinking (§6). The covertly bourgeois standard of 'disinterest' has been much discussed recently, but the more directly Kantian politics of taste have always been a vital question for Heaney's own work, because the possibility of disinterestedness indicates an implicitly detached position where judgements can be made about proportions and construction of the whole. Drawing on the story of Jesus delaying, then averting, the stoning of an adulterous woman by writing in the sand, Heaney has called the act of writing itself a pause, a 'break with the usual life' of accusation and judgement.[15] Ironically, the supposedly non-political act of artistic taste itself would in Heaney's case protest against the compulsory division of Northern Irish politics and its denial that anyone could stand outside one side or the other. For Owen, though, standing outside the situation is exactly what the civilian population must not be allowed to do (and in Heaney's defence, it should be added that in poems such as 'Whatever you Say, Say Nothing' and section VIII of 'Station Island', he has not failed to explore his own unease about the complicity between his artistic taste and a refusal to tell the truth of the situation). Bad taste – in the Kantian sense – would be, for Owen, committed writing. And we know that Kantian disinterest is more or less the opposite of Owen's belief, because unexpectedly, he drafted a poem about it; there are only fragments left, but it is titled 'Beauty':

> The beautiful, the fair, the elegant,
> Is that which pleases us, says Kant,
> Without a thought of interest or advantage.
> [. . .]
> A shrapnel ball –
> Just where the wet skin glistened where he swam –
> Like a full-opened sea-anemone
> We both said 'What a beauty! What a beauty, lad!'
> I knew that in that flower he saw a hope
> Of living on, and seeing again the roses of his home.

There is more to this fragment than a simple redefinition of beauty for the wounded man's sake. Owen's rejection of Kantian disinterestedness in favour of the flagrantly interested applies to his own situation as an artist, too. For in the trenches, there is no disinterestedness possible, no self-removal from what one sees. Where Kant formulated the judgement of beauty as a way of reconciling the demands of necessity (in physical nature) and freedom (in moral action), Owen's 'beauty' comes from a situation where necessity and freedom are at each other's throats, and where disinterested contemplation is not possible. As Jean-Luc Nancy has pointed out, Kant's aesthetic citizen is implicitly independent and wealthy – disinterestedness implies no pressing needs – but for Owen, such independence is possible only as a betrayal, and he will not grant the luxury of such a refined position to himself, or to a civilian readership that wanted to distance itself from suffering.[16] Hence beauty in this poem is aesthetic (the sea-anemone comparison is not ironic in itself), interested in the possibility of escape for the soldier, and, simultaneously, grotesque. Owen's aesthetic risks the impossible collision of these reactions – too many rhymes, too many identifications – by refusing to balance or cut down, because that would imply some position of detached perspective, and to have such a perspective on the war is in some way to be out of it. This may be the reason why he takes such extraordinary risks in these lines from 'Insensibility':

> Having seen all things red
> Their eyes are rid
> Of the hurt of the colour of blood for ever.

'Seeing red' is a cliché which Owen grimly literalises in the manner of Sassoon, compressing bloodlust and bloodbath together. And yet there is a certain appalling jokiness to the pun, and in the next line, a shiveringly discordant pararhyme, red/rid. The simultaneous intensity and cool distance persists into the next line, too, where 'the hurt of the colour of blood' does not quite exorcise the ghost of the younger Owen, the would-be dandy in his purple slippers, wincing at the wrong shade of red. Indeed, such self-adoring sensitivity is what Owen undercuts with an incontrovertible reason for pain, but even to describe the traumatic in terms of the aesthetic is risky. Rather than deny the aesthetic, Owen insists upon its importance, but in such a way as to render him simultaneously shockingly detached and embarrassingly interested, in the Kantian sense. Owen's term for this mixture was 'pity', and exploring this term and its background involves more of the third area of conflict in Owen's life which remained hidden for so long, his sexuality.

### PITY AND SEXUALITY

'Insensibility' ends with a curse on the insensible that is also a plea for a particular kind of interested sensibility:

> By choice they made themselves immune
> To pity and whatever moans in man
> Before the last sea and the helpless stars;
> Whatever moans when many leave these shores;
> Whatever shares
> The eternal reciprocity of tears.

Pity, then, would be the opposite of unfeeling, and recalls Owen's famous Preface, that 'the Poetry is in the Pity'. In the light of the evidence for Owen's unmistakable interest in the aesthetic, therefore, it might be better to see this statement not as a disparagement of poetry but a resituation of it. Owen has not rejected poetry, only Poetry as an end in itself; poetry is now included within pity, which places his aesthetic in a peculiar nexus of interested feelings to do with art, compassion and sexuality.

James Najarian has helpfully drawn attention to the sexual element in Owen's 'pity', glossing the word as 'erotic sympathy' and deriving this balance of sympathy and sexuality from Owen's reading of Keats, in whom the sensuous means a forgetting of the borders of self, which is a prerequisite for sympathy.[17] By the 1890s, however, the sensuality Keats represented – where Beauty was Truth and that was all you needed to know – had become more than a generally erotic sentiment, for its Pateresque overtones had made the author something of an icon for the period's homophilic writers. John Addington Symonds wrote to Wilde praising the latter's 'Keatsian openness at all pores to beauty', and after his own death in Rome, was memorialised in the covertly homophile journal *The Artist* with an anonymous verse:

> Let each lay here in this grave a rose
> And breathe a prayer for England's dead,
> Keats and Shelley and Symonds, sleeping
> Here in the ancient city's keeping,
> Servants true of the Lord Erôs.[18]

Wilde himself famously admired Keats as a 'Priest of Beauty, slain before his time' and compared him to the martyred St Sebastian with the requisite curly hair and red lips.[19] Being a martyr to one's feeling for Beauty, however, is not quite the same as Keatsianly dissolving the borders of self, and Najarian's formula needs some refining when placed into the situation in which Owen himself was writing, adopted as a protégé of Robbie Ross and the survivors of the Wilde circle at Half-Moon Street. For in that context, the word 'pity' implies some notion of pain, since it had gained this sense strongly for Wilde while he had been in prison. In André Gide's memoir of Wilde (published in English in 1905, and in French before that), Wilde is reported as saying: 'Do you know, dear, that it's pity that kept me from killing myself? . . . What kept me from doing so was looking at the others, seeing that they were as unhappy as I, and having pity.'[20]

This could be taken in two different ways. Does it mean that Wilde simply stopped worrying about his own sorrows so much because he felt himself part of a common unhappiness? Or does Wilde realise that if he could pity them, then why could he not pity himself rather than hurt himself? Wildean pity is both, a fellow-feeling and a feeling for oneself in the face of suffering, and depends on the difference between the two, rather than a dissolution of borders. When another prisoner was punished, Wilde continued, 'as pity had entered my heart, I was afraid only for him; indeed, I was happy to suffer because of him . . . you don't know how sweet that can seem . . . to feel that we were suffering for each other'. Companionship in suffering is combined with a certain soulful sweetness, and such interested 'pity' also has an impact on Wilde's views about art. In the same passage, he repudiates a novelist he had formerly admired: 'Flaubert didn't want any pity in his work, and that's why it seems small and closed; pity is the side on which a work is open, by which it appears infinite.'[21]

Pity, then, is the opposite of artistic impersonality; it is the personal involvement of the artist in the work, and in *De Profundis*, it becomes the ideal mode of the artist. For pity is defined as imaginative sympathy for sorrow, and sorrow as the form of true art, and hence the thing that makes Christ the 'ideal artist':

Christ . . . took the entire world of the inarticulate, the voiceless world of pain, as his kingdom, and made of himself its eternal mouthpiece . . . his desire was to be to the myriads who had found no utterance a very trumpet through which they might call to Heaven. And feeling, with the artistic nature of one to whom Sorrow and Suffering were modes through which he could reach his conception of the beautiful . . . he makes himself the image of the Man of Sorrows.[22]

It is very possible Owen would have seen his own mission to speak for his men here; certainly he quotes from *De Profundis* on Christ in a letter written to his mother two months before drafting his Preface.[23] The difficulty of making a direct translation of *De Profundis* into Owen's poetic, though, is that at the same time as he is asserting sympathy for pain, Wilde is undercutting it by insisting that suffering is simply a mode of reaching the beautiful (he has earlier insisted that pain is true art because it has no object other than itself). This would be to insist with Kant that sympathy and aesthetics have no truck with one another, and elsewhere Wilde and Owen would insist that they do. Where they differ is that Owen's poetry lets pain remain pain even when conjoined with the aesthetic, where Wilde would simply turn pain into art, sentimentalising his 'pity' into aesthetics again. Eve Kosofsky Sedgwick has argued from Wilde's late work that pity and the sentimental becomes part of the 'epistemology of the closet' in 'the period from the 1880s through the First World War', because it is a feminine discourse of emotion played by men, centred around vicarious identification with images of the suffering male body.[24] Pity's oscillation between self-interest and sympathy thus marks all its devotion to other people with a stagily self-admiring, self-protecting consciousness essential to Wilde's depthless brand of camp, but perhaps homophilia in this period has more than one epistemology. For Owen was indeed interested in tear-stained feelings centred on the male body, but his situation was anything but vicarious: as with his *excess* of form, the war would ultimately make any theatricality of the situation testimony to its unbearableness.

This means that Owen's pity is a good deal more complex than straightforward 'sympathy', because it must therefore take place in the context of pain which cannot be safely bounded by aestheticising or sexualising it, although it may have elements of both in it. Take, for example, the fragment, 'I saw his round mouth's crimson', written at the same time as the defiant 'Apologia':

> I saw his round mouth's crimson deepen as it fell
> Like a sun, in his last deep hour;
> Watched the magnificent recession of farewell,
> Clouding, half gleam, half glower,
> And a last splendour burn the heavens of his cheek.
> And in his eyes
> The cold stars lighting, very old and bleak,
> In different skies.

To be sure, the ending is no celebration: as the 'different skies' are in fact the same skies without light, so his body is the same body but without life. But the brilliance is in the suggestion of the word 'indifferent' within 'in different', because as he watches the boy's eyes change, Owen is simultaneously half-aware of his own pain at not being responded to, at the indifference of death. And this half-suggestion wouldn't be so powerful unless Owen had previously been very interested in the boy: the 'heavens of his cheek' is more than simply part of the extended metaphor of sunset, and Owen is not watching the boy's crimson lips with a merely painterly eye. The dying boy is a protest, an aesthetic object, and an erotic one, and part of this poem's strangeness is that it is all three. Evidently, Owen is horrified, but he appears to make the boy an aesthetic spectacle, a beautiful sunset, gleaming and glowering, without evident irony, and this aesthetics is merged with eroticism. There is undoubtedly 'pity' in the fact that the boy is dying, but if Najarian is right, and pity extends to erotic interest about the splendour of his cheek or lip colour, then pity must embrace eros, art and death. He claims that Owen's message in 'Hercules and Antaeus' is that 'erotic bonds between men prevent recurring violence' (25), but pity's connotations of sorrow and suffering in the war poems would imply that pity's erotic bonds between men must in fact occur *within* the context of violence, which is perhaps a way to approach Owen's controversial poem 'Greater Love':

> Red lips are not so red
> As the stained stones kissed by the English dead.
> Kindness of wooed and wooer
> Seems shame to their love pure.
> O Love, your eyes lose lure
> When I behold eyes blinded in my stead!

The phrase 'Greater love' acts as a bridge between conventional soldierly sacrifice and Owen's complex eroticisation of it, so that the rejection of conventional romance is less a rejection of eros than its transference into an all-male context. Owen's Shakespearian pun on 'kindness' indicates that the wooed and wooer are heterosexual, and then inverts the homoerotic 'shame' onto that couple ('shame' is Douglas's rhyme-word for the love that dare not speak its name, of course). Here, desire appears not as a positive counter to death, but inseparably one with it:

> Your slender attitude
> Trembles not exquisite like limbs knife-skewed,
> Rolling and rolling there
> Where God seems not to care;
> Till the fierce love they bear
> Cramps them in death's extreme decrepitude.

Owen's rejection of 'your slender attitude' does not manage to dissociate itself from an aesthetic and erotic preoccupation with the refined; the Grecian Urn-derived 'attitude' is both, as is 'exquisite', another favourite homophilic word from Pater to *Dorian Gray*.[25] And nor can this mixture be separated from the soldiers' death-throes, for it is the 'fierce love' that cramps them, as if love were a bayonet-blade or shrapnel slice. The precise agony of the combination of grotesque and comradely in 'hearts made great with shot', where swelling with love, being a hero and bursting with bullets become the same thing, depends on no one strand predominating. Such a mixture has made many critics shiver, nevertheless, because although the poem seems to be a reply to Swinburne's 'Before the Mirror' and Wilde's *Salomé*, it is by no means a repudiation of them. On the contrary, their decadent themes of exquisite pain and erotic wounds are here simply made real, and such a paradoxical, twin insistence on the aestheticised-erotic *and* death in battle is what makes this poem neither straightforward reportage nor sexual game-playing. What would be in bad taste would be to suggest that any one of the elements in 'pity' has managed to absorb or ground the others; that the aesthetic and erotic can safely be explained by the pain of the war (which would not do Owen justice as an experimental, homophile poet); that Owen makes his war experience only into a aesthetic poem (which would imply a vicious detachment on Owen's behalf), or that it makes the dying soldiers nothing but participants in Owen's psychosexual theatre. Adrian Caesar believes something like the latter when he claims the mixture of pain and pleasure in war poetry is derived from Swinburne, and in a wider sense

from Christian culture's assumption that pleasure and guilt are inseparable – in other words, that Owen links his love with pain because he felt
guilty about homosexual feelings.[26] But as I have argued above, this
would follow Wilde by turning pain into something else, which Owen
refuses to do. Swinburne's sadomasochism is always to do with role-
playing, but Owen had no choice but to be himself in the war, however
impossible that self was.

Being himself, in fact, is a much better reason why Owen could not but
link sexuality and pain. Owen loved his men and Owen was leading those
men to their deaths: to love them was to be with them, to be with them as
an officer was to be complicit in killing them. Owen needs no psychosexual guilt to hurt him, because his situation does it for him, as in 'Arms and
the Boy', with its bayonet, 'famishing for flesh', and 'bullet-heads / Which
long to nuzzle in the heart of lads'. Paul Fussell maintained that there is a
'displaced eroticism' here, but the bullet and the bayonet are exactly the
place where Owen's eroticism must emerge.[27] Indeed, Owen seems to
have acknowledged the alignment of killing with homosexuality in this
poem, for he classified the poem under the section-title, 'Protest – the
unnaturalness of weapons', and as Victorian society's instinctive response
to homoeroticism *and* the keyword of his anti-Wordsworthian aesthetic,
'unnatural' was one of Wilde's favourite terms. In fact, Owen consistently
makes specific parallels between the homophilic situation and the community of soldiers in which he found himself. The parallel between the
shared unspeakable truth of soldiers and the Half-Moon Street set is
evident in Dorian Gray's favourite word, 'curious', which appears in
'Smile, Smile, Smile' as the coded smile of 'secret men who know their
secret safe'. Similarly, the conscripts in 'The Send-Off' disappear 'so
secretly, like wrongs hushed-up'; and they may 'mock what women meant
/ Who gave them flowers' in more ways than one. In 'Strange Meeting'
the famous line, 'I am the enemy you killed, my friend' paraphrases
Wilde's 'The Ballad of Reading Gaol' where 'each man kills the thing
he loves'. Moreover, the unknown speaker's 'piteous' greeting shadows
Dante's Brunetto Latini, who was in Hell for sodomy; like 'curious',
'strange' itself, the poem's most important word, is also one of Wilde's
synonyms for the peculiar combination of aesthetic and homosexual
feeling. As the speaker says, 'I went hunting wild / After the wildest
beauty in the world'. But to argue that these are coded references to a
hidden truth about Owen's homosexuality would be to miss the point
entirely, for Owen's sexuality is not the *real* meaning of his poems, which
the war then overlaid; rather, it intensifies the conflicts he felt and

understood in others, and remains inseparable from the soldier he was. Illegal desire and death irresistibly combine in a letter to the one person who might understand this dilemma, Sassoon, where he writes wryly, 'I desire no more *exposed flanks* of any sort for a long time.'[28] They reoccur when he reports that officers resent the way women adore him, but 'the dramatic irony was too killing': well, indeed.[29] Owen's sexuality is part of the complex of 'pity', and 'pity' is inseparable from suffering, as well as from his aesthetics, so that his poems embody the conflict they relate. That the erotic, the aesthetic and the deadly can run through the same two or three lines at a time is part of their overall protest, a protest manifest in the ambiguity in the famous phrase 'The pity of war; the pity War distilled'. Pity is the emotion that War concentrates and intensifies into undreamt-of sympathy, and at the same time that which War distils off and dissipates, so that no one feels anything. War does both, and the incompatibilities of feeling in 'pity' are not merely a result of the impossible situation that Owen was placed in, which to reconcile was to remove himself from. They are also partly a response to the terror of 'Insensibility', that the war will make Owen the poet unfeeling, when to feel *anything* is to be alive. Owen's argument against war is, simply, that feeling pain is a more primary reality than reason, tactics, justice or metaphysics, and none of them are worth it. Intensity of feeling is therefore more important than detached discrimination of feelings, and Owen's poetry goes over the top, loading on the rhymes, alliterations, puns, sensuality and horror, because such intense excess insists against neutrality. This disjunction between lyric form and its content may be bad aesthetics, and entirely opposed to the unifying, autonomous ideals of Owen's modernist contemporaries, but in his case it was indispensable; for the lurid sentiment with which his work persistently flirts (see 'A Tear Song', composed within weeks of 'Dulce et Decorum Est'), for the declaration of the unavowable (love or pain) which that sentiment witnesses to, and for any dealings with the traumatic. While Eliot was reasserting a poetic that aimed to eliminate any externality in the name of better emotional discipline, Owen's poetry would suggest that the truth of certain feelings might depend on maintaining it.

# Notes

## INTRODUCTION

1 Peter Finch, 'The Poetry Wars are Not Over Yet', in *The Writer's Handbook 2003*, ed. Barry Turner (London: Macmillan, 2002), pp. 118–46 (p. 118).

2 *The Nation's Favourite Poems* (London: BBC Books, 1996).

3 For example, Andrew Motion, *Edward Thomas* (London: Hutchinson, 1981), p. 7. The attempt to shape public taste for poetry on a modernist paradigm is evident in F. R. Leavis, *New Bearings in English Poetry* (London: Chatto & Windus, 1932) and continues in revisionist studies such as C. K. Stead's *The New Poetic* (London: Hutchinson, 1964) and Robert Ross, *The Georgian Revolt* (Carbondale: Southern Illinois University Press, 1965).

4 T. S. Eliot, 'Reflections on *Vers Libre*', *New Statesman*, 3 March 1917, pp. 518–19. T. S. Eliot, 'Tradition and the Individual Talent', in his *Selected Essays* (London: Faber & Faber, 1951), pp. 14–21.

5 See Peter Nicholls, *Modernisms* (Basingstoke: Macmillan, 1995) and Steve Giles, *Theorizing Modernism: Essays in Critical Theory* (London: Routledge, 1993).

6 Ross, *The Georgian Revolt*, p. 243.

7 Thomas Hardy, *The Life and Work of Thomas Hardy*, ed. Michael Millgate (London and Basingstoke: Macmillan, 1984), p. 422; Ezra Pound, letter to T. C. Wilson, 30 October 1934, in *Selected Letters of Ezra Pound, 1907–1941*, ed. D. D. Paige (London: Faber & Faber, 1971), p. 248, T. S. Eliot, *After Strange Gods* (Faber & Faber, 1934), p. 55.

8 In *A Tribute to Wilfred Owen*, ed. T. J. Walsh ([Birkenhead]: Birkenhead Institute, 1964), p. 28; *Letters on Poetry from W. B. Yeats to Dorothy Wellesley*, ed. Dorothy Wellesley (Oxford: Oxford University Press, 1940), p. 113.

9 Cf. Stan Smith, *The Origins of Modernism: Eliot, Pound, Yeats and the Rhetorics of Renewal* (London: Harvester Wheatsheaf, 1994).

10 Leonard Diepeveen, *The Difficulties of Modernism* (New York: Routledge, 2003), p. 12.

11 Arthur Waugh, 'The New Poetry', *Quarterly Review* 226 (1916), 365–86 (pp. 369, 366, 370).

12 Ezra Pound, 'Drunken Helots and Mr Eliot', *Egoist* 4 (1917), 72–4, repr. in *Ezra Pound's Poetry and Prose: Contributions to Periodicals*, ed. Lea Baechler,

James Longenbach and A. Walton Litz, 10 vols. (New York: Garland, 1991), II, p. 206 (henceforth *EPP*); T. S. Eliot, *The Use of Poetry and the Use of Criticism* (London: Faber & Faber, 1933), p. 72.

13 Dominic Hibberd, *Harold Monro: Poet of the New Age* (London: Palgrave, 2003), p. 169.

14 *Selected Letters of Ezra Pound to John Quinn, 1915–1924*, ed. Timothy Materer (Durham, NC: Duke University Press, 1991), pp. 152–3.

15 Lascelles Abercrombie, *Lyrics and Unfinished Poems* (Newtown, Montgomeryshire: Gregynog Press, 1940).

16 Ezra Pound, 'Harold Monro', *Criterion* 11 (1932), 581–92 (p. 590), *EPP*, V, 363.

17 A more nuanced account is found in David Perkins's *History of Modern Poetry, 1: From the 1890s to the High Modernist Mode* (Cambridge, MA: Belknap, 1976), p. 135, which distinguishes between modern and modernist poets.

18 W. B. Yeats, *Essays and Introductions* (London: Macmillan, 1961), p. 522.

19 Occult Notebook entry of 1914, quoted in Roy Foster, *W. B. Yeats, A Life*, I: *The Apprentice Mage, 1865–1914* (Oxford: Oxford University Press, 1997), p. 519; Yeats, *Essays and Introductions*, p. 509.

20 *A Critical Edition of Yeats's 'A Vision' (1925)*, ed. George Mills Harper and Kelly Hood (London: Macmillan, 1978), p. 28.

21 Cf. Fran Brearton, *The Great War in Irish Poetry* (Oxford: Oxford University Press, 2000), pp. 50–5, against the approach taken by Edna Longley, *Poetry in the Wars* (Newcastle upon Tyne: Bloodaxe, 1986), pp. 10–16. The problem of transcendental form and intransigent Irish history is also addressed throughout Peter McDonald's *Serious Form: Poetic Authority from Yeats to Hill* (Oxford: Clarendon Press, 2002).

22 T. S. Eliot, 'London Letter', *Dial* 70 (1921), 448–53 (p. 453).

23 Philip Larkin, 'It Could Only Happen in England', in his *Required Writing* (London: Faber & Faber, 1983), pp. 216–17, and cf. Andrew Motion, *Philip Larkin* (London: Methuen, 1982), p. 29. John Lucas blames Robert Graves as well in *Starting to Explain* (Nottingham: Trent Books, 2003).

24 Philip Hobsbaum, *Tradition and Experiment in English Poetry* (London: Macmillan, 1979), p. 291. J. P. Ward, *The English Line: Poetry of the Unpoetic from Wordsworth to Larkin* (London: Macmillan, 1991) presents a more sober case.

25 Eliot, 'Tradition and the Individual Talent', p. 15.

26 Graham Hough, *Image and Experience* (London: Duckworth, 1960), pp. 59–70. For modernism's relation to place, see *The Locations of Literary Modernism*, ed. Alex Davis and Lee M. Jenkins (Cambridge: Cambridge University Press, 2000).

27 Edward Thomas, 'The Newest Poet', *Daily Chronicle*, 23 November 1909, p. 3; T. S. Eliot, 'Reflections on Contemporary Poetry, I', *Egoist* 4 (1917), 118–19. Gabriel Josipovici has suggested that Larkin's public dislike of foreign poetry was also because he associated xenophilia with posing ('The Singer on the Shore', *PN Review* 27 (2001), 16–20).

28 Letter of 19 May 1914, in *Selected Letters of Edward Thomas*, ed. R. George Thomas (Oxford: Oxford University Press, 1995), p. 93.

29 Pierre Bourdieu, 'The Historical Genesis of a Pure Aesthetics', in *The Field of Cultural Production: Essays on Art and Literature*, ed. Randal Johnson (New York: Columbia University Press, 1993), p. 266.

30 *Classical and Romantic German Aesthetics*, ed. J. M. Bernstein (Cambridge: Cambridge University Press, 2003), p. xvi.

31 Walter Benjamin, 'The Concept of Criticism in German Romanticism', in his *Selected Writings*, 3 vols. (Cambridge, MA: Belknap, 1996–2002), I : *1913–1926* (1996), ed. Marcus Bullock and Michael W. Jennings, pp. 116–200 (p. 174).

32 G. W. F. Hegel, *Aesthetics*, trans. by T. M. Knox, 2 vols. (Oxford: Clarendon, 1975), II, p. 1023. Simon Jarvis relates this idealist theory to New Historicism in 'Prosody as Cognition', *Critical Quarterly* 40 (1998), 3–17.

33 Jacques Derrida, 'Che cos'è la poesia?', in *Points. . .*, ed. Elizabeth Weber, trans. Peggy Kamuf et al. (Stanford, CA: Stanford University Press, 1995), pp. 288–99 (p. 295).

34 Derek Attridge, *The Rhythms of English Poetry* (London: Longmans, 1982).

## CHAPTER 1 INSIDE AND OUTSIDE MODERNISM

1 1798 text from *Lyrical Ballads and Other Poems, 1797–1800*, ed. James Butler and Karen Green (Ithaca, NY: Cornell University Press, 1992).

2 Ibid., p. 745.

3 See Michael Bell, *Sentimentalism, Ethics and the Culture of Feeling* (London: Palgrave, 2000), p. 108.

4 *The Collected Works of Samuel Taylor Coleridge*, ed. Kathleen Coburn (Princeton, NJ: Princeton University Press, 1969–), 7: *Biographia Literaria*, ed. James Engell and W. Jackson Bate (1983), II, pp. 68–9. References in brackets are to volume II of this edition.

5 *Collected Letters of Samuel Taylor Coleridge*, ed. E. L. Griggs, 6 vols. (Oxford: Oxford University Press, 1956–71), II, p. 812.

6 F. Schiller, *On The Aesthetic Education of Man in a Series of Letters*, ed. Elizabeth M. Wilkinson and L. A. Willoughby (Oxford: Clarendon, 1967), especially letter 27; Immanuel Kant, *Critique of Judgement*, trans. Werner S. Pluhar (Indianapolis: Hackett, 1987), p. 306.

7 F. Schiller, 'Kallias or Concerning Beauty: Letters to Gottfried Körner', repr. in *Classical and Romantic German Aesthetics*, ed. J. M. Bernstein (Cambridge: Cambridge University Press, 2003), pp. 145–83 (p. 167).

8 *Lyrical Ballads*, pp. 750, 754.

9 See Paul Hamilton, *Coleridge's Poetics* (Oxford: Blackwell, 1983) and Michael Kooy, *Coleridge, Schiller and Aesthetic Education* (London: Palgrave, 2002).

10 *Lyrical Ballads*, p. 345.
11 Samuel Taylor Coleridge, *Collected Works of Samuel Taylor Coleridge*, ed. Kathleen Coburn (London: Routledge & Kegan Paul, 1969–), 5: *Lectures on Literature 1808–1819*, ed. R. A. Foakes (1987), I, p. 495.
12 Nigel Leask, *The Politics of Imagination in Coleridge's Critical Thought* (Basingstoke: Macmillan, 1988).
13 Donald Wesling, *The New Poetries: Poetic Form since Coleridge and Wordsworth* (London: Associated University Presses, 1985), p. 64.
14 Ezra Pound, 'Prolegomena', *Poetry Review* 1 (1912), 72–6 (p. 73), *EPP*, I, p. 60.
15 Ezra Pound, 'Affirmations, IV. As for Imagisme', *New Age* 16 (1915), 349–50 (p. 349), *EPP*, II, p. 9.
16 Ezra Pound, 'T. S. Eliot', *Poetry* 10 (1917), 264–71 (p. 267); *EPP*, II, p. 249.
17 Coleridge, *Collected Works*, 12: *Marginalia*, ed. George Whalley (1980), I, p. 377.
18 Pound, 'As for Imagisme', p. 349, *EPP*, II, p. 9.
19 Ezra Pound, 'Books Current', *Future* 2 (1918), 188–90 (p. 188), *EPP*, III, p. 115.
20 T. S. Eliot, 'The Function of Criticism', in his *Selected Essays* (London: Faber & Faber, 1951), p. 23.
21 Lecture entitled 'The Origins: What is Romanticism?' repr. in Ronald Schuchard, *Eliot's Dark Angel* (New York: Oxford University Press, 1999), p. 27.
22 Cited in Joy Grant, *Harold Monro and the Poetry Bookshop* (London: Routledge & Kegan Paul, 1967), p. 143.
23 Harold Monro, 'The Imagists Discussed', *Egoist* 2 (1915), 77–80 (p. 78).
24 May Sinclair, 'Two Notes', *Egoist* 2 (1915), 88.
25 Ezra Pound and Frank Flint, 'Imagisme', *Poetry* 1 (1913), 198–200 (p. 199).
26 See Michael H. Levenson, *A Genealogy of Modernism* (Cambridge: Cambridge University Press, 1984), p. 95.
27 T. S. Eliot, 'London Letter', *Dial* 70 (1921), 448–53 (p. 451).
28 Harold Monro, 'The Future of Poetry', *Poetry Review* 1 (1912), 10–13 (p. 10).
29 Harold Monro, 'Freedom', *Poetry Review* 1 (1912), 59–60 (p. 59).
30 Ezra Pound, 'Vorticism', *Fortnightly Review*, 1 September 1914, pp. 461–71 (p. 467), *EPP*, I, p. 281; Ezra Pound, 'The Serious Artist, IV', *New Freewoman* 1 (1913), 213–14 (p. 214), *EPP*, I, p. 202.
31 Pound, 'The Serious Artist, III – Emotion and Poesy', *New Freewoman* 1 (1913), 194–5 (p. 195) *EPP*, I, p. 199.
32 Maurice Browne, 'The Poetry of Wilfrid Wilson Gibson', *Poetry Review* 1 (1912), 15–18 (pp. 15, 17).
33 F. S. Flint, 'Reviews', *Poetry Review* 1 (1912), 28–9 (p. 28).
34 Lascelles Abercrombie, 'The Function of Poetry in the Drama', *Poetry Review* 1 (1912), 108–19 (pp. 108, 112).
35 Ezra Pound, 'A Few Don'ts by an Imagiste', *Poetry* 1 (1913), 200–6 (p. 200), *EPP*, I, p. 120; Pound, 'Vorticism', p. 464, *EPP*, I, p. 278.

36 Frank Flint, review of Pound's *Ripostes*, in *Poetry and Drama* 1 (1913), 61; Flint, 'The Poetry of H. D.', *Egoist* 2 (1915), 72–3 (p. 73).
37 Pound, 'Prolegomena', p. 73, *EPP*, I, p. 60.
38 Richard Aldington, 'Free Verse in England', *Egoist* 1 (1914), 351–2 (p. 351).
39 Abercrombie, 'The Function of Poetry', p. 112.
40 Sinclair, 'Two Notes', 88.
41 W. W. Gibson, 'Some Thoughts on the Future of Poetic-Drama', *Poetry Review* 1 (1912), 119–22 (p. 122).
42 Rupert Brooke, Review of *Fires*, in *Poetry and Drama* 1 (1913), 58–60 (pp. 58, 59).
43 Pound, 'Prolegomena', 73, *EPP*, I, p. 60.
44 Review of *Eve and Other Poems*, in *Poetry and Drama* 1 (1913), 370–1.
45 Walter de la Mare, 'The Poems of Ralph Hodgson', unsigned review, *Times Literary Supplement*, 7 October 1915, p. 342; Ezra Pound, 'The Approach to Paris . . . V', *New Age* 13 (1913), 662–4 (p. 662), *EPP*, I, p. 181.
46 Harold Monro, 'New Books', *Poetry and Drama* 2 (1914), 176–84 (p. 178).
47 Richard Aldington, 'Modern Poetry and the Imagists', *Egoist* 1 (1913), 201–3 (p. 202); Pound, 'Vorticism', p. 463, *EPP*, I, p. 277.
48 Monro, 'New Books', p. 179.
49 Frank Flint, review of *A Boy's Will*, in *Poetry and Drama* 1 (1913), 250.
50 Pound, 'Reviews', *Poetry* 2 (1913), 72–4 (p. 72), *EPP*, I, p. 138; Frost, letter of 17 July 1913 to Thomas B. Mosher, *in Selected Letters of Robert Frost*, ed. Lawrance Thompson (London: Jonathan Cape, 1965), p. 84.
51 *The Collected Writings of T. E. Hulme*, ed. Karen Csengeri (Oxford: Clarendon, 1994), p. 80.
52 Pound, 'Vorticism', p. 462, *EPP*, I, p. 273; *Lyrical Ballads*, pp. 744, 755, 747.
53 T. S. Eliot, 'The Music of Poetry', in *On Poetry and Poets* (London: Faber & Faber, 1957), p. 31.
54 Monro, 'The Imagists Discussed', 77.
55 Ezra Pound, 'The Rev. G. Crabbe, LL.B', *Future* 1 (1917), 110–11 (p. 110), *EPP*, II, p. 188.
56 Pound, 'Prolegomena', p. 73, *EPP*, I, p. 60.
57 Aldington, 'Free Verse in England', p. 351.
58 Ezra Pound, 'Breviora', *Little Review* 5 (1918), 23–4, *EPP*, III, p. 197.
59 Ezra Pound, 'The Serious Artist, III', pp. 194–5, *EPP*, I, 200.
60 *Lyrical Ballads*, p. 756.
61 Pound, 'Books Current', p. 190, *EPP*, III, p. 116.
62 T. E. Hulme, 'A Lecture on Modern Poetry', in his *Collected Writings*, pp. 49–56 (pp. 53, 54).
63 T. S. Eliot, 'A Commentary', *Criterion* 2 (1924), 231.
64 Levenson, *A Genealogy of Modernism*, pp. 95–102; R. Shusterman, *T. S. Eliot and the Philosophy of Criticism* (London: Duckworth, 1988), pp. 30–6.
65 T. E. Hulme, 'Romanticism and Classicism', in his *Collected Writings*, pp. 59–73 (p. 61).
66 *The Works of John Ruskin*, ed. E. T. Cook and Alexander Wedderburn, 39 vols. (London: George Allen, 1903–12), IV (1903), p. 236.

67 Coleridge, *Lectures on Literature*, II, p. 278.

68 Henri Bergson, *Introduction to Metaphysics*, trans. T. E. Hulme (London: Macmillan, 1913), p. 6. The translation was in fact Flint's.

69 Pound, 'Affirmations, IV', p. 350, *EPP*, II, p. 9.

70 Bergson, *Introduction to Metaphysics*, p. 3.

71 Pound, 'A Few Don'ts', p. 200, *EPP*, I, p. 120.

72 See John T. Gage, *In the Arresting Eye: The Rhetoric of Imagism* (Baton Rouge: Louisiana State University Press, 1981).

73 John Middleton Murry, 'Art and Philosophy', *Rhythm* I (1911), 9–12 (pp. 9, 12).

74 John Middleton Murry, 'Reviews', *Rhythm* I (1911), 35.

75 *The Letters of Rupert Brooke*, ed. Geoffrey Keynes (London: Faber & Faber, 1968), p. 419.

76 T. E. Hulme, 'Bergson Lecturing', in his *Collected Writings*, pp. 155–6.

77 Robert Ferguson, *The Short Sharp Life of T. E. Hulme* (London: Allen Lane, 2002), p. 99.

78 Humphrey Carpenter, *A Serious Character: The Life of Ezra Pound* (London: Faber & Faber, 1988), p. 114; Pound, 'Books Current', 311–12, *EPP*, III, p. 252.

79 *Blast* I (1914), 8; editorial, *Little Review* 4 (1917) [3] – 6, *EPP*, II, p. 197; Ezra Pound, 'The Yeats Letters', *Poetry* 11 (1918), 223–5, *EPP*, III, p. 8.

80 See James Longenbach, *Stone Cottage: Pound, Yeats and Modernism* (New York: Oxford University Press, 1988) and Frank Lentricchia, *Modernist Quartet* (Cambridge: Cambridge University Press, 1994).

81 Max Stirner, *The Ego and his Own*, ed. James T. Martin, trans. Steven T. Byington (New York: Dover, 1973), p. 37.

82 Ezra Pound, 'Provincialism the Enemy, IV', *New Age* 21 (1917), 308–9, *EPP*, II, p. 251.

83 Ezra Pound, 'Affirmations, VI. Analysis of this Decade', *New Age* 16 (1915), 409–11 (p. 411), *EPP*, II, p. 17.

84 See Jean-Luc Nancy, *The Sense of the World*, trans. Jeffrey S. Librett (Minneapolis: University of Minnesota Press, 1997), p. 72.

85 Frank Kermode, *Romantic Image* (London: Routledge & Kegan Paul, 1957), p. 157.

86 Hulme, 'Romanticism and Classicism', p. 80; Pound, 'Vorticism', p. 466, *EPP*, I, p. 280.

87 Marc Redfield, *Phantom Formations: Aesthetic Ideology and the Bildungsroman* (Ithaca, NY: Cornell University Press, 1996), p. 18.

88 Ezra Pound, Canto XVI, *The Cantos* (London: Faber & Faber, 1986), p. 71; Matthew Arnold, preface to first edition of *Poems* (1853) in *Complete Prose Works of Matthew Arnold*, ed. R. H. Super, 10 vols. (Ann Arbor: University of Michigan Press, 1960–77), I: *On the Classical Tradition* (1960), pp. 5–6. See also Kenneth Daley, *The Rescue of Romanticism; Walter Pater and John Ruskin* (Athens: Ohio University Press, 2001).

89 Full sources and influences are given in Coleridge, *Lectures on Literature*, II, p. 399.

90  F. Schiller, *On the Aesthetic Education of Man*, pp. clxvi ff.
91  Kooy, *Coleridge, Schiller and Aesthetic Education*, pp. 59–64.
92  Schiller, *On the Naïve and Sentimental*, repr. in *Friedrich Schiller: Essays*, ed. W. Hinderer and Daniel O. Dahlstrom, trans. Daniel O. Dahlstrom (New York: Continuum, 1993), p. 185.
93  T. S. Eliot, 'Swinburne as Poet', in *Selected Essays*, p. 327.
94  Pound and Flint, 'Imagisme', p. 199.
95  Ezra Pound, 'Affirmations, II. Vorticism', *New Age* 16 (1915), 277–8 (p. 278), *EPP*, II, p. 5; T. S. Eliot, 'Seneca in Elizabethan Translation', in *Selected Essays*, p. 68; T. S. Eliot, 'The Metaphysical Poets', in *Selected Essays*, p. 287.
96  Schiller, *On the Naïve and Sentimental*, p. 229.
97  Walter Pater, 'The School of Giorgione', in *The Renaissance* (London: Macmillan, 1910), pp. 130–54 (p. 135).
98  Pound, 'As for Imagisme', p. 350, *EPP*, II, p. 9.
99  Hulme, 'Romanticism and Classicism', p. 69; Schiller, *On the Naïve and Sentimental*, p. 199.
100  Schiller's uncertainty is discussed in Kooy, *Coleridge, Schiller and Aesthetic Education*, p. 15.
101  Pound and Flint, 'Imagisme', p. 199, *EPP*, I, 119.
102  Letter to Felix Schelling, 8 July 1922, in *Selected Letters of Ezra Pound, 1907– 1941*, ed. D. D. Paige (London: Faber & Faber, 1971), p. 178.
103  Ezra Pound, 'The Approach to Paris. . .V', *New Age* 13 (1913), 662–4 (p. 662), *EPP*, I, p. 181.
104  Text taken from *Des Imagistes* (London: Poetry Bookshop, 1914).
105  T. E. Hulme, 'Bergson's Theory of Art', in his *Collected Writings*, p. 193.
106  Sinclair, 'Two Notes', p. 88.
107  Letter of 28 October 1913, in *The Letters of D. H. Lawrence*, ed. James T. Boulton, 7 vols. (Cambridge: Cambridge University Press, 1979–93), II: *1913–16*, ed. with George J. Zytaruk (1981), p. 46.
108  Text taken from Masefield's *Collected Poems* (London: Heinemann, 1923).
109  Texts from Gibson's *Collected Poems* (London: Macmillan, 1926).
110  Letter of 10 November 1915, Berg Collection of English and American Literature, New York Public Library, Astor, Lenox and Tilden Foundations (hereafter Berg Collection).
111  Edward Thomas, 'John Masefield and Wilfred Gibson', *Bookman*, November 1914, 51–2 (p. 51).
112  Edward Thomas, *Walter Pater* (London: Martin Secker, 1913), p. 202.
113  Rupert Brooke, untitled paper on Shakespeare, Notebook M/6, Brooke Collection, King's College, Cambridge; Rupest Brooke, 'Democracy and the Arts', repr. in Timothy Rogers, *Rupert Brooke: A Reappraisal and Selection*, (London: Routledge & Kegan Paul, 1971), pp. 98–9.
114  G. E. Moore, *Principia Ethica* (Cambridge: Cambridge University Press, 1971), p. 201.
115  Letter of 19 October 1916, *Selected Letters of Edward Thomas*, ed. R. George Thomas (Oxford: Oxford University Press, 1995), p. 132.

116 T. S. Eliot, 'Reflections on Contemporary Poetry, I', *Egoist* 4 (1917), 118–19 (p. 118).

117 T. S. Eliot, 'Observations', *Egoist* 5 (1918), 69.

118 Harriet Monroe and Alice Corbin Henderson, *The New Poetry: An Anthology* (New York: Macmillan, 1917), p. xxxix.

119 T. S. Eliot, 'Reflections on Contemporary Poetry, III', *Egoist* 4 (1917), 151.

120 T. S. Eliot, 'Reflections on Contemporary Poetry, IV', *Egoist* 6 (1919), 39–40 (p. 39).

121 T. S. Eliot, 'Tradition and the Individual Talent', in his *Selected Essays*, pp. 17, 16.

122 Ezra Pound, 'Harold Monro', *Criterion* 11 (1932), 581–92 (p. 590), *EPP*, V, p. 363.

123 *Some Imagist Poets* (Boston, MA: Houghton Mifflin, 1916), p. vi. The preface was actually written by Richard Aldington.

124 Pound, 'Harold Monro', p. 363.

125 Reproduced in Schuchard, *Eliot's Dark Angel*, p. 21.

126 Interview in *Writers at Work: The Paris Review Interviews*, selected by Kay Dick (Harmondsworth: Penguin, 1972), p. 119.

127 T. S. Eliot, 'The Possibility of a Poetic Drama', in *The Sacred Wood* (London: Methuen, 1920), p. 63.

128 Rémy de Gourmont, *Selected Writings*, ed. and trans. Glenn S. Burne (Ann Arbor: University of Michigan Press, 1966), p. 96.

129 Ibid., p. 99.

130 Walter Pater, 'Style', in *Appreciations* (London: Macmillan, 1910), p. 19. Louis Menand discusses its relevance to Pound throughout *Discovering Modernism* (New York: Oxford University Press, 1987).

131 Eliot, 'Tradition and the Individual Talent', p. 15.

132 T. S. Eliot, *Knowledge and Experience in the Work of F. H. Bradley* (London: Faber & Faber, 1964), p. 146.

133 Friedrich Schlegel, *Critical Fragments* 60, in *Friedrich Schlegel's* Lucinde *and the Fragments*, trans. Peter Firchow (Minneapolis: University of Minnesota Press, 1971), p. 150; *Athenaeum Fragments* 116, in ibid., p. 175.

134 Schlegel, *Critical Fragments* 42, in ibid., p. 148.

135 *Ideas* 95, in ibid., p. 250.

136 Eliot, 'The Function of Criticism', p. 23.

137 Schlegel, *Critical Fragments* 103, p. 154; *Athenaeum Fragments* 116 (my italics), p. 175. Schlegel also anticipates Eliot when he maintains that disparate poetic ideas come together by the sudden 'chemical' operation of the poet's wit, and that an impersonal detachment is necessary for poetry, for 'in order to write well about something, one shouldn't be interested in it any longer' (*Athenaeum Fragments* 366, p. 221; *Critical Fragments* 37, p. 146).

138 Walter Benjamin, 'The Concept of Criticism in German Romanticism', in his *Selected Writings*, ed. Michael W. Jennings, 3 vols. (Cambridge, MA: Belknap, 1996–2002): I, *1913–1926*, ed. Marcus Bullock and Michael W. Jennings (1996), 116–200 (pp. 181–3); Philippe Lacoue-Labarthe and Jean-Luc Nancy, *The Literary Absolute*, trans. Philip Barnard and Cheryl

Lester (Albany: State University of New York Press, 1988), p. 11; Maurice
Blanchot, 'The Athenaeum', in *The Infinite Conversation*, trans. Susan
Hanson (Minneapolis: University of Minnesota Press, 1993), 351–9 (p. 359);
Paul de Man, 'The Rhetoric of Temporality', *Blindness and Insight*, 2nd edn
(London: Routledge, 1983), 187–228 (pp. 220–2); Rodolphe Gasché,
foreword to Schlegel's *Philosophical Fragments*, trans. Peter Firchow
(Minneapolis: University of Minnesota, 1991), p. xiii.

139 Cf. Anne Janowitz's comments on Eliot in 'The Romantic Fragment', in *A Companion to Romanticism*, ed. Duncan Wu (Oxford: Blackwell, 1998), 442–51.
140 Schlegel, *Lucinde and the Fragments*, p. 189.
141 T. S. Eliot, 'A Brief Introduction to the Method of Paul Valéry', in Paul Valéry, *Le Serpent*, trans. Mark Wardle (London: Cobden-Sanderson, 1924), p. 12.
142 M. A. R. Habib, *The Early T. S. Eliot and Western Philosophy* (Cambridge: Cambridge University Press, 1999), p. 198; Lacoue-Labarthe and Nancy, *The Literary Absolute*, p. 12.
143 T. S. Eliot, 'Critical', in *The Collected Poems of Harold Monro*, ed. Alida Monro (London: Cobden-Sanderson, 1933), xiii–xiv.
144 Eliot, 'Tradition and the Individual Talent', p. 17.
145 Coleridge, *Lectures on Literature*, I, p. 495.
146 De Gourmont, 'The Problem of Style', in *Selected Writings*, p. 128.
147 Pound, editorial, *Little Review* 4 (1917), 6, *EPP*, II, p. 197.
148 Eliot, 'London Letter', p. 450.
149 Giorgio Agamben, *The End of the Poem: Studies in Poetics*, trans. Daniel Heller-Roazen (Stanford, CA: Stanford University Press, 1999), p. 109.
150 Theodor Adorno, *Aesthetic Theory*, ed. Gretel Adorno and Rolf Tiedemann, ed. and trans. Robert Hullot-Kentor (New York: Continuum, 2002), p. 146.
151 *Selected Poems of Ezra Pound* (London: Faber & Gwyer, 1928), p. x.
152 Jacques Derrida, 'Che cos'è la poesia?', in *Points. . .*, ed. Elizabeth Weber, trans. Peggy Kamuf and others (Stanford, CA: Stanford University Press, 1995), pp. 288–99.
153 Coleridge, *Lectures on Literature*, I, p. 495.
154 Coleridge himself conceded this (*Lectures on Literature*, I, p. 358) but insisted that we still know an ash tree throughout all local variations of its form. This would make the organic poem an affair of genre rather than a unique self-relation.

CHAPTER 2   EDWARD THOMAS IN ECSTASY

1 Robert Ross, *The Georgian Revolt* (Carbondale: Southern Illinois University Press, 1965), p. 99; A. Walton Litz and Lawrence Rainey, 'Ezra Pound', in *The Cambridge History of Literary Criticism*, 9 vols. (Cambridge: Cambridge University Press, 1989–), VII: *Modernism and the New Criticism*, ed. A. Walton Litz, Louis Menand and Lawrence Rainey (2000), pp. 57–92 (p. 73).
2 Ross, *The Georgian Revolt*, pp. 110, 155–6.

3  F. R. Leavis, *New Bearings in English Poetry* (London: Chatto & Windus, 1932), pp. 68–9.
4  *Selected Letters of Edward Thomas*, ed. R. George Thomas (Oxford: Oxford University Press, 1995), p. 118; review reprinted in *A Language Not to be Betrayed: Selected Prose of Edward Thomas*, ed. Edna Longley (Manchester: Carcanet, 1981), p. 112.
5  Thomas *Selected Letters*, p. 118.
6  Thomas, *Selected Prose*, p. 114; 'New Numbers', in Thomas, *Selected Letters*, p. 106.
7  Thomas, *Selected Prose*, pp. 112, 116.
8  Ibid., pp. 105–6.
9  Ibid., p. 125.
10  Edward Thomas, 'More Georgian Poetry', *The Bookman*, April 1913, p. 47.
11  Thomas, *Selected Letters*, p. 93.
12  The text and title of this and all subsequent poems is taken from *The Collected Poems of Edward Thomas*, ed. R. George Thomas (Oxford: Clarendon Press, 1978).
13  Eleanor Farjeon, *Edward Thomas: The Last Four Years* (London: Oxford University Press, 1958), p. 154. Stan Smith expands its significance in '"Literally, For This": Metonymies of National Identity in Thomas, Yeats and Auden', in *Locations of Literary Modernism*, ed. Alex Davis and Lee M. Jenkins (Cambridge: Cambridge University Press, 2000), pp. 113–34.
14  'The Attempt', repr. in Thomas, *Selected Prose*, p. 261.
15  Farjeon, *Edward Thomas*, pp. 17, 18.
16  Ibid., pp. 32, 38.
17  Ibid., 43, 58.
18  Two holograph notebooks marked 'Fiction (Incomplete)', signed and dated Feb 25, 1914 and April 7, 1913 [i.e. 1914], Berg Collection, New York Public Library.
19  [Ecstasy], 'The History of Men is the History of Ecstasy', Holograph draft of an essay [1913], Berg Collection. All quotations are taken from the MS: R. George Thomas has reproduced a portion of the shorter and substantially different TS version in his *Edward Thomas: A Portrait* (Oxford: Clarendon Press, 1985), pp. 254–5.
20  T. S. Eliot, 'Tradition and the Individual Talent', in his *Selected Essays* (London: Faber & Faber, 1951), p. 17.
21  This passage has been cancelled and some words are very difficult to make out. In the first line, 'Humour' might be 'stupor'; in the third, 'tendencies' is my conjecture for an illegible word, and in the fourth 'humanity' might be 'luminosity'.
22  *Lyrical Ballads and Other Poems, 1797–1800*, ed. James Butler and Karen Green (Ithaca, NY: Cornell University Press, 1992), p. 351.
23  Ibid. The 'Ecstasy' essay notes that Wordsworth was fascinated by distraction.
24  Edward Thomas, *Keats* (London: T. C. & E. C. Jack, 1914), pp. 57, 53, 54.
25  MS entitled 'An Essay on Passion in Contemporary Fiction', [Essays] (6), Berg Collection.

26 Walter Pater, *The Renaissance* (London: Macmillan, 1910), pp. ix–x.

27 Ezra Pound, 'I Gather the Limbs of Osiris', *New Age* 10 (1912), 224–5 (p. 224), *EPP*, I, 53. Pound acknowledged his borrowing in the 1910 introduction to his translations of Cavalcanti, reprinted in *Translations of Ezra Pound*, ed. Hugh Kenner (London: Faber & Faber, 1953), p. 18.

28 Ezra Pound, 'The Rev. G. Crabbe, LL.B', *Future* I (1917), 110–11 (p. 110), *EPP*, II, p. 188.

29 Edward Thomas, *Walter Pater* (London: Martin Secker, 1913), pp. 93–4.

30 Walter Pater, 'Style', *Appreciations* (London: Macmillan, 1910), p. 34.

31 Ezra Pound, 'The Serious Artist, IV', *New Freewoman* I (1913), 214, *EPP*, I, p. 202; Ezra Pound, 'The Approach to Paris. . .V', *New Age* 13 (1913), 662–4 (p. 662), *EPP*, I, p. 181.

32 Thomas, *Selected Prose*, pp. 125, 118, 119.

33 Ibid., pp. 117, 121, 123.

34 Ibid., pp. 113, 114.

35 Ibid., pp. 107, 105.

36 Clive Scott, *Vers Libre: The Emergence of Free Verse in France, 1886–1914* (Oxford: Clarendon Press, 1990), pp. 15, 18.

37 Thomas, *Walter Pater*, p. 211.

38 Thomas, *Selected Letters*, p. 93.

39 Thomas, *Selected Prose*, p. 128.

40 Letter to John Bartlett, 4 July 1913, in *Selected Letters of Robert Frost*, ed. Lawrance Thompson (London: Cape, 1965), p. 80.

41 Edward Thomas, *Feminine Influence on the Poets* (London: Martin Secker, 1910), p. 76. Love-poetry, the chapter explains, is also inextricable from nature-poetry.

42 Walter de la Mare, 'The Dreams of Men', *Times Literary Supplement*, 18 October 1917, p. 502.

43 Thomas, *Walter Pater*, p. 78.

44 J. W. Haines, *In Memoriam Edward Thomas*, Green Pastures series (London: Morland Press, 1919), p. 14.

45 Edward Thomas, *The South Country* (London: Dent, 1909), p. 7.

46 Ibid., p. 4.

47 Edward Thomas, *The Icknield Way* (London: Constable, 1913), vi.

48 Thomas, *The South Country*, pp. 64–5.

49 Ibid., pp. 254, 253.

50 Thomas, *The Icknield Way*, p. 143.

51 Edward Thomas, *The Country*, ed. Mary Stratton (London: Batsford, 1913), pp. 35, 36, 37.

52 Edward Thomas, *Maurice Maeterlinck* (London: Methuen, 1911), p. 159.

53 Thomas, *The Country*, p. 39.

54 Thomas, *The South Country*, pp. 75, 85.

55 Raymond Williams, *The Country and the City* (London: Chatto & Windus, 1973), pp. 259, 255.

56 Thomas, *The Country*, pp. 25–6.
57 William James, *Talks to Teachers on Psychology; and to Students on Some of Life's Ideals* (London: Longmans, 1903), p. 245.
58 Edward Thomas, *The Happy-Go-Lucky Morgans* (London: Duckworth, 1913), pp. 47, 59, 49.
59 Edward Thomas, *The Heart of England* (London: Dent, 1906), p. 2; Thomas, *The South Country*, p. 252.
60 Edward Thomas, *The Childhood of Edward Thomas: A Fragment of Autobiography* (London: Faber & Faber, 1938), p. 56.
61 Thomas, *Selected Prose*, p. 130.
62 Arthur Symons, 'In Praise of Gypsies', *Journal of the Gypsy Lore Society* n.s., 1 (1908), 296–9 (p. 296).
63 Arthur Symons, 'Reviews', *JGLS* 1 (1908), 281.
64 E. O. Winstedt, 'Gipsy "civilisation"', *JGLS*, 1 (1908), 319–49 (p. 345).
65 Edward Thomas, *George Borrow: The Man and his Books* (London: Chapman & Hall, 1912), p. 319.
66 'Field Notes' 67 [n.p.], Berg Collection.
67 Derek Attridge, *Poetic Rhythm* (Cambridge: Cambridge University Press, 1995), p. 157.
68 H. P. [Henry Playford] Text taken from Thomas D'Urfey, *Wit and Mirth, or, Pills to Purge Melancholy*, 4th edn., 6 vols. (London: W. Pearson for J. Tonson, 1719–20), V (1719), p. 319. George Farquhar's alternative version in *The Recruiting Officer* (1719) is a call to enlist; John Gay's *The Beggar's Opera* (1728) transforms it into a love-song.
69 Hollows are sites of torture and death in 'The Hollow Wood' and Morris's 'The Hollow Land', which Thomas had recently reviewed. There may be echoes too of Hardy's 'After a Journey', where the ghostly wife is 'scanned across the dark space wherein I have lacked you'.
70 Field Notes 67 [n.p.], Berg Collection.
71 Robert Frost, letter to Grace W. Conkling, repr. in William Cooke, 'Elected Friends: Robert Frost and Edward Thomas', *Poetry Wales* 13:4 (1978), 22–3 (p. 23).
72 Text taken from *Robert Frost: Collected Poems, Prose and Plays* (New York: Library of America, 1995).
73 Thomas, *Selected Letters*, p. 114.
74 Cf. Frank Lentricchia, *Modernist Quartet* (Cambridge: Cambridge University Press, 1994), pp. 74–6.
75 Thomas, *The Icknield Way*, p. 2.
76 Thomas, *Feminine Influence on the Poets*, p. 85.
77 Thomas, *Selected Letters*, p. 146.
78 Leavis, *New Bearings*, p. 69.
79 Jean-Luc Nancy, *The Inoperative Community*, ed. Peter Connor, trans. Peter Connor, Lisa Garbus, Michael Holland and Simona Sawhney (Minneapolis: University of Minnesota Press, 1991), p. 19.
80 Thomas, *The Country*, p. 55.

CHAPTER 3 WALTER DE LA MARE'S IDEAL READER

1 Walter de la Mare, 'Books and Reading' [II], *Saturday Westminster Gazette*, 22 February 1919, p. 8.
2 'The Poet of Spoon River', unsigned review, *Times Literary Supplement*, 21 September 1916, p. 451.
3 'The Quintessential', unsigned review, *Times Literary Supplement*, 12 August 1915, p. 268.
4 Ezra Pound, 'Vorticism', *Fortnightly Review*, 1 September 1914, pp. 461–71 (465), *EPP*, I, p. 279.
5 De la Mare, 'The Quintessential'.
6 Walter de la Mare, '*The Spirit of Romance*', *Saturday Westminster Gazette*, 22 October 1910, p. 12.
7 Walter de la Mare, 'Mr. Pound's Canzoni', *Saturday Westminster Gazette*, 19 August 1911, p. 12.
8 'Life Desiring Life', unsigned review, *Times Literary Supplement*, 2 October 1919, p. 527.
9 Walter de la Mare, 'How to Read Contemporary Poetry', *Everyman*, 17 May 1919, p. 133.
10 'Doggerel', unsigned review, *Times Literary Supplement*, 21 August 1913, p. 341.
11 Letter of August 1918, cited in Theresa Whistler, *Imagination of the Heart* (London: Duckworth, 1993), p. 288.
12 Iona and Peter Opie, *The Oxford Dictionary of Nursery Rhymes* (Oxford: Oxford University Press, 1951), p. 3.
13 Walter de la Mare, 'Flowers in Poetry', repr. in *Pleasures and Speculations* (London: Faber & Faber, 1940), pp. 200–32 (p. 231). Cf. Thomas's letter to de la Mare dated 16 May 1911, MS.Eng.Lett.622, Bodleian Library, Oxford.
14 Walter de la Mare, 'Magic and Poetry', TS lecture (n.d. but c. 1910), Literary Papers of Walter de la Mare, Bodleian Library, Oxford [n.p.].
15 Juliet Dusinberre, *Alice to the Lighthouse: Children's Literature and Radical Experiments in Art* (London: Macmillan, 1987), p. 22.
16 Edward J. O'Brien, 'The Younger Bards', *Poetry* 6 (1915), 188–96; 'A Review of Contemporary Art', *Blast* 2 (1915), 38–47 (p. 46).
17 Text of de la Mare's 'adult' verse taken from his *Collected Poems* (London: Faber & Faber, 1979).
18 Walter de la Mare, 'Meaning and Poetry', lecture (n.d.), Literary Papers of Walter de la Mare, p. 7.
19 Walter de la Mare, 'Craftsmanship', lecture (n.d.), Literary Papers of Walter de la Mare, p. 2.
20 Walter de la Mare, 'Poetry in Prose', *Proceedings of the British Academy* 21 (1935), 241–321 (pp. 246, 257).
21 Ibid., p. 257.
22 De la Mare, 'Craftsmanship', p. 22.
23 Text of de la Mare's 'children's' verse taken from his *Collected Rhymes and Verses* (London: Faber & Faber, 1978).

24 Literary Papers of Walter de la Mare, lecture, p. 13. Labelled 'Craftsmanship in Poetry' and marked as 'old', the TS is itself a reincorporation of parts of 'Poetic Technique', dated 1920.
25 Ibid., p. 5.
26 'Doggerel', p. 341.
27 See Giorgio Agamben, *The End of the Poem: Studies in Poetics*, trans. Daniel Heller-Roazen (Stanford, CA: Stanford University Press, 1999), p. 111.
28 W. H. Auden, 'Walter de la Mare', in *Forewords and Afterwords* (London: Faber & Faber, 1973), 384–94 (p. 389).
29 Ibid.
30 Adam Phillips, *The Beast in the Nursery* (London: Faber & Faber, 1998), p. 45.
31 Walter de la Mare, 'Books for Children', Literary Papers of Walter de la Mare, paginated 2 but not in sequence.
32 Walter de la Mare, 'The English Lyric', *Times Literary Supplement*, 2 October 1913, pp. 405–6.
33 Ezra Pound, 'In Metre', *New Freewoman* 1 (1913), 113, *EPP*, I, p. 152.
34 Nicolas Abraham, *Rhythms: On the Work, Translation and Psychoanalysis*, collected and presented by Nicholas T. Rand and Maria Torok, trans. Benjamin Thigpen and Nicholas T. Rand (Stanford, CA: Stanford University Press, 1995), p. 70.
35 Sigmund Freud, 'The Uncanny', *Penguin Freud Library*, trans. James Strachey, ed. Angela Richards and Albert Dickson (Harmondsworth: Penguin, 1990–3), XIV: *Art and Literature*, ed. Albert Dickson (1990), pp. 336–76 (p. 364).
36 Ibid., p. 340.
37 Although Freud claimed that *The Interpretation of Dreams* was based on 'a portion of my own self-analysis' (Preface to the Second Edition, repr. in *Penguin Freud Library*, IV: *The Interpretation of Dreams*, ed. Angela Richards (Harmondsworth: Penguin, 1991), p. 47.)
38 Neil Hertz, 'Freud and the Sandman', in *The End of the Line* (New York: Columbia University Press, 1985), pp. 97–121 (p. 99). S. S. Towheed emphasises another sense of the text's own uncanniness in 'R. L. Stevenson's Sense of the Uncanny: "The Face in the Cheval-Glass"', *English Literature in Transition* 42 (1999), 23–38 (pp. 23–5).
39 Freud, 'The Uncanny', p. 341.
40 V. C. F. Rost, *Deutsch–Griechisches Wörterbuch* (Göttingen: Bandenhöf & Ruprecht, 1837); H. Schenkl, *Deutsch–Griechisches Schul-Wörterbuch* (Leipzig: Teubner, 1897).
41 Freud, 'The Uncanny', p. 361.
42 Freud, 'The Uncanny', p. 376 and 'Three Essays on the Theory of Sexuality', *Penguin Freud Library*, VII: *On Sexuality*, ed. Angela Richards (Harmondsworth: Penguin, 1991), p. 147, n. 1.
43 F. R. Leavis, *New Bearings in English Poetry* (London: Chatto & Windus, 1932), pp. 52–4.

44 Robert M. Pierson, 'The Metre of "The Listeners"', *English Studies* 45 (1964), 373–81.
45 Letter to Georgina Sime, 7 February 1944, cited in Whistler, *Imagination of the Heart*, pp. 203–4.


CHAPTER 4 THE SIMPLICITY OF W. H. DAVIES

1 Letter of 9 December 1906, in *Edward Thomas: Letters to Gordon Bottomley*, ed. R. George Thomas (London: Oxford University Press, 1968), p. 128.
2 Edward Thomas, 'A Poet at Last', *Daily Chronicle*, 21 October 1905, p. 3.
3 Sybil Hollingdrake, 'The True Traveller', *Poetry Wales* 18:2 (1982), 25–44 (p. 35).
4 Edward Thomas, 'A Poet and Mr Shaw', *Daily Chronicle*, 23 April 1908, p. 3.
5 Edward Thomas, 'A Poet by Birth', *Daily Chronicle*, 4 November 1908, p. 3.
6 Edward Thomas, review of *Farewell to Poesy*, *Morning Post*, February 1910, repr. in R. George Thomas, '"Immortal Moments": Edward Thomas and W. H. Davies', *Poetry Wales* 18:2 (1982), 57–66 (p. 63).
7 Louis Menand, *Discovering Modernism* (New York: Oxford University Press, 1987), p. 41.
8 'New Lamps for Old', unsigned review, *Times Literary Supplement*, 6 November 1913, p. 506.
9 Ezra Pound, 'William H. Davies, Poet', *Poetry* 11 (1917), 99–102 (pp. 100, 102).
10 F. Schiller, 'On the Naïve and Sentimental', in *Friedrich Schiller: Essays*, ed. W. Hinderer and Daniel O. Dahlstrom, trans. Daniel O. Dahlstrom (New York: Continuum, 1993), pp. 196–7.
11 T. S. Eliot, 'Critical', in *The Collected Poems of Harold Monro*, ed. Alida Monro (London: Cobden-Sanderson, 1933), p. xiv.
12 Cited in *A Language Not to be Betrayed: Selected Prose of Edward Thomas*, ed. Edna Longley (Manchester: Carcanet, 1981), p. 113.
13 Thomas, 'A Poet and Mr Shaw', p. 3.
14 Text of this and all subsequent poems from Davies's *Collected Poems* (London: Cape, 1928).
15 J. C. Squire, 'W. H. Davies', *New Statesman*, 16 December 1916, p. 255.
16 Ibid., p. 254, 255.
17 George Bernard Shaw, preface to W. H. Davies, *The Autobiography of a Super-Tramp* (London: Fifield, 1908; repr. London: Cape, 1926), p. ix.
18 Walter de la Mare, 'Doggerel', unsigned review, *Times Literary Supplement*, 21 August 1913, p. 341.
19 Eleanor Farjeon, *Edward Thomas: The Last Four Years* (Oxford: Oxford University Press, 1958), p. 13.
20 Labour Camps: Report of the Departmental Committee on Vagrancy, 1906.
21 Josiah Flynt, *Tramping with Tramps* (London: T. Fisher Unwin, 1900), Edmond Kelly, *The Elimination of the Tramp* (New York: Putnams, 1908). Sterilisation: W. H. Dawson, *The Vagrancy Problem* (London: King, 1910).
22 Daniel Defoe, *Moll Flanders* (London: Simpkin, Marshall, Hamilton, Kent, 1924), p. xii.

23 Jack London, *People of the Abyss* (London: Isbister, 1903), pp. 60, 126.
24 Everard Wyrall, *The Spike* (London: Constable, 1909), pp. 14, 15.
25 R. C. K. Ensor, 'Tramping as a Tramp', *Independent Review* 4 (1904–5), 102–18 (p. 105).
26 Mary Higgs, *Glimpses into the Abyss* (London: King, 1906), p. 267.
27 Helen Thomas, *A Memory of W H Davies* (Edinburgh: Tragara Press, 1973). (unpaginated).
28 Davies, *The Autobiography of a Super-Tramp*, p. 203.
29 Richard Stonesifer, *W. H. Davies: A Critical Biography* (London: Cape, 1963), p. 41.
30 Davies, *The Autobiography of a Super-Tramp*, pp. 167–8.
31 Ibid., pp. 67, 232–4.
32 Cited in Fiona Pearson, 'W. H. Davies and Contemporary Artists', *Poetry Wales* 18:2 (1982), 73–9 (p. 76.)
33 Bart Kennedy, *Wander Pictures* (London: Cassell, 1906), p. 4; Bart Kennedy, *A Tramp Camp* (London: Cassell, 1906), p. 200.
34 Kennedy, *Wander Pictures*, pp. 2, 4–5.
35 C. F. G. Masterman, *The Condition of England* (London: Methuen, 1909; new edn., 1960), pp. 139–40.
36 *The Tramp* 2 (1910), p. 1.
37 Jack London, 'Road Kids and Gay Cats', *The Tramp* 2 (1910), 30–6 (p. 36).
38 Harry Roberts, 'The Art of Vagabondage', *The Tramp* 1 (1910), 22–6 (p. 25).
39 M. E. M. Donaldson, 'An Attractive Corner of Inverness-shire', *The Tramp* 1 (1910), 299–301 (p. 299).
40 Scudamore Jarvis, 'The Caravan', *The Tramp* 1 (1910), 155–8 (p. 155).
41 Arthur Ransome, 'On the Road in France', *The Tramp* 1 (1910), 142–6 (p. 142).
42 J. Crawford Flitch, 'On Foot in Mallorca', *The Tramp* 1 (1910), 503–7 (p. 504).
43 Kennedy, *Wander Pictures*, p. 252.
44 Margaret Sackville, 'The New Forest', *The Tramp* 1 (1910), 83–7 (p. 86).
45 Discussed in Anne Wallace, *Walking, Literature and English Culture* (Oxford: Clarendon Press, 1993).
46 Letter dated 12 June 1909, Walpole Collection, King's School, Canterbury.
47 W. H. Davies, *Later Days* (London: Cape, 1925; repr. Oxford: Oxford University Press, 1985), pp. 15, 16.
48 Higgs, *Glimpses into the Abyss*, p. 82.
49 Dawson, *The Vagrancy Problem*, p. 51.
50 Thomas Holmes, *London's Underworld* (London: Dent, 1912), p. 56.
51 Cited in Rachel Vorspan, 'Vagrancy and the New Poor Law in Late Victorian and Edwardian England', *English Historical Review* 92 (1977), 59–81 (p. 76).
52 Pound, conversation with Richard Stonesifer, in *W. H. Davies*, p. 120.
53 Helen Thomas, *A Memory of W H Davies*.
54 Letter of 12 June 1909, Walpole Collection.

55 Philip Larkin, 'Freshly Scrubbed Potato', in his *Required Writing* (London: Faber & Faber, 1983), p. 166.
56 Michael Cullup, 'Recovering W. H. Davies', *PN Review* 47 (1985), 36–8.
57 Edward Thomas, 'The Natural Poet', *Bookman*, May 1910, pp. 80–1.
58 Pound, 'William H. Davies, Poet', p. 99.
59 F. S. Flint, 'Recent Verse', *New Age* 4 (1908), 95–7 (p. 96).
60 T. S. Eliot, 'Reflections on Contemporary Poetry, III', *Egoist* 4 (1917), 151.
61 Thomas, 'The Natural Poet', p. 80.
62 *Shorter Lyrics of the Twentieth Century* (London: Poetry Bookshop, 1922), p. 7.
63 T. S. Eliot, *The Varieties of Metaphysical Poetry*, ed. Ronald Schuchard (London: Faber & Faber, 1993), p. 211.

## CHAPTER 5 HARDY'S INDIFFERENCE

1 Text of all Hardy's poems taken from the *Collected Poetic Works of Thomas Hardy*, ed. Samuel Hynes, 3 vols. (Oxford: Clarendon Press, 1984).
2 *The Literary Notebooks of Thomas Hardy*, ed. Lennart A. Björk, 2 vols. (Basingstoke: Macmillan, 1985), I, 27.
3 Thomas Hardy, *The Life and Work of Thomas Hardy*, ed. Michael Millgate (London and Basingstoke: Macmillan, 1984), p. 324.
4 Repr. in Michael Millgate, *Thomas Hardy: A Biography* (Oxford: Oxford University Press, 1982), p. 89.
5 *Thomas Hardy's Public Voice*, ed. Michael Millgate (Oxford: Clarendon, 2001), p. 197.
6 D. H. Lawrence, *Study of Thomas Hardy and Other Essays*, ed. Bruce Steel (Cambridge: Cambridge University Press, 1985), p. 91.
7 Hardy, *Life*, p. 182.
8 *Lyrical Ballads and Other Poems, 1797–1800*, ed. James Butler and Karen Green (Ithaca, NY: Cornell University Press, 1992), p. 745.
9 See Matthew Campbell, *Rhythm and Will in Victorian Poetry* (Cambridge: Cambridge University Press, 1999), pp. 212–16.
10 Millgate, *Thomas Hardy*, p. 373.
11 Letter of 1 November 1918, in *The Collected Letters of Thomas Hardy*, ed. Richard L. Purdy and Michael Millgate, 7 vols. (Oxford: Clarendon, 1978–88), V: *1914–1919* (1985), p. 284.
12 Letter of 17 June 1921, in *The Letters of Emma and Florence Hardy*, ed. Michael Millgate (Oxford: Clarendon, 1996), p. 177.
13 Letter of 6 November 1918, Thomas Hardy Memorial Collection, Dorset County Museum, Dorchester (hereafter DCM).
14 Letter to de la Mare, 15 October 1919, in Hardy, *Collected Letters*, V, p. 331. Letter of 5 March 1928, in *Letters of Emma and Florence Hardy*, p. 274. Hardy, *Life*, p. 480.
15 Theresa Whistler, *The Imagination of the Heart* (London: Duckworth, 1993), pp. 312, 313.

16 Russell Brain, *Tea with Walter de la Mare* (London: Faber & Faber, 1957), p. 31.
17 Walter de la Mare, 'Mr. Hardy's Lyrics', *Times Literary Supplement*, 27 November 1919, pp. 681–2.
18 Edward Thomas, *A Literary Pilgrim in England* (London: Methuen, 1917), p. 149.
19 Letter from Helen Thomas (n.d. but internal evidence suggests 1920), DCM.
20 Edward Thomas, 'Time's Laughingstocks', *Morning Post*, 9 December 1909, p. 2.
21 Edward Thomas, 'Mr Hardy's New Poems', *Daily Chronicle*, 7 December 1909, p. 3.
22 Edward Thomas, 'Thomas Hardy of Dorchester', *Poetry and Drama* 1 (1913), 180–4 (p. 180).
23 Lytton Strachey, 'Mr Hardy's New Poems', *New Statesman*, 19 December 1914, pp. 269–71. See also John Bayley, *An Essay on Hardy* (Cambridge: Cambridge University Press, 1978), p. 10; Samuel Hynes, *The Pattern of Hardy's Poetry* (Chapel Hill: University of North Carolina, 1961), p. 63.
24 Letter of 18 March 1915, DCM.
25 Letter of 5 October 1913, in Hardy, *Collected Letters*, IV: *1909–1914* (1984), p. 307.
26 Letter of 21 March 1915, DCM.
27 Letter of 17 April 1916, in Hardy, *Collected Letters*, V, pp. 156–7.
28 Hardy, *Life*, p. 323.
29 Peter Robinson, *In the Circumstances: About Poetry and Poets* (Oxford: Clarendon Press, 1992), pp. 60–1.
30 Hardy, *Thomas Hardy's Public Voice*, p. 250.
31 Hardy, *Life*, p. 239.
32 Hardy, *Thomas Hardy's Public Voice*, p. 199.
33 Hardy, *Life*, p. 361.
34 James Richardson, *Thomas Hardy: The Poetry of Necessity* (Chicago: University of Chicago Press, 1977), p. 22.
35 Hardy, *Life*, p. 153.
36 Ibid., p. 409.
37 Arthur Schopenhauer, *The World as Will and Representation*, trans. E. F. J. Payne, 2 vols. (New York: Dover, 1966), II, pp. 357–8.
38 Hardy, *Literary Notebooks*, II, p. 39, taken from Schopenhauer, *World as Will and Representation*, II, p. 434.
39 Robert Rethy, 'The Metaphysics of Nullity', *Philosophy Research Archives* 12 (1986), 357–86; Cheryl Foster, 'Ideas and Imagination', in *The Cambridge Companion to Schopenhauer*, ed. Christopher Janaway (Cambridge: Cambridge University Press, 1999), pp. 213–51 (p. 224).
40 Hardy, *Literary Notebooks*, II, p. 107.
41 Thomas Hardy, *The Dynasts* (London and Basingstoke: Macmillan, 1978), I.V.iv.99 (p. 147).

42 Hardy, *Literary Notebooks*, II, p. III; Eduard von Hartmann, *Philosophy of the Unconscious*, 3 vols. in 1 (1884; repr. London: Routledge, 2000), I, pp. 246–7.

43 Hardy, *The Dynasts*, Fore Scene, lines 2–5 (p. 21).

44 Letter of 26 December 1920, *Letters of Emma and Florence Hardy*, p. 171.

45 Walter Benjamin, *The Origins of German Tragic Drama*, trans. John Osborne (London: New Left Books, 1977), p. 137.

46 See Howard Caygill, *Walter Benjamin: The Colour of Experience* (London: Routledge, 1998), p. 59 and 'Benjamin, Heidegger and the Destruction of Tradition', in *Walter Benjamin's Philosophy: Destruction and Experience*, ed. Andrew Benjamin and Peter Osborne, 2nd edn. (Manchester: Clinamen Press, 2000), pp. 1–30 (pp. 10–21).

47 De la Mare, 'Mr. Hardy's Lyrics', p. 681; Edward Thomas, *In Pursuit of Spring* (London: Thomas Nelson, 1914), p. 196.

48 Edmund Gosse, *Some Diversions of a Man of Letters* (London: Heinemann, 1919), pp. 252–3; Hardy, *Life*, p. 265.

49 Hardy, *Literary Notebooks*, II, pp. 127–8.

50 Hardy, *The Dynasts*, Fore Scene (pp. 27–8).

51 Hardy, *Life*, p. 218.

52 See Josh Cohen, 'Unfolding: Reading after Romanticism', in *Walter Benjamin and Romanticism*, ed. Andrew Benjamin and Beatrice Hanssen (London: Continuum, 2002), pp. 98–108.

53 Thomas, 'Mr Hardy's New Poems', p. 3.

54 Jahan Ramazani, *The Poetry of Mourning: The Modern Elegy from Hardy to Heaney* (Chicago: Chicago University Press, 1994), p. 50.

55 Millgate, *Thomas Hardy*, p. 470.

56 Postcard to Amy Lowell, 2 October 1914, in *Selected Letters of Ezra Pound, 1907–1941*, ed. D. D. Paige (London: Faber & Faber, 1971), p. 40; *Confucius to Cummings*, ed. Ezra Pound and Marcella Spann (New York: New Directions, 1964), pp. 325–9.

57 Letter of 31 March 1921, DCM. Reproduced in Patricia Hutchins, 'Ezra Pound and Thomas Hardy', *Southern Review* 4 (1968), 90–104 (p. 99).

58 Pound, *Selected Letters*, p. 248.

59 Louis Menand, *Discovering Modernism* (New York: Oxford University Press, 1987), p. 23.

## CHAPTER 6 GOING OVER THE TOP: THE PASSIONS OF WILFRED OWEN

1 Texts of all Owen's poems are taken from volume I of *Wilfred Owen: The Complete Poems and Fragments*, ed. Jon Stallworthy, 2 vols. (London: Chatto & Windus, 1983).

2 Allyson Booth, *Postcards from the Trenches: Negotiating the Space between Modernism and the First World War* (Oxford: Oxford University Press, 1996),

p. 6; Trudi Tate, *Modernism, History and the First World War* (Manchester: Manchester University Press, 1998), p. 5.

3 Jane Goldman, *Modernism, 1910–1945: Image to Apocalypse* (London: Palgrave, 2004), pp. 88–9.

4 *Selected Letters of Wilfred Owen*, ed. John Bell (Oxford: Oxford University Press, 1998), p. 351.

5 Ibid., p. 360.

6 Dominic Hibberd, *Owen the Poet* (Basingstoke: Macmillan, 1986), pp. 182–3.

7 Merryn Williams, *Wilfred Owen* (Bridgend: Seren, 1993), p. 141.

8 Fran Brearton plausibly sees it as a pre-emptive strike against his readership's likely expectations (*The Great War in Irish Poetry* (Oxford: Oxford University Press, 2000), p. 55).

9 Craig A. Hamilton, 'Genetic Criticism and Wilfred Owen's Revisions to "Anthem for Doomed Youth" and "Strange Meeting"', *English Language Notes* 38 (2001), 61–71.

10 Douglas Kerr speculates on Owen's modernism in *Wilfred Owen's Voices* (Oxford: Clarendon Press, 1993), p. 10.

11 Owen, *Selected Letters*, p. 322.

12 Seamus Heaney, *The Government of the Tongue* (London: Faber & Faber, 1986), pp. xiv, xv.

13 Keith V. Comer, *Strange Meetings: Walt Whitman, Wilfred Owen and the Poetry of War*, Lund Studies in English 91 (Lund: Lund University Press, 1996), p. 155.

14 Immanuel Kant, *Critique of Judgement*, trans. Werner S. Pluhar (Indianapolis: Hackett, 1987), p. 53.

15 Heaney, *The Government of the Tongue*, p. 108. On criticism of Kantian aesthetics, see Paul de Man, *Aesthetic Ideology*, ed. Andrzej Warminski (Minneapolis: University of Minnesota Press, 1996); Terry Eagleton, *The Ideology of the Aesthetic* (Oxford: Blackwell, 1990); and the replies in *The New Aestheticism*, ed. John Joughin and Simon Malpas (Manchester: Manchester University Press, 2003).

16 Jean-Luc Nancy, 'Of the Sublime', in J.-F. Courtine et al., *Of the Sublime: Presence in Question*, trans. Jeffrey S. Librett (Albany: State University of New York Press, 1993), p. 31.

17 James Najarian, ' "Greater Love": Wilfred Owen, Keats and a Tradition of Desire', *Twentieth-Century Literature* 47 (2001), 20–38 (p. 28).

18 Quoted in Richard Ellmann, *Oscar Wilde* (London: Hamish Hamilton, 1987), p. 139; *The Artist and Journal of Home Culture*, 1 April 1893, p. 120.

19 Ellmann, *Oscar Wilde*, p. 71.

20 André Gide, *Oscar Wilde* (London: Kimber, 1951), p. 35.

21 Ibid.

22 Oscar Wilde, *De Profundis*, repr. in *Complete Works of Oscar Wilde* (London: HarperCollins, 1999), p. 1031.

23 Owen, *Selected Letters*, p. 316.

24 Eve Kosofsky Sedgwick, *The Epistemology of the Closet* (London: Penguin, 1994), pp. 146–51 (p. 146).
25 *Contra* Najarian, '"Greater Love"', p. 33.
26 Adrian Caesar, *Taking it Like a Man: Suffering, Sexuality and the War Poets* (Manchester: Manchester University Press, 1993).
27 Paul Fussell, *The Great War and Modern Memory* (Oxford: Oxford University Press, 2000), p. 160.
28 Owen, *Selected Letters*, p. 353 (italics Owen's).
29 Ibid., p. 360.

# Index

Pound, Ezra, 1, 2, 28
  Davies and 130, 141, 145
  de la Mare and 119
  Hardy, praise for 5, 45, 180–181
  individualist views 39–41, 54
  poetic form and 24–25, 53–54, 60
  relations with Georgian poets 6, 27–34,
    64, 146
  Schiller, influence of 42
  Wordsworth and 32–34, 74
  *works*:
    'The Approach to Paris...V' 46
    'Credo' 24
    'Imagisme' ('A Few Don'ts') 45–47
    'Prolegomena' 6, 27, 29
prosody and agency 12–13, 23

rhetoric 6–7, 7–12, 34, 51–52, 181
  modernist poetry and 59–61
*Rhythm* 6, 38, 140
Richardson, James 157
Ross, Robert H. 8
Rossetti, Christina G., 112, 175
Ruskin, John 37

Schiller, Friedrich, 26
  *Aesthetic Education* 20, 21, 41
  *Kallias* (Letters to Körner) 20
  *On the Naïve and Sentimental* 41–45, 56, 131
Schlegel, A. W. 41
Schlegel, F. 26, 41, 56–58, 63, 169
Schopenhauer, Arthur 159–161, 162
sentimentalism 18
Shusterman, Richard 34
Sinclair, May 27, 31, 48
Squire, J. C. 4, 5
Stead, C. K. 8
Stirner, Max 40
Surrealism 111, 146
Symons, Arthur 96, 166

Thomas, Edward 2, 4, 31
  appears alongside modernists 28, 146
  auditory poetic 85–88
  Brooke, opinion of 51
  Davies and 129–130, 144, 146
  enlisting 99–105
  free verse and 7, 60, 65, 78, 79
  Frost and 85, 95, 99–100, 101–103
  Georgian poets and 4, 50–51, 64–65, 77–78
  Hardy, relations with 153, 154, 166
  Imagism, criticism of 76, 77
  Keats, criticism of 73
  Lawrence, criticism of 65, 78
  Pater and 50, 73–78, 84–85, 86, 106

Pound, criticism of 11, 77
  speech and 84–86
  suburbia in 91–92
  superfluousness and 92–93, 102
  tramping/homelessness in 33, 88–89, 93, 95, 98
  Verlaine and 12
  Wordsworth and 95, 102
  *works*:
    'After You Speak' 83–84
    'As the Team's Head Brass' 103–106
    'The Ash Grove' 82–83
    'Aspens' 70
    'Beauty' 81
    *The Childhood of Edward Thomas* 68, 94
    'Ecstasy' [MS] 68–70, 75–76, 80, 88
    'The Gypsy' 95–98
    'Home [1]' 89
    'Home [2]' 86, 89–90
    'Home [3]' 89
    'I Never Saw that Land Before' 66–67
    'The Lane' 90, 100
    'Liberty' 73, 100–101
    'Man and Dog' 98–99
    'The New Year' 94–95
    'Old Man' 70–71
    'Over the Hills' 80–81
    'The Penny Whistle' 93–94
    'Rain' 71–73
    'Roads' 101–103
    'The Signpost' 67, 100
    'Song [3]' 103
    'The Unknown Bird' 87–88
    'The Wasp Trap' 82
    'When we two walked' 81
    'Words' 78–80
Tradition (literary term) 8, 25–26
*Tramp, The* 138–140
tramping and vagrancy, attitudes to 134–136,
  140–141

Walcott, Derek 1, 2
*Wheels* (Edith Sitwell) 4
Wilde, Oscar 194–195
  *see also* Owen, Wilfred
Williams, Raymond 92
Wordsworth, William 8, 11, 32–34
  Preface to *Lyrical Ballads* 15, 20–21, 32, 43
  on repetition 71, 72
  'Simon Lee' 15–18, 22–23

Yeats, John B. 39
Yeats, William Butler 11
  dislike of Owen 5, 10
  *A General Introduction for my Work* 9–10
  *A Vision* 10, 60